COMPUTER
PROGRAMMING
AND ARCHITECTURE
The VAX-11

COMPUTER PROGRAMMING AND ARCHITECTURE
The VAX-11

Henry M. Levy
Richard H. Eckhouse, Jr.

Digital Press

Printed in U.S.A.

1st Printing, April 1980

Documentation Number EY-AX008-DP-001

LIBRARY OF CONGRESS
CATALOGING IN PUBLICATION DATA

Levy, Henry M.   1952-
  Computer Programming and Architecture - - The VAX-11

  Bibliography: p.
  Includes index
  1. VAX-11 (Computer) - - Programming. 2. Assembler
Language (Computer program language). 3. Computer
architecture. 1. Eckhouse, Richard H., 1940-
joint author. 2. Title.
QA 76.8.V37   001.64.'2   80-14409

ISBN 0-932376-07-X

Trademarks

Digital Equipment Corporation: DEC, DECUS, PDP, UNIBUS,
VAX, DECnet, DECsystem-10, DECSYSTEM 20, DECwriter,
DIBOL, EduSystem, IAS, MASSBUS, PDT, RSTS, RSX, VMS, VT.

IBM: System 360/370, Series 1.

Control Data Corporation: CYBER.

In memory of Samuel J. Levy

Contents

Foreword

Understanding today's computers requires a systems viewpoint. Relentless advances in semiconductor components open the opportunity to integrate higher levels of the systems architecture into the basic hardware. Thus, we should not approach computer structures without examining software needs.

This text is unique in addressing hardware structures and assembly language programming, while also describing the interfaces and mechanics of an operating system; it introduces the full range of fundamental hardware and software structures. Another noteworthy aspect of this book is its use of a practical, modern computer system that contains process support as well as virtual memory. Using the VAX-11, the authors have raised a host of topics and problems encountered by programmers and operating systems.

I highly recommend this book to those looking for a readable, practical introduction to the fundamentals of hardware and software computer structures.

Samuel H. Fuller
Technical Director
Digital Equipment Corporation

Preface

This book is for those who wish to understand the architecture and operation of computer systems. We believe that the best way to understand a computer's architecture is to use it, and the best way to use the architecture is to program at the assembly level. Once the basic assembly language concepts of addressing and instruction execution are mastered, one can begin to consider more advanced concepts such as data structures, Input/Output programming, and features for operating system resource management. The operating system support features, however, are a part of the architecture seen by the operating system, as opposed to the programmer-visible interface.

Therefore, this book is divided into two parts. The first half of the book, Chapters 1 through 6, is concerned with the architecture of a computer as seen by the assembly language programmer. The reader is first presented with the basics of computer organization and arithmetic. More complex concepts, including data-types and data structures, are then developed along with their manipulation by assembly language programming. The computer used to illustrate the concepts discussed is the VAX-11 manufactured by Digital Equipment Corporation.

Chapter 1 begins with a discussion of the differences between architecture and implementation. It also presents a brief review of number systems.

Chapter 2 introduces basic computer structures: memories, processors, and I/O devices. It first covers the machine-independent concepts of memory addressing, instruction execution cycles, and data representation, proceeding to describe the VAX-11 and its data-types and instructions. By the end of the chapter, the reader should be able to code simple machine language instructions using simple addressing.

Chapter 3 presents more advanced addressing and instruction techniques. The reader is shown how VAX-11 instructions are represented in memory. At this stage, the reader should then be able to code small routines using more complex instructions and varied addressing modes.

Chapter 4 develops more advanced control structures such as loops, subroutines, and stacks for storage and linkage. The use of macros to simplify assembly programming is also described.

Chapter 5 concludes the VAX-11 assembly language section with more sophisticated instructions and the manipulation of complex data structures such as lists, queues, and trees. By this point, the reader should thoroughly understand how to manipulate data types and data structures to solve problems.

Chapter 6 allows the reader to contrast his or her general knowledge of the VAX-11 architecture to that of three other architectures: the IBM System 370, the CDC Cyber, and the IBM Series 1. The material in this chapter focuses on the instruction encoding and memory addressing of these machines. In addition, the material provides some insight into the architectural tradeoffs made in designing each one.

The second half of the book, Chapters 7 through 11, considers the more sophisticated architectural support of an operating system and the strategies used by an operating system to manage hardware resources. These chapters examine that part of the architecture and implementation not usually seen by the applications programmer.

The VAX-11 physical I/O system is introduced in Chapter 7. The nature of I/O devices is explained, and simple examples of programmed I/O device control are presented.

Chapter 8 examines the architecture that supports the operating system. It develops the need for sharing of resources and deals with the VAX-11 process structure, the use of access modes, the implementation of virtual memory, and the handling of interrupts and exceptions.

In Chapter 9 we examine how an operating system uses the architectural support described in Chapter 8. The VAX/VMS operating system is used as an example, along with discussions of general operating system strategies.

Chapter 10 describes the interfaces and utilities provided for the user by an operating system.

Chapter 11 concludes with an examination of the implementation of a particular member of an architectural family. The discussion covers features transparent to the programmer, such as the cache, translation buffer, and instruction buffer. It shows the tradeoffs available to the hardware designer in producing a cost-effective implementation while still meeting the architectural constraints.

The book is intended for the programmer with some experience in a high level language, such as Pascal or FORTRAN. Of course, the language is not nearly as important as the ability to construct algorithms that yield computer programs. An understanding of basic data structures is also expected.

We do not intend to make the reader a sophisticated assembly language programmer. Rather, we expect the reader to emerge with a sound understanding of computer organization, memory addressing, program execution, and the fundamentals of one particular architecture. An awareness of the purpose of an operating system and the support it requires from the underlying hardware should also crystallize.

Therefore, while the story is told with the VAX-11 as the main character, we believe the book is generally applicable to the understanding of any computer system. The techniques developed should enable a programmer to quickly master any new machine encountered. It should also aid the programmer in assessing the strengths and weaknesses of a particular architecture relative to the VAX-11.

Acknowledgements

We would like to thank the reviewers for their valuable comments. In particular, Steve Beckhardt, Tom Dopirak, Sandy Kaplan, Art Karshmer, Larry Kenah, Ed Lazowska, Victor Lessor, and Carol Peters (along with a number of reviewers who remain anonymous) provided us with much valuable feedback. We also appreciate the support of the staff of Digital Press who were instrumental in starting us on the book. We would also like to thank Digital Equipment Corporation for its support, especially Gordon Bell, Jim Bell, Sam Fuller, and Bill Strecker. Finally, we would like to thank the VAX-11 architects, VAX-11/780 implementors, and VAX/VMS operating system group for making the last few years so interesting.

Hank Levy
Dick Eckhouse

COMPUTER
PROGRAMMING
AND ARCHITECTURE
The VAX-11

PART ONE

THE USER ARCHITECTURE

Chapter 1

Architecture and Implementation

There are two major levels at which we usually examine any computer system: architecture and implementation. It is important to understand the distinction, since we often refer to these terms.

The *architecture* of a computer system is the user-visible interface: the structure and operation of the system as seen by the programmer. *Implementation* is the construction of that interface and structure from specific hardware (and possibly software) components. There can be several different implementations of an architecture, each using different components, but each providing exactly the same interface to the user.

For example, let's examine the architecture of a piano. The definition of a piano's architecture is the specification of the keyboard, as shown in Figure 1-1a. The keyboard is the user (player) interface to the instrument. It consists of 88 keys, 36 black keys and 52 white keys. Striking a key causes a note of a specified frequency to be played. The size and arrangement of the keys are identical for all piano keyboards. Therefore, anyone who can play the piano can play any piano.

There are many implementations of the piano, as shown in Figure 1-1b. The implementation is concerned with the materials used to build the instrument. The kinds of wood used, the selection of ivory or plastic keys, the shape of the instrument, and so forth, are all implementation decisions made by the piano builder. Regardless of the implementation decisions made, however, the final product can be played by any piano player.

3

a.   Piano keyboard architecture.

b.   Piano implementations.

Figure 1-1.   Architecture and implementation of the piano.

In a computer system, the architecture consists of the programming interface: the instruction set, the structure and addressing of memory, the control of I/O devices, etc. There can be several implementations of an architecture, for example, one with vacuum tubes, one with transistors, and one with large scale integrated circuits. Clearly, each of these implementations would have different size, cost, and performance characteristics. However, a program that runs on one machine would run on all of the machines following the architecture.

ORGANIZATION OF THE BOOK

In this book, we deal primarily with the architecture of one computer system: the VAX-11. A typical VAX-11 configuration is shown in Figure 1-2. We learn about the VAX-11 architecture by using it, and to use it we must become assembly language programmers. As assembly language programmers, we learn how to directly control the operation of the hardware system. We also gain a better understanding of how high level language programs are translated by the compiler and executed.

Figure 1-2.   Typical VAX-11 computer system.

The first half of this book, then, develops the basics of assembly language programming on the VAX-11. First, the elementary concepts of processors, memories, and instruction execution are introduced. Later we develop the more sophisticated addressing techniques, and build an instruction repertoire suitable for problem solving. Then, we see how the VAX-11 instruction set is used to manipulate more complex data structures.

Later, we use the concepts developed through the VAX-11 to examine the instruction set architectures of three other machines: the IBM 360/370, the Control Data Corporation Cyber, and the IBM Series 1. This material provides an interesting basis for comparison and helps solidify the material already learned.

Finally, the last part of the book deals with the VAX-11 architectural features used by the operating system. We show how the VAX-11 supports the resource management activities of the operating system, and how the VAX/VMS operating system uses these facilities. In the last chapter, we examine the implementation of the VAX-11, and the choices available to the hardware designer in producing a cost-effective machine.

REVIEW OF NUMBER SYSTEMS

Before beginning our examination of computer structures, it is worthwhile to review the basics of number systems. Throughout the book we will use numbers in decimal, binary, and hexadecimal number systems. Therefore, the reader should be comfortable with these representations, and with converting from one to the other. However, some readers may wish to skip this section. For those who need additional reading in this area, references are provided at the end of the chapter.

Number Systems

All data stored within the computer are represented in binary form. However, when dealing with the contents of computer memory, we usually represent the contents using base 8, 10, or 16. The value of a unit is the same regardless of the base used to represent it; however, different bases are suitable for different applications. In particular, bases 8 (*octal*) and 16 (*hexadecimal* or hex) are useful for looking for patterns of bits within a word, while base 10 is useful for understanding the *decimal* value of a word.

In the weighted numbering system, the value of a numeral depends upon its position in a number; for example, in base 10:

$$
\begin{aligned}
347 = 3 \times 100 &= 300 \\
+ 4 \times 10 &= 40 \\
+ 7 \times 1 &= \underline{7} \\
&347
\end{aligned}
$$

The value of each position in a number is its *positional coefficient*. The second factor or power of the base is called the digit-position weighting value, weighting value, or simply *weight*.

Using the positional coefficients and weighting values, we can express any weighted number system in the following generalized form:

$$X = x_n w_n + x_{n-1} w_{n-1} + \ldots + x_1 w_1 + x_0 w_0 + x_{-1} w_{-1} + \ldots + x_{-m} w_{-m}$$

where

$$w_i = r^i \, (r^i = \text{weighting values and } r = \text{radix or base})$$

and

$$0 \leqslant x_i \leqslant r - 1 \, (x = \text{positional coefficients})$$

This formalism makes it clear that the largest value of a positional coefficient is always one less than the base value. Thus, for base 2 (binary) the largest coefficient is one; for base 10 (decimal) it is nine. Although this may seem intuitively obvious, it is not uncommon for the novice programmer and even some old-timers to write illegal numbers while coding programs, for instance, 10853 in base 8 or 102 in base 2. Equally confusing are bases greater than 10, in which positional coefficients are denoted by letters rather than numbers. In hexadecimal, for example, the letters A through F are used to represent the numerical values 10 through 15, respectively.

Examples of writing the full formal expressions for weighted number systems follow:

$$140 = 1 \times 10^2 + 4 \times 10^1 + 0 \times 10^0 \text{ (base 10)}$$

$$= 1 \times 2^7 + 0 \times 2^6 + 0 \times 2^5 + 0 \times 2^4 + 1 \times 2^3 + 1 \times 2^2 + 0 \times 2^1$$
$$+ 0 \times 2^0 \text{ (base 2)}$$

$$= 2 \times 8^2 + 1 \times 8^1 + 4 \times 8^0 \text{ (base 8)}$$

$$= 8 \times 16^1 + C \times 16^0 \text{ (base 16)}$$

In other words,

$$140_{10} = 10001100_2 = 214_8 = 8C_{16}$$

Although these examples assume a positive radix, negative radices are also possible. For example, assuming a radix of –3, the value 140 may be expressed as

$$140_{10} = 2 \times (-3)^4 + 1 \times (-3)^3 + 1 \times (-3)^2 + 2 \times (-3)^1 + 2 \times (-3)^0$$

$$= 21122_{-3}$$

It is even possible to conceive of non-weighted number systems—and such systems do exist—such as "Excess – 3" and "2 out of 5," but discussion of these systems is beyond the scope of this book.

Binary and Hexadecimal Representation

Because of the inherent binary nature of computer components, all modern digital computers are based on the binary number system. However, no matter how convenient the binary system may be for computers, it is exceedingly cumbersome for human beings. Consequently, most computer programmers use base 8 or base 16 representations instead, leaving it to the various system components—assemblers, compilers, loaders, etc.—to convert such numbers to their binary equivalents. Modern assemblers also permit decimal numbers, both integer and real (floating-point), to be input directly, a useful convenience for most applications programs.

Base 8 or octal and base 16 or hexadecimal representations of binary numbers are not only convenient but also easily derived. Conversion simply requires the programmer to separate the binary number into 3-bit (octal) or 4-bit (hexadecimal) groups, starting with the least significant digit and replacing each binary group with its equivalent. Thus, for the binary number 010011100001,

$$010 \quad 011 \quad 100 \quad 001_2 = 2341_8$$

and

$$0100 \quad 1110 \quad 0001_2 = 4E1_{16}$$

This process is performed so naturally that most programmers can mentally convert visual representations of binary numbers (computer displays) to their octal or hexadecimal representation without conscious effort. Special pocket calculators that operate in both octal and hexadecimal are available for use as an aid in debugging programs. Fortunately, the tools of the assembly language programmer, the program listings, linker maps (showing the locations of variables and modules), and dumps (displays of the contents of memory), are expressed in at least octal or hexadecimal. The programmer need not be concerned with bits and binary numbers unless he or she chooses to be. However, when examining the bit patterns that make up the different data elements within the computer, the programmer has no alternative. In the next section, we examine these patterns.

Negative Numbers

For any base, there are three common ways to represent negative numbers. Negative binary numbers, for example, can be represented in *sign magnitude, one's complement,* or *two's complement* form. One might ask, therefore, which form a computer would use in performing arithmetic calculations.

Sign magnitude numbers are represented by treating the most significant bit as the sign bit, and the remaining bits as the magnitude. Therefore the 6-bit representation of ± 18 would be:

$$+18_{10} \quad 010010_2$$
$$-18_{10} \quad 110010_2$$

Addition and subtraction require a consideration of both the signs of the numbers to be added as well as the relative magnitudes in order to carry out the required operation.

Complement form for negative numbers takes advantage of the continuum of representation. While the most significant bit remains the sign bit, the representation of the magnitude is different for negative and positive numbers. The one's complement representation is formed by taking the positive number and inverting all the bits. The two's complement representation is formed by adding one to the one's complement representation. For example, the 6-bit representations of ± 18 are:

$$+18_{10} \quad 010010_2$$
$$-18_{10} \quad 101101_2 \quad \text{One's complement form}$$
$$-18_{10} \quad 101110_2 \quad \text{Two's complement form}$$

Sign magnitude form is rejected in favor of complement form because it is more complex to add or subtract numbers using sign magnitude arithmetic. Thus, the choice of form for negative binary numbers is really between one's and two's complement representations. In reality, this choice is frequently one of the designer's preference. Generating one's complement numbers is easier than generating the two's complement form. Moreover, from the computer hardware point of view, it is more "uniform" to build a one's than a two's complement adder. On the other hand, one's complement notation has two representations of zero, both a positive and a negative zero:

$$0000 \quad 0000_2 \quad \text{Zero}$$
$$1111 \quad 1111_2 \quad \text{Minus zero in one's complement}$$

whereas only one zero exists in two's complement form:

$$0000 \quad 0000_2 \quad \text{Zero}$$
$$1111 \quad 1111_2 \quad \text{One's complement}$$
$$+1 \quad \text{Plus one}$$

discarded → 1) $0000 \quad 0000_2$ Two's complement of zero

Mathematically speaking, it is inconvenient to have two representations for zero. It is also more difficult to test for zero, an operation performed frequently on computers. As a result, most machines today use two's complement notation to represent negative numbers.

Forming the complement of a hexadecimal number may seem strange at first. Compared with binary, where one simply "inverts" the bits, hexadecimal complementation requires a subtraction (and an addition of one for the two's complement result). For example,

3C8E	Original number
B271	One's complement
+1	
B272	Two's complement

Fortunately, as with all such techniques, familiarity comes with use.

After this brief digression, we can now turn our attention to the general structure of computer systems and the architecture of the VAX-11. We will find that an understanding of hexadecimal and binary number systems is helpful to our understanding of computer concepts.

REFERENCES

The material of this chapter is rather general in nature and may be supplemented by reading Eckhouse and Morris (1979) and Foster (1976) for a discussion of number systems. Number systems are also covered in Ralston's book (1971) and a concise history of computing can be found there. More about computer architecture and organization can be found in the several books by Bell et al (1971, 1979), Burr and Smith (1977), Foster (1976), Hamacher et al (1978), Hellerman (1973), Stone (1975) and Tannenbaum (1976). Strecker's article (1978) and the book by Bell, Mudge, and McNamara give a concise history of the PDP-11 and the evolution of the VAX-11/780.

EXERCISES FOR CHAPTER 1

1. Describe the architecture of a typewriter. What parts of the typewriter are not part of the architecture? What are some implementation differences among different typewriters?

2. Why do you think that it is important to precisely define a computer's architecture?

3.   Why do you think that different computer manufacturers build computers with different architectures? What does this imply about the importance of high level languages? Why is there a need for standardizing high level languages?

4.   What range of integers can be represented in a 12-digit unsigned binary number? In a 12-digit two's complement signed number?

5.   Is 10234 a legal value in base 8? base 16? base 5? base 4? Express the value 10234_5 in base -3.

6.   Convert 101010101_2 into hexadecimal and octal. Convert $10A34_{16}$ into octal and decimal. Convert both values into their binary two's complement form.

Chapter 2

Computer Structures and Elementary VAX-11 Programming

Depending on the nature of the application and the language chosen, programming a computer requires different levels of understanding. For most programmers writing in Pascal, for example, the computer appears to be a machine that executes Pascal statements and manipulates high level data structures. The structure of the underlying hardware is invisible.

In this chapter, we will introduce the fundamentals needed by the assembly language programmer. To program at the assembly level, we need a thorough understanding of the structure of a computer system, the process of program execution, and the nature of memory addressing. Once we have this foundation, we can begin to focus on the basics of instructions and elementary programming for a particular machine.

COMPUTER STRUCTURES

Most general purpose computers have the same basic structure, consisting of the high speed primary *memory*, the arithmetic and control unit (typically called the *central processing unit* or CPU), and the peripheral *input* and *output* devices (the I/O system). One or more *buses* (described in more detail later) move data between these components. Although there are other components of interest, these are the units that are directly visible to the machine-level programmer and are part of the user architecture. Figure 2-1 shows an organizational representation of this basic structure.

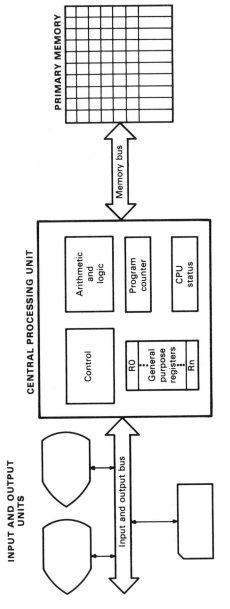

Figure 2-1.   Basic computer structure.

The Memory

The memory of a computer is a repository for both instructions and data. Memory may be implemented by any device that can retain two or more distinguishable states that can be set and sensed. All common memories are composed of two-state devices that can be used to represent the values zero and one. Hence, each device—such as a magnetic core, a semiconductor flip-flop, or a two-sided coin—can represent one binary digit, or *bit*.

Bits in memory are arranged as an array of information units with each information unit composed of a fixed number of bits. Each information unit resides in a distinct location in memory, and each location is capable of holding one such unit, as shown in Figure 2-2.

All memories share two organizational features:

1. Each information unit is the same size.

2. An information unit has a numbered address associated with it by which it can be uniquely referenced.

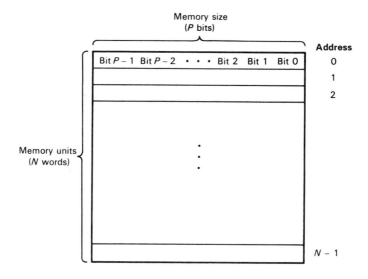

Figure 2-2.   Memory organization.

Thus, we say that a memory unit is characterized by two things:

1. An *address*, which is its relative position in memory.

2. The *contents*, which is a number that is physically stored at the particular location in memory.

As Figure 2-3 shows, memory can be viewed as a large one-dimensional array, $M(i)$, where each element of the array contains one unit (word) of information. The index, i, is the address of the unit. Using its address, we can determine the contents of any unit. However, it is important to remember the difference between the address of a unit, i, and the contents of the unit, $M(i)$.

When a computer is designed, the size of its information units is chosen according to the applications for which the computer is intended. On many machines, each information unit is known as a *word*. Word sizes typically range from 8 bits on microprocessors to 64 bits on large computers. A word is usually divided into a number of *bytes*; each byte can represent one character. Machines designed for administrative data processing, in which information to be processed includes names and English letters as well as numbers, are often *byte addressable*. In these machines the byte is the basic

Array M	Address (index)	Contents
M (0)	0	M (0)
M (1)	1	M (1)
. . .		
M (i)	i	M (i)
. . .		
M ($N-1$)	$N-1$	M ($N-1$)

Figure 2-3. Memory as an array.

information unit, and each byte has a unique address by which it can be accessed. On the other hand, *word addressable* machines are generally used for scientific calculations in which large numbers are manipulated and precise numerical results are required.

The key difference between byte and word machines is the size of the smallest addressable information unit. For a byte machine, this unit is one byte, that is, a unit of information capable of holding a small number or representing a letter of the alphabet or digit. For a word machine, the smallest addressable unit is one word, a unit of information capable of holding several characters or a large number. Words can often be subdivided into a fixed number of characters or digits. In a true word machine, however, we can reference only the collection, not the individual characters. Thus, the value of the subdivision is its storage efficiency.

The *address space* is the set of all addresses, or the number of distinct information units that a program can reference. The size of the address space is determined by the number of bits used to represent an address. An address is usually less than or equal to the word size for a given machine. Minicomputers have typically used 16-bit addresses, yielding 2^{16} or 65,536 unique memory locations. However, programmers quickly discovered that 16 bits of address were insufficient for representing large data structures or solving complex problems. The VAX-11, with 32-bit addresses, allows for a memory address space of 2^{32} or 4,294,967,296 unique addresses and therefore for much larger programs and data structures.

The Central Processing Unit

The central processing unit is the brain of the computer. The CPU is capable of fetching data from and storing data into memory. It requests instructions from memory and executes them, performing arithmetic and logic operations specified by the instructions. The CPU can manipulate addresses as well as data. In addition, the processor can examine a memory location and follow different program paths depending on its value. Finally, the CPU can execute instructions that initiate input and output operations on peripheral devices.

Internal to the CPU are a number of *registers* that provide local, high speed storage for the processor. These registers can be used to hold program data and to address memory. Some computers have different sets of registers to perform different functions, for example, to address arrays or to represent floating-point numbers; others have general purpose registers that can be used for any function.

Also internal to the CPU are one or more status words that describe the state of the processor, the instruction being processed, any special conditions that have occurred, and the actions to take for special conditions.

Instruction Execution

A computer is controlled by a *program*, which is composed of a sequence of *instructions*. Each instruction specifies a single operation to be performed by the CPU. Instructions can be classified in several basic categories:

1. *Data movement* instructions move data from one location in memory to another, or between memory and I/O devices.

2. *Arithmetic* instructions perform arithmetic operations on the contents of one or more memory locations, e.g., add the contents of two locations together, increment the contents of a location.

3. *Logical* instructions perform logic operations such as AND, OR, EXCLUSIVE OR.

4. *Comparative* instructions examine the contents of a location or compare the contents of two memory locations.

5. *Control* instructions change the dynamic execution of a sequence of instructions by causing program execution to be transferred to a specified instruction, either unconditionally or based on the result of a comparative, arithmetic, or logical instruction.

Instructions are stored in memory along with the data on which they operate. The processor fetches an instruction from memory, interprets what function is to be performed, and executes the function on its operands. Each computer has its own representation of instructions, but all instructions are composed of two basic components:

1. An *operation code* (opcode) that specifies the function to be performed, e.g., Add, Subtract, Compare.

2. One or more *operand specifiers* that describe the locations of the information units on which the operation is performed. These information units are the *operands* of the instruction.

An instruction in memory can occupy several consecutive words (or bytes): one for the operation code and, optionally, several more for the operand addresses. For instance, an instruction to add the contents of memory location 100 to memory location 200, shown symbolically as

ADD   100,200

may be represented in computer memory as follows:

ADD operation code	Instruction word 0 (opcode)
100	Instruction word 1 (first operand address)
200	Instruction word 2 (second operand address)

.
<next instruction>
.
.

The processor executes a program by fetching and interpreting instructions. The location (memory address) of the next instruction to be executed is held in a special internal CPU register called the *program counter* (PC). When the program is loaded into memory, the PC is loaded with the address of the first instruction. Using the PC, the CPU fetches this instruction, along with any operand specifiers. The operands themselves are then fetched, the operation is performed, and any results generated are stored back in memory. Figure 2-4 shows the complete cycle of fetching, interpreting, and executing an instruction.

Note that each time an instruction is fetched, the PC is modified to point to the next instruction. Thus, the processor executes instructions one after another. Some instructions, like "branch" (the machine-level GO TO), affect the flow of control by explicitly changing the contents of the PC so that a new location, not the next one in sequence, is taken to be the one containing the next instruction to be executed. Otherwise, instructions are fetched and executed sequentially from memory.

A computer program, then, consists of two parts: instructions and data. When loaded into memory, each instruction and each data element is located at a unique address. Looking at the program as a string of words or bytes, we are unable to differentiate data from instructions because both are

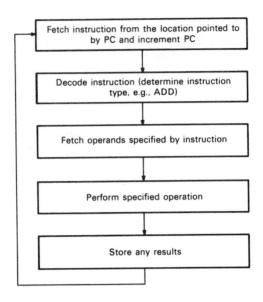

Figure 2-4.   Instruction execution.

merely strings of numbers coded in binary. We are also unable to differentiate data-types because integers, floating-point numbers, character strings, etc. are represented as strings of binary numbers, too. Only in context does the program have meaning.

The key to making sense of the string of numbers representing a program is the starting address of that program, since this tells the CPU where to find the first instruction to execute. The first instruction in the program can be located anywhere in the memory of the computer. The programmer specifies the starting address of the program by means of a directive to the language translator or the program loader. (In a high level language, this is the main program or procedure.) When the operating system loads the program into memory, it transfers control to this initial instruction by making sure that the initial contents of the PC "point to" the address of the starting instruction. As each instruction and operand is fetched in sequence, the PC is incremented so that it points to the next byte or word to be fetched.

The Input/Output System

Connected to the processor and memory are several input and output devices. The I/O devices allow the processor to communicate with humans, with other processors, and with secondary storage devices that are slower than main memory but larger in capacity.

The most common devices are magnetic tapes, magnetic disks, terminals, and line printers. Magnetic tapes and disks provide large online or backup storage for programs and data. These devices are usually capable of transferring large blocks of data directly to primary memory. In contrast, the processor must feed or retrieve one character at a time to or from most terminal devices.

Because all these devices are slow compared to the execution speed of a modern CPU, the systems are designed to overlap processing with I/O. That is, the processor begins an I/O operation on a device and then continues executing program instructions. Later, the processor can check at a convenient time to see if the operation is complete, or the device can signal when it is done.

One or more data buses can be used to interconnect the CPU, memory, and I/O devices. Early minicomputers had two (or more) buses, one to connect the memory to the CPU, another to connect I/O devices to the CPU. A later refinement was embodied in the PDP-11 Unibus, which used only one bus for all transfers between I/O devices, memory, and the CPU. Figure 2-5 shows some alternatives in the interconnection of the CPU, memory, and I/O devices.

Whether there is one bus or several, the purpose remains the same: to carry address, data, and control signals between the devices connected to the bus. The address and control signals specify the device and function to be performed on the data. The bus is like a common highway for computer information flow. Any device connected to it can place information onto the highway; conversely, any can take information from it. The bus thus provides an efficient means for passing information between the functional units connected to it.

INTRODUCTION TO THE VAX-11

The VAX-11 is a general purpose digital computer. The VAX machine was designed to extend the addressing capabilities of the PDP-11, hence the name VAX for Virtual Address eXtension. Although some VAX-11 instructions resemble those of the PDP-11, the VAX-11 is an entirely new system architecture.

Because both software and hardware engineers designed the VAX-11, the VAX architecture contains many high level features that support operating systems and compiler code generation. The VAX-11 instruction set currently includes over 240 instructions, and over 20 formats for operand

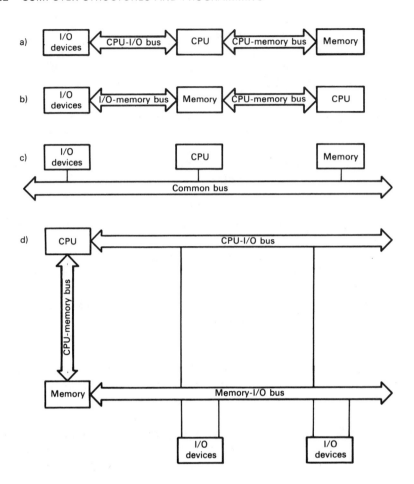

Figure 2-5. Alternative bus structures.

specifiers, called addressing modes. This flexibility enables the programmer to select instruction and addressing combinations that are both space- and time-efficient. Thus, algorithms implemented with the VAX-11 instruction set architecture are generally compact (compared to the same algorithm implemented on other architectures, including the PDP-11), and fast (compared to programs running on other machines using the same hardware technology).

Figure 2-6 shows the organizational structure of the VAX-11/780 computer system, the first implementation of the VAX-11 architecture. While

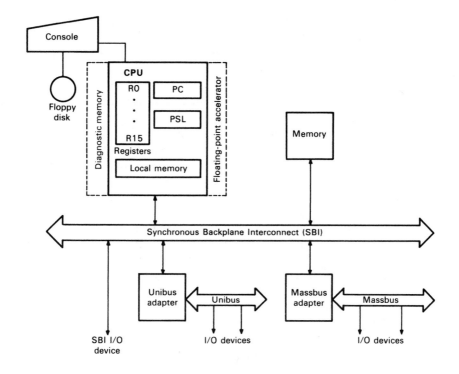

Figure 2-6.   VAX-11/780 organizational structure.

resembling the structure of the general computer shown in Figure 2-1, the VAX-11 is somewhat "richer" in that additional components serve to increase its capabilities and speed. Some of these components, such as the floating-point accelerator that increases the speed of some VAX-11 instructions, do not affect the way the machine is programmed. Such components are said to be *transparent* to the programs that execute on the machine. As part of the hardware implementation, these will be covered in a later chapter. However, here we will briefly describe those components that concern the programmer.

The VAX-11/780 CPU shown in the center of Figure 2-6 is the master controller of the VAX system. The processor contains sixteen 32-bit general purpose registers that provide high speed local storage for programs. Several of these registers have special uses, and one is used as the Program Counter. Also internal to the CPU is the 32-bit Processor Status Longword (PSL) that contains information about the processor and the current state of the program being executed. The PSL is composed of two 16-bit words. The lower 16 bits, called the Program Status Word (PSW), contain information about the user program and are accessible to the user. The upper 16 bits contain privileged processor information and can be modified only by the operating system. Thus, the user program can examine and change program state information, but processor state is protected from user modification.

The common bus connecting the CPU, memory, and I/O buses is called the Synchronous Backplane Interconnect (SBI). Through this bus, all input and output devices are connected so that they can communicate with each other, as well as with the CPU and memory. Indeed, it is possible for I/O devices to send and receive data between themselves and memory without processor intervention.

Special *controllers* are used to attach devices other than the CPU to the SBI. These controllers interpret the SBI bus signals for proper data flow. For example, through the SBI, the memory controllers allow the CPU to access up to 8 million bytes of main memory. In addition, the controller forces the memory to read and write 64 bits of data at a time. Each memory controller can also buffer up to four memory requests. With this buffering, the CPU can issue a write request and continue processing without waiting for the write to complete. A memory controller is a specialized device that serves both to connect memory to the SBI and to use memory efficiently.

In a complementary way, the Massbus and Unibus adapters are controllers that connect existing, standard I/O equipment to the SBI in an efficient manner. These adapters allow existing devices to be connected to the VAX-11 system without change, thereby offering benefits in development cost and time. Devices can thus be made immediately available for a new machine by providing an interface between the new computer bus and the existing I/O buses. In fact, future implementations of the VAX-11 could be built with a backplane other than the SBI. As long as Massbus and Unibus adapters are developed for other backplanes, the same devices could be used on those implementations.

VAX-11 INFORMATION UNITS AND DATA-TYPES

We have already described byte addressable and word addressable machines. In the context of that discussion, it is appropriate to say that the VAX-11 is a byte-oriented computer. The basic information unit on the VAX-11 is the 8-bit byte. However, the instruction set is also capable of operating on a number of other information units formed by groups of bytes and bits. The multiple-byte units are the 16-bit *word* (two bytes), the 32-bit *longword* (four bytes), and the 64-bit *quadword* (eight bytes) shown in Figure 2-7. Each of these information units is formed by a sequence of contiguous bytes. The unit is always addressed by the low order byte of the group. Note that the bits within any information unit are numbered from the least significant bit, bit 0 on the right, to the most significant bit or leftmost bit, bit 7, 15, 31, or 63 for byte, word, longword, or quadword.

Another information unit found in the VAX-11 is the variable-length *bit field*. The bit field is different in that the basic addressable unit is based on a length measured not in bytes but in bits. A bit field can be from 0 to 32 contiguous bits in length and can be located arbitrarily with respect to the beginning of a byte. To describe a bit field, three attributes are required: (1) a *base address* (A) of a particular byte in memory chosen as a reference point for locating the bit field; (2) a *bit position* (P) that is the starting location of the field with respect to bit 0 of the base address byte; and (3) a *size* (S) giving the length of the bit field in bits. For example, Figure 2-8 shows a bit field with base address A, bit position P, and size S.

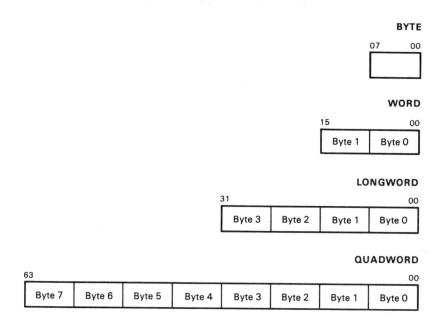

Figure 2-7.   VAX-11 information units.

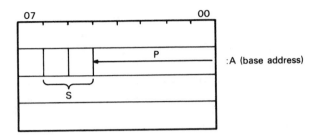

Figure 2-8.   Variable-length bit field.

Bit fields are commonly used to pack multiple information fields tightly together. For example, Boolean values (sometimes called "flags") can be packed eight per byte. In this context, bit field instructions allow the programmer to manipulate fields smaller than a byte.

The byte, word, longword, and quadword are the fundamental information units of the VAX-11. Built on these information units are *data-types*, which are interpretations of the bits contained in the units. All information units contain a string of binary digits, but a unit can represent an integer, a letter of the alphabet, a real number, and so forth. The VAX-11 processor is capable of manipulating a great variety of data-types. The choice of data-type allows the programmer (or the compiler) to produce very compact programs using those data-types most closely tailored to his or her needs. There is also a full set of instructions for converting easily from one data-type to another, which reduces the complexity of many programs.

Integers

Integers are represented as both unsigned binary numbers and two's complement signed numbers, and may be stored in byte, word, longword, or quadword elements. The choice of storage representation for an integer determines both the maximum value of the number to be stored and the efficiency of the representation (i.e., the number of bits used effectively). Table 2-1 shows the numeric range for the various integer sizes. The VAX-11 has a complete set of instructions for adding, subtracting, dividing, multiplying, complementing, and shifting integers, although quadword arithmetic is not fully supported.

A complete set of conditional *branch* instructions allows the programmer to alter the flow of control based on the result of previous arithmetic operations. Because the most significant bit of a two's complement number

Table 2-1. Integer Data-Types

Integer Type	Size	Range (Decimal)	
		Signed	Unsigned
Byte	8 bits	-128 to $+127$	0 to 255
Word	16 bits	-32768 to $+32767$	0 to 65535
Longword	32 bits	-2^{31} to $+2^{31}-1$	0 to $2^{32}-1$
Quadword	64 bits	-2^{63} to $+2^{63}-1$	0 to $2^{64}-1$

always indicates the sign, the hardware can easily test for positive or negative. The VAX-11 also has instructions for implementing arithmetic on unsigned integers larger than 64 bits (extended precision).

Floating-Point Numbers

Integers are useful for data representation and problem solution in many areas, but they often lack the dynamic range necessary for a variety of scientific applications. Although integers represent the data with sufficient precision, the magnitude of the data or intermediate results may exceed the range defined by the width of the data word. A *floating-point* number, like an integer, is a sequence of contiguous bits in memory. The bits, however, are interpreted as having two distinct parts, the *fraction* (or mantissa) and the *exponent*. That is, the floating-point number might be stored in a computer word as

S	*m*	S	*n*
	Exponent		Fraction

and is interpreted as $\pm 0.n \times 2^{\pm m}$ where *n* represents the bits in the fraction field and *m* represents the bits in the exponent field. Note that we have arbitrarily allocated two sign bits to allow positive and negative fractions and exponents. It is more common, however, to assign only one sign bit to a word. Thus, a different representation is used in which the most significant bit of the word is the sign of the fraction and the exponent is represented as a positive (*biased*) value. In other words, although the exponent is a positive number in the range 0 through *m* – 1, half of the exponent range (0 to *m*/2) is used to represent negative numbers while the other half (*m*/2 to *m* – 1) represents positive numbers.

The floating-point conventions used in the VAX-11 are based on the PDP-11 formats for reasons of compatibility. In the VAX-11, *single precision* floating-point numbers are stored within four contiguous bytes and addressed by the byte containing bit 0. Bit 15 of the longword designates the sign of the number, while an 8-bit exponent separates the high or most significant part of the fraction from its sign. The low part of the fraction is stored in the remaining 16 bits. VAX-11 single precision floating-point numbers are stored as shown:

1. The fraction is expressed as a 24-bit positive fraction, where $0.5 \leqslant$ fraction $\leqslant 1$, with binary point positioned to the left of the most significant bit. Since this bit must be 1 if the number is nonzero, it is not stored. This effectively enables the fraction to be stored in 23 bits. This form is called a *normalized* fraction.

2. The exponent is stored as a biased 8-bit positive integer. That is, when 128 is subtracted from the exponent, the result represents the power of 2 by which the fraction is multiplied to obtain the true value of the floating-point number.

3. The sign of the number is positive when S, the sign bit, is 0, and negative when $S = 1$.

A floating-point number represented by the 32-bit word is described by the equation

$$X = (1 - 2 \times S) \times \text{fraction} \times 2^{(exponent - 128)}$$

where

$$2^{-128} = 2.939 \times 10^{-39} \leqslant X < 2^{127} = 1.701 \times 10^{38}$$

The bits devoted to the fraction assure about seven decimal digits of precision; a second 32-bit word can be appended to the fraction to yield about 16 decimal digits of precision in *double precision* floating-point numbers, which require eight contiguous bytes. Note that if the exponent = 0 and $S = 0$, the number X is assumed to be 0.0 regardless of the value of the fraction.

Alphanumeric Characters

Although all information units contain binary numbers, *alphanumeric characters* can be represented by inventing a numeric code for each character. In the VAX-11, the American Standard Code for Information Interchange (*ASCII*) is used. The ASCII character set includes both upper and lower case alphabetic characters, the numerics (0–9), punctuation marks, and special control characters. Shown in Table 2-2, the ASCII code was

Table 2-2.   ASCII Character Encoding

Hex Code	ASCII Char	Hex Code	ASCII Char	Hex Code	ASCII Char	Hex Code	ASCII Char
00	NUL	20	SP	40	@	60	`
01	SOH	21	!	41	A	61	a
02	STX	22	"	42	B	62	b
03	ETX	23	#	43	C	63	c
04	EOT	24	$	44	D	64	d
05	ENQ	25	%	45	E	65	e
06	ACK	26	&	46	F	66	f
07	BEL	27	'	47	G	67	g
08	BS	28	(	48	H	68	h
09	HT	29	)	49	I	69	i
0A	LF	2A	*	4A	J	6A	j
0B	VT	2B	+	4B	K	6B	k
0C	FF	2C	,	4C	L	6C	l
0D	CR	2D	–	4D	M	6D	m
0E	SO	2E	.	4E	N	6E	n
0F	SI	2F	/	4F	O	6F	o
10	DLE	30	0	50	P	70	p
11	DC1	31	1	51	Q	71	q
12	DC2	32	2	52	R	72	r
13	DC3	33	3	53	S	73	s
14	DC4	34	4	54	T	74	t
15	NAK	35	5	55	U	75	u
16	SYN	36	6	56	V	76	v
17	ETB	37	7	57	W	77	w
18	CAN	38	8	58	X	78	x
19	EM	39	9	59	Y	79	y
1A	SUB	3A	:	5A	Z	7A	z
1B	ESC	3B	;	5B	[	7B	{
1C	FS	3C	<	5C	\	7C		
1D	GS	3D	=	5D	]	7D	}
1E	RS	3E	>	5E	^	7E	~
1F	US	3F	?	5F	—	7F	DEL

developed by the American National Standards Institute (ANSI) to allow the connection of computers and peripherals by different manufacturers. Therefore, all ASCII character-oriented peripherals, such as line printers and terminals, will output an *A* when the ASCII code for *A* is presented.

Figure 2-9 shows the ASCII representation for the alphanumeric string "VAX-11." Note that each character uses one byte of storage, or two hex digits. The string is referenced by the address of the first byte, the one containing the character *V*, at symbolic address STRING.

The VAX-11 has instructions to manipulate strings of contiguous bytes, called character string instructions. A character string has two attributes: an address and a length in bytes (or characters). On the VAX-11, character strings can be from 0 to 65,535 bytes in length.

Decimal Strings

In addition to binary representations, numbers can be represented within the computer as a string of decimal digits. Numbers are usually entered in ASCII format and converted to binary for arithmetic operations. For some applications, however, it may be more convenient to operate in a decimal format. This is often true in a business application (COBOL) environment, where programs require only simple computations.

The VAX-11 supports two forms of decimal strings. In one form known as *numeric string*, each digit occupies one byte. Numeric strings can be in *leading separate* or *trailing numeric* format depending on whether the sign appears before the first digit or superimposed on the last digit. The second decimal form, known as *packed decimal*, packs two decimal digits per byte.

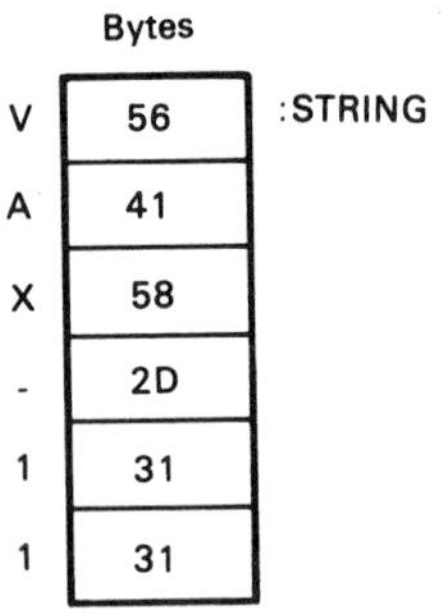

Bytes

V	56	:STRING
A	41	
X	58	
-	2D	
1	31	
1	31	

Figure 2-9. ASCII representation of the string "VAX-11."

Table 2-3.   Decimal String Representation

Digit or Sign	Decimal Value	Hex Value
0	0	0
1	1	1
2	2	2
3	3	3
4	4	4
5	5	5
6	6	6
7	7	7
8	8	8
9	9	9
+	12	C
−	13	D

Table 2-3 shows the format for a packed decimal string. A packed decimal string is composed of a sequence of bytes in memory, with each byte divided into two 4-bit *nibbles*. Each nibble contains a representation for one of the decimal digits. The last nibble contains a representation of the sign of the number. For example, the packed decimal string representation for the number −11780 is shown in Figure 2-10.

A decimal string is specified by two attributes: the address of the first byte of the string (shown as DECIMAL in Figure 2-10) and the length specified as the number of digits (not bytes) in the string. The VAX-11 has instructions to perform arithmetic operations on decimal strings and to convert decimal strings to other formats. For some simple operations on

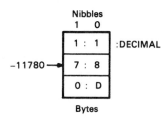

Figure 2-10.   Decimal string representation of −11780.

numbers entered in ASCII, it is easy and efficient to convert from ASCII to a decimal string, perform the operation, and convert back to ASCII for output.

Data-Type Summary

We have reviewed a number of ways to represent information within a computer. Although only binary values are contained in memory, we can place almost any interpretation we wish on the contents because the computer instruction set recognizes and operates on a number of interpretations. Selecting the correct representation depends on the intended application and its requirements. Figure 2-11 shows the data-types supported by the VAX-11.

Interestingly, we can take the same information and represent it in many different ways. Figure 2-12 shows how the number 11780 can be represented by four different data-types: packed decimal string, longword integer, single floating, and ASCII string. Each representation is shown as a string of hexadecimal bytes.

In the same way that we represent alphabetic letters by encoding them, we can also encode machine instructions. However, we would still refer to the machine instructions by their binary codes if it were not for the symbolic assembler that lets us use memory assisting names, or *mnemonics*, in place of

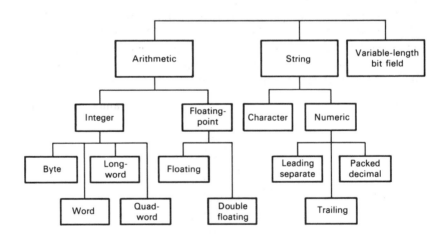

Figure 2-11.   VAX-11 data-types.

the codes. In Chapter 3, we will look at the actual VAX-11 encodings. For now, however, it is only necessary to understand the basic instructions in their symbolic form.

USING ASSEMBLY LANGUAGE

You are probably familiar with one or more high level languages such as Pascal, FORTRAN, or PL/I. For these languages, programs are coded in an algebraic English-like style. A language translation program called a *compiler* reads the high level language program (called the *source* program) and translates it into a machine language program (called the *object* program). Because the language can express concepts not directly executable by the computer hardware, the compiler often generates many machine instructions for a single source language statement.

One major advantage of high level languages, besides the ease with which they can express algorithms, is their machine independence. They hide the specifics of the hardware machine and instruction set. Nonetheless, there are still a number of reasons why understanding machine language programming is valuable. First, it gives us a better appreciation for computer architecture and the way a computer functions. Understanding how

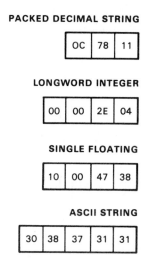

Figure 2-12.   Representations of the number 11780.

the hardware works allows us to write better high level language programs. Second, there are still a few applications, usually involving careful manipulation of specific hardware features of a particular computer, for which the machine language level of programming is required. For example, the parts of an operating system that manage memory and input/output devices may be written in machine language. If one's goal is to develop a basic understanding of the machine, then a knowledge of machine language is worthwhile.

Of course, we would not want to code instructions for a computer in their binary machine language form for several reasons. The chance of making errors would be extremely high because binary is inconvenient to use. In addition, since instructions specify operand addresses, inserting an extra instruction or data item would change the ordering of all succeeding addresses, requiring massive changes to those instructions referencing them within the modified program.

Assembly language solves these problems by allowing us to specify machine operations using symbolic names for memory locations and instructions. A program called the *assembler* translates the assembly language program into binary machine code, just as the compiler translates the high level source program into binary machine code. The assembler does all the work of remembering the values of symbols and the addresses of data elements. However, unlike the high level language, each assembly language instruction corresponds to exactly one machine instruction.

Assembler Statement Types

The process of programming in assembly language is one of using imperative, declarative, and control statements to specify both what is to be produced and how it is to be produced.

1.   *Imperative* statements are the actual machine instructions in symbolic form (e.g., ADD for the add instruction, CMP for the compare instruction, MOV for the move instruction).

2.   *Declarative* statements are used to control assignment of storage for various names, input/output, and working areas. These are not really instructions but rather are reservations of space, definitions of symbols, and assignments of contents to locations (e.g., .LONG to initialize a longword, .BLKW to reserve a block of words).

3. *Control* statements are instructions directed to the assembler to allow the programmer to have some control over portions of the assembly process.

We will use these statement types casually in the following discussion without giving careful definitions or precise meanings. Basically, we are concerned with understanding computer architecture and organization and will therefore leave the actual details of assembly language programming to the *VAX-11 Macro Language Reference Manual.*

VAX-11 Instruction Format

A VAX-11 instruction is specified by an operation code and from zero to six operand specifiers. The assembly language format of an instruction is

```
LABEL:  OPCODE SPECIFIER1,SPECIFIER2,...        ; COMMENT
```

where

1. LABEL is an alphanumeric symbol that can be used to refer to the address of the instruction.

2. OPCODE is a mnemonic (symbolic name) for one of the VAX-11 instructions.

3. SPECIFIER is the symbolic name or specification for the address of an operand.

4. COMMENT is an English language description of the function of the instruction.

The label and comment fields are optional, and the number of required specifiers is determined by the opcode.

To understand the form of VAX-11 instructions and to prepare for the addressing fundamentals of Chapter 3, a simple subset of the VAX-11 instruction set is given in Table 2-4. These instructions, the ones most commonly used by beginning programmers, include one-, two-, and three-operand instructions.

To understand how instructions operate, it will be helpful to examine a simple longword Add instruction that sums two 32-bit longwords in memory. We can specify the locations of the operands to be added by their addresses. For instance, the instruction

```
ADDL   200,204
```

causes the longword stored at location 200 to be added to the longword stored at location 204. The result for two-operand arithmetic instructions is always stored at the second operand address. That is, the contents of location 204 are modified by this instruction.

Suppose that memory locations 200 and 204 contain the following values before the execution of the ADDL instruction:

Address	Contents
200	1765
204	23
208	152

Table 2-4. Simple VAX-11 Instructions

Name	Symbolic Form		Operation
Move Longword	MOVL	A,B	Copy the contents of the longword at address A into the longword at address B.
Move Address of Longword	MOVAL	A,B	Move the address of longword A into the longword at address B.
Clear Longword	CLRL	A	Zero the longword at address A.
Add Longwords	ADDL	A,B	Sum the longwords at locations A and B and store the result in B.
Add Longwords (3 operands)	ADDL3	A,B,C	Sum the longwords at locations A and B and store the result in the longword at address C.
Subtract	SUBL	A,B	Subtract the longword at address A from the longword at address B, storing the result in location B.
Increment	INCL	A	Add one to the longword at address A.
Decrement	DECL	A	Subtract one from the longword at address A.
Compare	CMPL	A,B	Compare the longwords at locations A and B. This evaluates the quantity $(B) - (A)$.

Following the execution of ADDL 200,204 instruction, the contents of memory will appear as follows:

Address	Contents
200	1765
204	1788
208	152

The VAX-11 also allows three-operand forms of most arithmetic operations. If we wish to preserve the contents of locations 200 and 204 and store the results in location 208, we would instead code

```
ADDL3   200,204,208
```

Table 2-4.   Simple VAX-11 Instructions (Cont.)

Name	Symbolic Form	Operation
Test	TSTL A	Evaluate the longword at location A. This compares the contents of A to zero.
Branch Equal	BEQL X	Branch to X if the result of an arithmetic operation, compare, or test was equal to zero.
Branch Not Equal	BNEQ X	Branch if the result was not equal to zero.
Branch Less Than	BLSS X	Branch if the result was less than zero.
Branch Less Than or Equal	BLEQ X	Branch if the result was less than or equal to zero.
Branch Greater Than	BGTR X	Branch if the result was greater than zero.
Branch Greater Than or Equal	BGEQ X	Branch if the result was greater than or equal to zero.
Jump	JMP X	Branch unconditionally to location X.

Following the execution of this instruction, the contents of memory would appear as follows:

Address	Contents
200	1765
204	23
208	1788

We usually do not specify addresses numerically. Instead, we assign symbolic names to the data locations and let the assembler keep track of the numeric values. A symbolic name is created by labelling a particular line of code or data. The resulting symbolic address, or label, provides a means of referencing the location.

In VAX-11 Macro, the assembly language for the VAX-11, the notation LABEL: at the beginning of a line creates a symbol and equates it to the address of that statement. VAX-11 Macro also has declarative statements, called pseudo-operations or *pseudo-ops* because they do not generate instructions, that allocate and initialize data locations. For example, the statement

```
A:      .LONG   5
```

causes the assembler to allocate a 32-bit longword of memory and initialize it with the value 5. The symbol A is given the value of the address of the longword.

Using symbolic labels, the previous Add example could be coded as shown below:

Address	Assembly Statement		
200	A:	.LONG	1765
204	B:	.LONG	23
208	C:	.LONG	152
.		.	
.			
.		.	
400		ADDL3	A,B,C

The addresses shown to the left appear only for the sake of this example and are not part of the instructions coded by the programmer. The assembler does all the work of remembering addresses, providing the programmer with a symbolic way to reference them.

It is important to remember that the symbols A, B, and C represent the *addresses* of three longwords, not the values stored there. The value of the symbol A in the preceding example is 200, while the value of the longword stored at location 200 is 1765. This is quite different from the concept of a symbol A in most high level languages where the symbol and its value are synonymous. When programming in assembly language, always keep in mind the distinction between an address and the data stored at that address.

THE FUNCTIONS OF A SYMBOLIC ASSEMBLER

As we have said, the VAX-11 assembler performs the clerical task of translating the symbolic assembly language program into the binary machine language program. To translate a symbolic assembly program, the assembler performs the following functions:

1. It generates a *symbol table* containing the values of all user-defined labels and symbols.

2. It maintains a *location counter* that tells where the next instruction or data item will be placed in memory.

3. It translates the symbolic instruction names and operand specifiers into binary machine code (called the *object program*).

4. It produces a listing for the programmer, showing the instructions and data and how they are translated and assigned to unique memory locations.

To understand how an assembler works, it is most helpful to look at the mechanisms it utilizes in performing the translation process. These mechanisms include the location counter, the definition and use of symbols, storage allocation, expression evaluation, and control statements.

The Location Counter

Programs are generally written on the assumption that successive instructions are stored in successive memory locations. While it is common to have decision statements or instructions that alter the flow of control from one statement to the next, programmers normally write blocks of statements in which the implicit flow of control is sequential. Consequently, most instructions do not include an address field in which the address of the next instruction to be executed is given.

Since it is implied that instructions are to be executed in sequence, they must be stored that way in memory. Then, when the program counter is automatically incremented between instructions, it necessarily points to the next instruction in memory that is to be executed after the previous one is completed. Analogous to the CPU's program counter, the assembler maintains a location counter to keep track of where the next byte of instruction or data will be placed.

The assembler usually assumes that the first byte of a program will be placed in the first location of memory, e.g., at address zero. As the assembler reads instruction and data specifications from the source program, it translates and outputs each byte to the object program. The location counter is incremented as each byte is output; thus, it always points to the address at which the next byte will be placed.

In VAX-11 Macro, the period (.) is the symbol for the location counter. When used in the operand field of an assembler directive, it represents the address of the current byte. For example,

```
MANGO:  .LONG   .                    ; refers to location MANGO
```

causes the assembler to place the address of the location MANGO in the longword at MANGO. In general, it is preferable to use labels rather than to reference bytes through the location counter because the resulting program is easier to read and because the use of the period can lead to errors. For example, the statements

```
MANGO:  .LONG   MANGO
        .LONG   MANGO
```

and

```
MANGO:  .LONG   .
        .LONG   .
```

are not equivalent. In the first set, both longwords are initialized to the address of MANGO. In the second set, the second longword refers to its own address which is MANGO+4.

Symbols

A symbol is a string of alphanumeric characters. It can contain any of the characters of the alphabet (both upper and lower case), the digits 0 through 9, and the special symbols period (.), underline (__), and dollar sign ($). A symbol can be up to 15 characters long, e.g., A__LONG__SYMBOL, but its first character can not be a digit.

A symbol can be defined in two ways. First, a symbol is defined when it is used as a label. For example, the source line

```
OAK:    SUBL    LEAF,TREE               ; defoliate
```

defines the symbol OAK. The assembler equates OAK with the address at which the instruction will be assembled, i.e., the value of the location counter.

The second way a symbol is defined is by direct assignment using the equal sign (=). For example, the statements

```
SIX = 6
COUNT = 50
ARRAYSIZE = 100
```

equate the symbols with the specified values. Such assignments are provided for programming convenience and documentation. They do not generate any machine code.

Symbols that are defined as labels (by following them with a :) or by direct assignment (by equating them with a value through the = sign) are local to the program in which they are defined. To specify a symbol that can be referenced globally (i.e., outside of the current program), the notations :: and == are used.

Constants

The assembler interprets all constants as decimal integers. However, a unary operator can be used to specify a constant in another radix or representation, as shown in Table 2-5. For example, the statement

```
BYTE_OF_ONES = ^XFF
```

equates the symbol BYTE—OF—ONES to hexadecimal value FF. To define an ASCII constant, a delimiter character must be placed before and after the string. All of the statements

```
ABC = ^A/ABC/
ABC = ^A.ABC.
ABC = ^ADABCD
```

equate the symbol ABC to the ASCII equivalent of the three characters ABC.

Table 2-5.   Assembler Unary Operators

Operator	Representation
^ B	Binary
^ D	Decimal
^ O	Octal
^ X	Hexadecimal
^ A	ASCII
^ F	Floating-Point

Storage Allocation

The allocation of storage for data is provided by declarative statements or assembler *directives,* some of which are listed in Table 2-6. These directives exist for initializing bytes, words, longwords, etc., and for allocating large blocks of storage. For instance, the statement

```
NUMBERS: .BYTE   1,2,3
```

stores three bytes of data containing the integers 1, 2, and 3 into consecutive bytes and defines the label NUMBERS as the address of the byte containing the 1. The statement

```
LIST:   .LONG   156,718,0
```

stores the integers 156, 718, and 0 into consecutive 32-bit longwords.

To allocate large blocks of storage without specifying the contents of each element, the .BLKx directive is used, where *x* specifies the size of each element in the block. The statements

```
        ARRAYSIZE = 50
ARRAY:  .BLKW   ARRAYSIZE
```

allocate 50 words of contiguous storage. As a convenient feature of the assembler, the storage space is automatically initialized to zero.

Expressions

Expressions are combinations of terms joined by binary operators. A term can be either a numeric value or a defined symbol. The binary operators are shown in Table 2-7.

Table 2-6.   Assembler Storage Allocation Directives

Directive			Meaning
label:	.BYTE	value_list	Store specified values in successive bytes in memory at symbolic address "label."
label:	.WORD	value_list	Store specifed values in successive words in memory.
label:	.LONG	value_list	Store specified values in successive longwords in memory.
label:	.QUAD	value_list	Store specified values in successive quadwords in memory.
label:	.ASCII	/string/	Store ASCII representation of the delimited character string in successive bytes in memory.
label:	.ASCIC	/string/	Store ASCII representation of the delimited character string in successive bytes in memory, following a byte that contains the number of characters in "string."
label:	.ADDRESS	address_list	Store the 32-bit addresses of the specified locations in memory.
label:	.BLKB	count	Reserve a contiguous block of "count" bytes of memory at symbolic address "label." The bytes are initialized to zero.
label:	.BLKW	count	Reserve a contiguous block of words.
label:	.BLKL	count	Reserve a contiguous block of longwords.
label:	.BLKQ	count	Reserve a contiguous block of quadwords.

Table 2-7.   Assembler Binary Operators

Operator	Example	Meaning
+	$A + B$	Sum of A and B.
−	$A - B$	Difference of A and B.
×	$A \times B$	Product of A and B.
/	A / B	Integer quotient of A and B.
@	$A @ B$	Arithmetic shift of A by B bits. If B is positive, A is shifted left, and zeros are shifted into the low order bits. If B is negative, A is shifted right and the high order bit of A is duplicated in the high order bits.
&	$A \& B$	Logical AND of A and B.
!	$A ! B$	Logical OR of A and B.
\\	$A \backslash\backslash B$	Logical EXCLUSIVE OR of A and B.

The expression and all terms are evaluated as 32-bit values. The expression is processed left to right, with no operator precedence. However, angle brackets (<>) can be used to change the order of evaluation. For example,

$$A + B \times C \qquad \text{and} \qquad A + <B \times C>$$

have different values.

Angle brackets can be nested, as in the expression

$$<<A ! B> @ - C>$$

Expressions can be used anywhere within the program that values are used. As a result, all of the following uses of expressions are legal:

```
.LONG   35*<7+6>
.BLKB   ARRAYSIZE*4
LENGTH = 4*8*ARRAYSIZE
```

Control Statements

There are four assembler control statements frequently used in this text. The title directive,

```
.TITLE module_name    comment
```

defines the name of the program module and contains a comment string that is printed on the top line of each page of the listing. The subtitle directive,

```
.SBTTL comment
```

contains a comment string to be printed on the second line of each listing page. The .TITLE directive is always the first line of the module, while the .SBTTL directive is used before each routine within a module. The assembler also uses the subtitle declarations to produce a table of contents on the first page of the listing.

The program section directive,

```
.PSECT section-name
```

can be used, among other things, to separate instructions and data. Just as the title and subtitle directives serve to logically subdivide the program modules and submodules, the program section directive serves physically to subdivide the program into segments. Each segment is thus a physical entity with a set of unique labels and symbols. During the linking phase, the program segments are combined and references between them are resolved.

Finally, the end statement,

```
.END    label
```

informs the assembler that this is the last source line to be processed. The label operand of the .END statement tells the assembler the starting address for the translated program. When the program is executed, it will begin at the specified location. This is a label within the main program. If the module contains only subroutines and no starting point, the label is omitted.

The Listing

Figure 2-13 shows a typical listing produced by the VAX-11 Macro assembler. For each line in the listing, the assembler prints the following information:

1. A decimal line number for reference.

2. The source line from the source input program.

3. The hexadecimal address at which the first byte generated from the source line will be placed (printed as an offset from the start of the program section).

4. The hexadecimal representation for the binary values to be placed in memory for data, or the generated machine code for an instruction.

The assembler also prints a symbol table at the end of the listing, giving the numeric value for each symbol used in the assembly language program.

The Assembly Process

Now that we've examined the syntax and semantics of assembly language, we will briefly describe the process of assembling a program. The assembly process is easily illustrated by examining a simple, two-pass assembler. The two-pass assembler earns its name by reading the source program twice. Two passes are required because all symbol values must be known before the translation can begin.

The objective of the assembler is to read the user's symbolic *source program* and to produce the binary *object program* and the listing. To do this, the assembler must be able to:

1. Remember the addresses and values of the symbols used in declarations and instructions.

2. Translate the symbolic operation names into binary opcodes.

3. Convert the symbolic operand specifiers into their binary forms.

The purpose of the first pass, then, is to build a *symbol table* containing the values of all labels and symbols defined in the program. For example, a symbol table for the program listed in Figure 2-13 might contain the following information:

Symbol Name	Value (hex)	Symbol Type
BOTTOM	68	Label (address)
BUFFER	0	Label
BUFSIZE	64	Symbol
CHAR	4	Symbol
COUNT	64	Label
INSBUF	70	Label
TOP	6C	Label

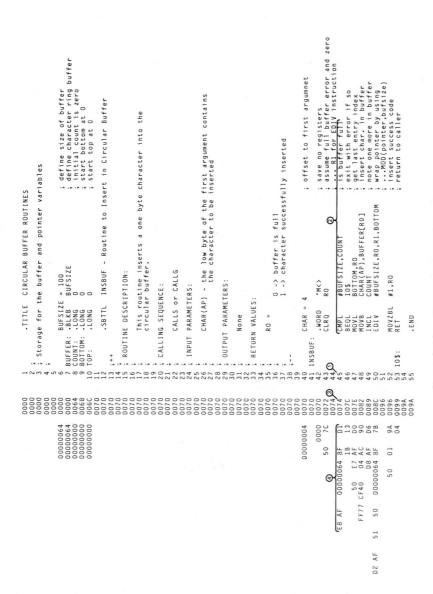

Figure 2-13.   Typical VAX-11 Macro listing.

Figure 2-14 shows the simplified flow of control for the assembler's first pass. As the figure shows, the first pass begins by setting the location counter to zero. As each line is read it is syntactically analyzed and interpreted to determine what type of statement it contains. If the line contains a label, the label is assigned the current value of the location counter and is stored in the symbol table. Equated symbols are placed in the symbol table with their specified values. If an instruction or storage space declaration is found, the assembler increments the location counter by the size of the instruction or allocated data.

The second pass is shown in Figure 2-15. During this pass, the assembler uses the symbol table to translate the program. Once again, the location counter is initialized to zero and the source program is read. The assembler composes a listing line for each source line consisting of the source text, the line number, location counter, and hex representation for any instruction or data. As each line is read, it is again analyzed for syntax and any errors are noted in the listing line. Label and symbol definitions are usually checked against the symbol table for consistency. If an instruction is found, the assembler uses the symbol table to find the values of any symbolic operand specifiers. The instruction is then assembled into binary from the opcode and specifiers, and is output to the object file. If a storage allocation declaration is found, the assembler outputs the initial values of the storage items to the object program.

Conventions for Writing Programs

As each programmer becomes comfortable with a new machine or language, he or she develops a personal style of programming. This style is exhibited in several areas, including:

1. The way programs are structured.
2. The algorithms used to solve common problems.
3. The instructions or language constructs chosen.
4. The format of the source program.
5. The language used in commenting the program.

The computer science shelves are now filled with books teaching the programmer how to structure or format programs and what language constructs to use and avoid. Since this information is readily available, it is not repeated here, but we will make some general comments about assembly language programming.

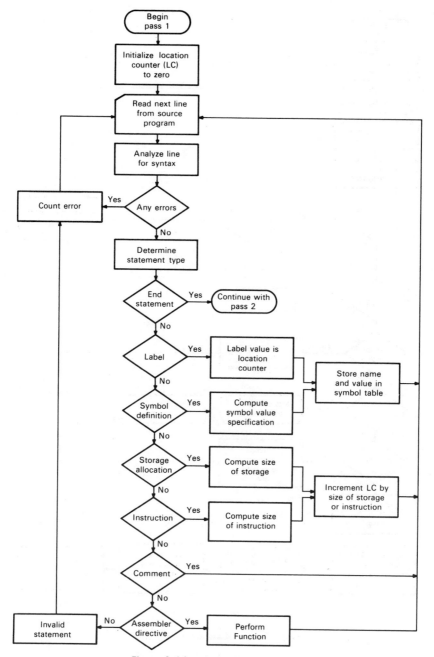

Figure 2-14.   Assembler pass one.

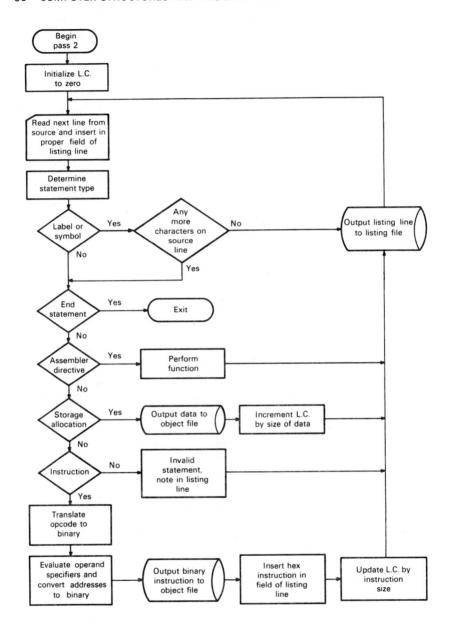

Figure 2-15.   Assembler pass two.

Most assembly language programs are systems programs; that is, they are part of a large collection of programs that provide service to computer users. The design and implementation of such programs comprise only a small fraction of their lifetimes. While a complicated program may require several years to implement, its use, maintenance, and updating may continue for more than a decade. In that time, a number of programmers are involved in using or modifying the program. Therefore, in designing or implementing a new program, a programmer should consider the following goals:

1. The program must solve the problem at hand.

2. It must communicate both the solution technique and the implementation details to the reader.

3. It must be easy to understand and modify.

These goals require that the program be clearly documented and described. On a machine with a rich instruction set such as the VAX-11, there is always a number of instructions suitable for a given situation. Luckily, the simplest solution to a problem is usually the easiest to understand and the most efficient. Thus, the programmer should try to select instructions and solution methods that are straightforward and easily comprehended.

The comments are as much a part of a program as are the instructions. It is not the number of comments that is important, particularly in assembly language, in which every line is usually commented, but the content of the comments. Each instruction should be followed by a comment describing the logical operation or, perhaps, the reason for performing the instruction. The comment explains how the instruction fits into the problem solution.

Block comments can be used to describe the flow or the logical function of a series of instructions and to break up a complicated section of code into smaller, comprehensible pieces. Form good programming habits now, and you will be rewarded the first time you try to modify your own programs.

SUMMARY

In this chapter, we have introduced the basic elements of the computer as seen by the assembly language programmer. The most important concepts to understand at this point are the instruction execution process and the addressing of memory. To be able to write assembly language programs, we must be comfortable with the fundamentals of computer operations.

The next chapter builds on this foundation by examining more complex addressing techniques. Our goal is to understand computers and this is best achieved by programming them.

REFERENCES

Many books have been written to give the basics of assembly language programming. Maurer's book (1977) is one of the few that is almost machine independent. Others, such as Abrams and Stein (1973), Chapin (1968), Gear (1974), Gill (1978), Hayes (1978), Katzan (1971), Stone (1975), Struble (1969), and Vickers (1971) focus on specific machines, particularly the IBM S/360 or S/370 and the DEC PDP-11. If one wants to read the manufacturer's "System Reference Manual," then the *VAX-11 Architecture Handbook* and the *VAX-11 Technical Summary* are the ones to read. Tannenbaum (1976) is also worth reviewing for its architectural musings on the PDP-11. The *VAX-11 Macro Language Reference Guide* gives the complete coverage of the assembly language for the VAX/VMS operating system.

EXERCISES FOR CHAPTER 2

1. Name the 3 major components of the computer system. Describe the function of each.

2. What is an address? In Figure 2-2, the last address is given as "$N - 1$." Why? If a memory unit has address 37, how many memory units precede it?

3. Compare and contrast the computer memory system to the human memory.

4. What is the address space? How is the size of the address space determined? If a machine has 4-bit addresses, how many addressable memory units are there? How are they numbered?

5. What are the parts of an instruction? Describe in detail the steps in the execution of an instruction. Why are instructions stored (and executed) sequentially in memory?

6. What are some of the characteristics of I/O devices? What are some of the differences between the bus organizations shown in Figure 2-5? How many buses does the VAX-11/780 have?

7. What are the information units on the VAX-11? What distinguishes an information unit from a data-type? What are the VAX-11 data-types and what is each data-type used for?

8. In Figure 2-9, if the "V" is stored in a byte with address 1248 (hex), what is the address of the byte containing the second "1"?

9. Give an example of a statement for a high level language (FORTRAN, Pascal, PL/I or ?) and its assembly language equivalent.

10. Why are special symbols used, such as ":" and ";", in writing an assembly language statement?

11. What happens when the following code segment is executed by the VAX-11 computer?

```
A:          .LONG   1948
B:          .LONG   13
C:          .LONG   1640
            .
            .
            .
            ADDL    A,B
            ADDL3   B,C,A
            ADDL    A,B
```

12. What occurs when

```
            ADDL3   A,A,A
```

is executed? What occurs when the two-statement program

```
HERE:       ADDL3   A,A,A
            JMP     HERE
```

is executed?

13. Suppose three longword memory locations are defined as follows:

Address	Assembly Statement		
308	X:	.LONG	20
30C	Y:	.LONG	9
310	Z:	.LONG	10

Show the contents of X, Y, and Z following the execution of the following instructions or groups of instructions. Assume for each case that the same initial contents of X, Y, and Z apply (i.e., X is 20, Y is 9, and Z is 10).

```
a.    MOVL     Y,X

b.    MOVAL    Y,X

c.    SUBL     Y,X

d.    SUBL     X,Y

e.    SUBL3    Y,X,Z

f.    INCL     Y
      SUBL3    Y,X,Z

g.    MOVAL    X,X
      MOVAL    Y,Y
      MOVAL    Z,Z

h.    SUBL     Z,X
      DECL     X
      MOVL     X,Y
```

14. Why can't a symbol begin with a digit? What's the advantage of equating a value to a symbol (e.g., SIX = 6)? Which takes more bytes of storage:

```
a.    SIX:   .BYTE

b.    SIX = 6
```

15. What hexadecimal numbers are stored in memory for the following statement?

```
.LONG   156,^D128,^A.12,3.,^X29,,^01234,3*5/4
```

16. Circle the block comments in the listing of Figure 2-13. What purpose do they serve?

Chapter 3

Instruction and Addressing Fundamentals

Armed with the basic information presented in the previous chapter, we can now expand our instruction repertoire to write assembly language solutions for typical computer problems. But an understanding of the instruction set alone is not enough to write sophisticated assembly language programs and to understand how digital computers function. Along with the instruction set, we need to become familiar with the various techniques for addressing memory. Once we have a firm grasp of addressing and instruction formation, we can examine the encoding of instructions and learn how instructions are represented in memory. Our examples and techniques will all be based on the VAX-11.

This chapter introduces simple programming examples and builds upon them to demonstrate more advanced techniques. Thus, the first examples may seem awkward in retrospect. As the instruction set is developed, however, more efficient operations are explained and contrasted to the earlier examples.

VAX-11 INSTRUCTION CHARACTERISTICS

One of the important considerations in evaluating an architecture is the correspondence between a machine's basic data-types and the operations (or instructions) that can be performed upon these data-types. For example, if a machine has byte, word, and longword integers, it should have an Add instruction that operates on each of these data-types in a uniform and consistent manner. If a longword can contain an integer or an address, these two objects should be treated differently. These are the types of issues one needs to consider when examining a particular machine.

It is not uncommon to find architectures in which it is not possible for all the addressing techniques to be used with all the data-types. Alternatively, some machines, like the PDP-11, treat addresses and data equally, and the instruction to load a register with an address is no different than the instruction to load it with a constant. While this is usually satisfactory, there may be times when the addressing specification must be evaluated dynamically at run time rather than at assembly time.

As we shall see when we consider generic instruction sets, the VAX-11 has a complete set of instructions that not only perform generic operations on the primitive data-types, but also allow for conversion from one data-type to another. In addition, the VAX-11 provides different instructions for manipulating numeric data-types and addresses. Finally, there are the testable results of instruction execution that can be used to determine the effect of an instruction. In this way, we can change the order of execution of a sequence of instructions and cause different instruction streams to be executed for different data.

Generic Operations

The VAX-11 has a relatively symmetric instruction set. That is, the general instructions can operate on any of the VAX data-types. Instruction names are formed by taking generic operations, like MOV or ADD, and appending the data-type of the operands, such as B, W, or L for byte, word, and longword integers. In addition, some instructions also exist in both two- and three-operand forms. We denote the two- and three-operand forms by appending a 2 or 3 to the instruction name following the data-type specifier. For the Add instruction, which has both two- and three-operand forms, we can construct the instructions

```
ADDB2
ADDB3
ADDW2
ADDW3
ADDL2
ADDL3
```

Because the two-operand forms are used more frequently, the VAX-11 Macro assembler allows us to drop the suffix 2 on these instructions.

Table 3-1 shows the general integer arithmetic and data manipulation instructions. For each instruction, note which data-types are available and how many operands can be used. The Move and Clear instructions can operate on quadword elements, as well as bytes, words, and longwords.

Some of these instructions are familiar from Chapter 2. We have also seen the Branch instructions that allow us to change program control flow. At this point it is appropriate to look at the branching mechanism in more detail.

Table 3-1. VAX-11 Generic Integer Instruction Set

Operation	Mnemonic	Data-Types	Number of Operands
Move data from one location to another.	MOV	B,W,L,Q	2
Clear location (set to zero).	CLR	B,W,L,Q	1
Move negative. Moves negated value of first operand to second operand.	MNEG	B,W,L	2
Move complemented. Moves the logical NOT of the source to the destination. This is the one's complement of the source, i.e., the values of all bits complemented.	MCOM	B,W,L	2
Increment location. Adds one to a data element.	INC	B,W,L	1
Decrement location. Subtracts one from a data element.	DEC	B,W,L	1
Add operands together. In the two-operand form, the result is stored in the second operand. In the three-operand form, the first two operands are added and stored in the third operand.	ADD	B,W,L	2,3

(continues)

Table 3-1. **VAX-11 Generic Integer Instruction Set (Cont.)**

Operation	Mnemonic	Data-Types	Number of Operands
Subtract operands. In the two-operand form, the first operand is subtracted from the second, and the result is stored in the second operand. In the three-operand form, the first operand is subtracted from the second and the result is stored in the third operand.	SUB	B,W,L	2,3
Multiply operands.	MUL	B,W,L	2,3
Divide second operand by the first.	DIV	B,W,L	2,3

Control Flow

Perhaps the single most powerful feature of any computer is its ability to make decisions, by which we mean the ability to perform different functions or to execute different program sections depending on conditions in the program. Generally, the computer does this simply by determining whether the result of an operation is positive, negative, or zero. The "conditional branch" instructions are used to transfer control to a different program section based on these results.

The symbolic format of a VAX-11 conditional branch instruction is

```
Bcondition   destination
```

where condition is a mnemonic that indicates for what conditions a branch to the destination is made. For the conditional branches to operate, status information must be saved following each instruction so that the succeeding instruction(s) can examine it. On the VAX-11, there are four bits of status information, called the condition codes, that reflect the outcome of the last instruction executed. These bits are part of the low word of the Processor Status Longword (PSL) register, which is called the Processor Status Word (PSW). Instructions such as Branch examine the condition codes to determine what action to take.

The condition codes and their functions are

- *N—Negative Bit.* This bit is set if the result of an instruction is negative and cleared if the result is positive or zero. For example, following a decrement instruction, the N bit is set if the decremented value is less than zero.

- *Z—Zero Bit.* This bit is set when the result of an instruction is exactly zero and is cleared otherwise. For instance, the Z bit is set following a decrement instruction if the location decremented contains a one before the instruction is executed.

- *V—Overflow Bit.* This bit is set following arithmetic operations if the result of the operation is too large to be represented in the data-type used.

- *C—Carry Bit.* This bit is set following arithmetic instructions in which a carry out of, or a borrow into, the most significant bit occurred.

The difference between overflow and carry is not always obvious. Overflow indicates that the result of an operation was too large for the data-type and that the destination operand contains an incorrect number. For example, in an integer add, if the operands are of the same sign but the result is of a different sign, then overflow occurred. In this sense, overflow destroys the sign bit. Suppose we wish to add the following *signed* 4-bit numbers:

```
   7      0111
 + 6      0110
 ----     ----
  13      1101
```

When interpreted in 2's complement form, the value of the signed 4-bit result is –3, so overflow occurred. The addition of two positive numbers yielded a negative result.

Carry, which is used for *unsigned* arithmetic, is (in the case of ADD) a carry out of the high order bit. Suppose we again add two unsigned 4-bit numbers:

```
 11        1011
+ 6        0110
────     ────────
 17     1  0001
        └─ Carry
```

There is a one-bit carry out of the most significant bit, so the C condition code would be set. This condition can be used to implement multi-precision arithmetic, and serves as input to the instructions Add With Carry (ADWC) and Subtract With Carry (SBWC).

The VAX-11 Programmer's Card in Appendix A shows how each instruction affects the condition codes. Some instructions set or clear condition codes based on the last arithmetic or logic result, some set or clear them unconditionally, and some leave them unaffected.

Because each byte, word, or longword can be used to represent either a signed or an unsigned integer, we must be careful to use the correct conditional branch instruction following a comparison or operation on integer quantities. Consider the following two bytes A and B:

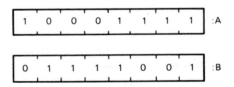

Which is larger? It depends, of course, on whether these bytes are being used to represent signed or unsigned 8-bit numbers. If the bytes are signed, then A is negative and B is larger. If the bytes are unsigned, A is larger.

Table 3-2 describes the two sets of conditional branches, those for signed and those for unsigned operands. It lists the instruction mnemonics and the conditions on which the branches are taken.

The Compare and Test instructions are used specifically to set the condition codes for program decision making and are usually followed by a conditional branch instruction. Each instruction can be used to test one item or compare two items of byte, word, longword, floating, or double floating data-type.

Table 3-2. VAX-11 Conditional Branch Instructions

Operation	Mnemonic	Branch Condition
Signed Branches		
Branch on Equal	BEQL	Z = 1
Branch on Not Equal	BNEQ	Z = 0
Branch on Less Than	BLSS	N = 1
Branch on Less Than or Equal	BLEQ	(N or Z) = 1
Branch on Greater Than	BGTR	(N or Z) = 0
Branch on Greater Than or Equal	BGEQ	N = 0
Unsigned Branches		
Branch on Equal Unsigned	BEQLU	Z = 1
Branch on Not Equal Unsigned	BNEQU	Z = 0
Branch on Less Than Unsigned	BLSSU	C = 1
Branch on Less Than or Equal Unsigned	BLEQU	(C or Z) = 1
Branch on Greater Than Unsigned	BGTRU	(C or Z) = 0
Branch on Greater Than or Equal Unsigned	BGEQU	C = 0

It is important to be careful in using conditional branches because different instructions affect the condition codes in different ways. When using a branch following a Compare, we are clearly testing the relationship between two data items. For instance, in the sequence

```
CMPL    A,B
BGTR    TARGET
```

the branch to TARGET is taken if A > B when A and B are treated as signed integers. In the sequence

```
CMPL    A,B
BGTRU   TARGET
```

the branch to TARGET is taken if A > B when A and B are treated as unsigned integers.

However, in the sequence

```
SUBL    A,B
BGTR    TARGET
```

the branch to TARGET is taken if *the result of the operation B–A is greater than zero*. Following an arithmetic instruction, the branches test the relationship of the result to zero. Therefore, the following three sequences are all identical in effect:

```
1.    SUBL    A,B
      CMPL    B,#0
      BGTR    TARGET

2.    SUBL    A,B
      TSTL    B
      BGTR    TARGET

3.    SUBL    A,B
      BGTR    TARGET
```

In example 1 above, the notation #0 means the value zero; # allows us to specify the operand value in the instruction instead of its address. From this, we see that the Test instruction (TSTL) simply compares an operand to zero. Following most arithmetic instructions, the test is superfluous because the condition codes are already set based on the result. Therefore, the Test is normally used to evaluate a data item that is not the result of the previous instruction.

OPERAND ADDRESSING TECHNIQUES

Unlike previous minicomputers in which the amount of addressable memory was very limited, the VAX-11 allows for 32-bit addresses. However, even though addresses are 32 bits, there are other methods for specifying operand addresses besides 32-bit values. These other methods, known as *addressing modes,* allow for more efficient representations of addresses within instructions. Addressing modes also simplify the manipulation of common data structures.

However an address is specified, the CPU must be able to locate or calculate the 32-bit operand address from the specification. This process is known as *effective address calculation,* and the result is the *effective address* of the operand.

In this section, we will examine the various addressing techniques for the VAX-11, and the method of effective address calculation associated with each. Along with the instructions already examined, these techniques will be used to demonstrate the solutions to common programming problems.

Simple Addressing

We have already seen simple address specification using symbolic labels in Chapter 2. In this direct addressing mode, the operand is specified by a name that represents the address of the operand. In programming, we often say then that the operand specifier "points to" the operand, or that the operand specifier is a *pointer.* This is shown diagramatically in Figure 3-1, where the operand specifier is the address of the operand. If we assume an instruction such as

```
CLRW    ABC
```

then the operand specifier is the address ABC, and the operand itself is the contents of the symbolically referenced location ABC.

As our first example of addressing, consider an array manipulation problem: to form the sum of two integer arrays, producing a third array. This summation could be expressed with a loop in a high level language, such as Pascal, as shown in Figure 3-2.

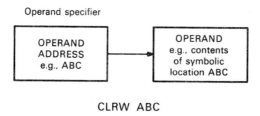

CLRW ABC

Figure 3-1.   Simple addressing.

```
const n = 50;
var i: integer;
    A: array[1..n] of integer;
    B: array[1..n] of integer;
    C: array[1..n] of integer;

begin
    for i := 1 to n do
        C[i] := A[i] + B[i] ;
end;
```

Figure 3-2.   High level integer array summation.

Each of the three arrays for our assembly language example, labelled A, B, and C in Figure 3-3, is composed of fifty 32-bit integer elements. Instead of using a loop as in the code in Figure 3-2, we first present a simple linear solution to the problem in Figure 3-4.

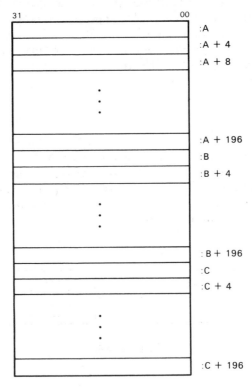

Figure 3-3.   Longword arrays.

```
A:        .BLKL   50              ; define array A of 50 longwords
B:        .BLKL   50              ; define array B
C:        .BLKL   50              ; define array C
          .
          .
          .
          ADDL3   A,B,C           ; C(1) = A(1) + B(1)
          ADDL3   A+4,B+4,C+4
          ADDL3   A+8,B+8,C+8
          .
          .
          .
          ADDL3   A+196,B+196,C+196 ; C(50) = A(50) + B(50)
          .
          .
          .
```

Figure 3-4.   Simple linear array sum example.

The program demonstrates a solution in which 50 three-operand Add Longword instructions are used to sum the elements of A and B into C. Since the elements added are longwords, we address every fourth byte. Notice that this introduces a typical programming problem: what is the address of the last element in an array of length N? Since the first element is at address A + 0, the last element is at A + 4 × (N − 1) for 4-byte longwords. That is, when the first symbolic address is zero, the last address is one less than the number of elements. The programmer must be careful to account for both endpoints.

Notice also that the VAX-11 memory is byte addressable. Each longword is specified by the address of its low order byte. Had the example in Figure 3-4 used an array of bytes instead of longwords, the following Add Byte instructions would be used:

```
ADDB3   A,B,C
ADDB3   A+1,B+1,C+1
ADDB3   A+2,B+2,C+2
.
.
.
```

For a 16-bit word array, the following Add Word instructions would be used:

```
ADDW3   A,B,C
ADDW3   A+2,B+2,C+2
ADDW3   A+4,B+4,C+4
.
.
.
```

In other words, the increment between array elements depends on the data representation and is a multiple of the base addressable unit, the byte. It is important to choose the appropriate Add instruction from the generic set of all Add instructions.

Immediate Mode

Programmers frequently need to specify constants in instructions. For example, there may be a need to add the integer 5 to a longword or to store the character A in memory. One way to do this is to allocate storage containing the constant, as shown below:

```
VALUE:  .LONG   5               ; constant value 5
        .
        .
        .
        ADDL    VALUE,A         ; add five to A
        .
        .
        .
```

Here the constant 5 is stored in memory at symbolic address VALUE. However, a more convenient and efficient notation is to use a literal in the instruction.

A *literal* is a constant or expression used in the instruction and stored as a part of the instruction rather than in a separate data location. The format for specifying a literal is #value, where value can be an expression. For example, to add five to the longword A, we can now write

```
        ADDL    #5,A
```

This is known as *immediate mode addressing* because the operand itself, not the operand address, is specified in the instruction. The number sign character (#) indicates to the assembler that what follows is the immediate operand for the instruction. Figure 3-5 shows pictorially that the first operand specifier is the operand itself for the instruction CMPW #100,R0.

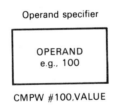

Operand specifier

```
OPERAND
e.g., 100
```

CMPW #100,VALUE

Figure 3-5.   Immediate mode addressing.

To further illustrate the use of literals, look at Figure 3-6, a program to form the sum of the integers between one and fifty. Instead of a linear solution, we use a loop to generate the values to be added.

Note that the loop counts downward from fifty instead of upward from zero. This technique recognizes the fact that the DECL instruction sets the condition codes, informing the control unit about the results of the last arithmetic operation just as the CMP instruction does. By performing the

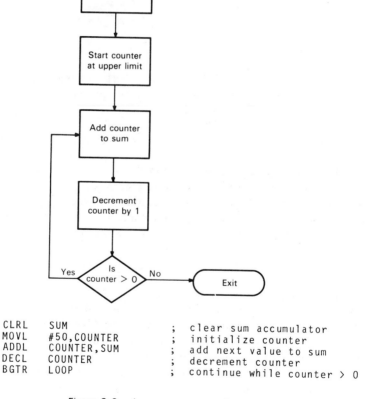

```
        CLRL   SUM                ;  clear sum accumulator
        MOVL   #50,COUNTER        ;  initialize counter
LOOP:   ADDL   COUNTER,SUM        ;  add next value to sum
        DECL   COUNTER            ;  decrement counter
        BGTR   LOOP               ;  continue while counter > 0
```

Figure 3-6.   Loop array summation.

additions in reverse order so that COUNTER counts down rather than up, it is unnecessary to use a CMP instruction to test for the upper limit. Instead, the program can test whether COUNTER is greater than zero after each iteration, and continue to loop as long as COUNTER is positive.

General Purpose Registers

A register is a high speed storage location that can be used for arithmetic, for addressing, and, as we shall see, for indexing arrays. Some early machines had only one register, called the *accumulator,* in which all arithmetic was done. Machines were structured this way because both memory and logic were extremely expensive. Since there was only one register, it was an implied operand in instructions. To perform the high level statement A: = A + B on such a machine would require the steps

```
LOAD    A            ; load accumulator with A
ADD     B            ; add B to accumulator
STORE   A            ; store accumulator result
                     ; ...back in A
```

On machines like the VAX-11 and PDP-11, all operations can be performed either in memory or in registers; the preceding steps can thus be written in memory-to-memory form as

```
ADDL    B,A          ; add B to A
```

There are still several good reasons, however, for including registers in these machines. First, registers on most current computers are used to supply a limited amount of high speed storage. On the VAX-11/780, for example, two-operand Add instructions like the one just shown execute several times faster if both operands are in registers, as in

```
ADDL    R0,R1        ; add register 0 to register 1
```

If a storage location is to be used for a large number of arithmetic operations within a routine, it may pay to first load its contents into a register, perform all the operations on it, then move it back to memory. A bigger payoff, however, comes when registers are used to simplify addressing of data structures such as arrays, as subsequent discussion will show.

The second, and often more important, feature of registers is that because there are few of them, they can be addressed using fewer bits. On the

VAX-11, for instance, there are sixteen 32-bit registers called R0, R1, . . . , R15. Because there are only 16 registers, each can be addressed in only 4 bits, compared to 32 bits that may be required to represent a memory address. This reduction in the size of operand addresses means a further increase in performance since fewer bytes are fetched from memory in order to interpret the instruction.

Not all sixteen registers are general purpose; four of them have special uses and should not be used for general programming. These four registers also have special names:

1.   R12, known as the argument pointer (AP), is used in the subroutine calling facility described in Chapter 4.

2.   R13, the frame pointer (FP), is also used in the subroutine calling facility.

3.   R14, the stack pointer (SP), is used in accessing the program's stack, a data structure also described in Chapter 4.

4.   R15 is the program counter (PC). On the VAX-11 and the PDP-11, the program counter is one of the general registers. As we shall see, this simplifies the encoding of some addressing modes.

The remaining registers, R0 through R11, are available for general programming use, and these registers can be used as operands in place of memory locations in almost all VAX-11 instructions.

Let us now re-examine the program shown in Figure 3-6. Instead of using memory locations for COUNTER and SUM, we use the registers R0 and R1 as shown.

```
;
; use R0 as SUM, R1 as loop COUNTER
;

        CLRL    R0              ; clear sum accumulator
        MOVL    #50,R1          ; initialize counter
LOOP:   ADDL    R1,R0           ; add next value to sum
        DECL    R1              ; decrement counter
        BGTR    LOOP            ; loop while counter > 0
```

A careful inspection of this code will reveal that replacing the memory locations with registers reduces the number of memory references by two orders of magnitude.

Any set of adjacent VAX-11 registers can be used as a 64-bit operand in a quadword instruction. The register pair is specified by the low order register number. For instance, the instruction

```
MOVQ    R3,R6
```

replaces the two-instruction sequence below:

```
MOVL    R3,R6
MOVL    R4,R7
```

This property is often used as an optimization technique by language compilers and assembly programmers. For example, the Clear Quadword (CLRQ) instruction can be used to zero two adjacent registers at one time.

Indirect Mode

Besides being used for arithmetic, registers, as well as memory locations, can be used to hold addresses of operands. Referencing an element through a register or memory location is called *indirect addressing.* This *deferred* mode of addressing can be combined with other modes, described later, to provide sophisticated addressing techniques.

Indirect addressing can be used in many ways. For example, it can assist the programmer in passing arguments to subroutines or in creating linked data structures. These capabilities exist because indirect addressing specifies the "address of the address of the operand" rather than the "address of the operand." Figure 3-7 indicates how indirect addressing implies that the operand is the "address of the address" by including another operand box to point to the actual operand. Assembler syntax for indicating deferred addressing is @ for indirect addressing through memory locations

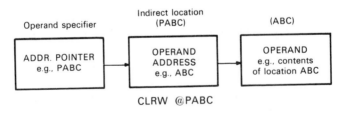

CLRW @PABC

Figure 3-7. Indirect addressing.

and ( ) for indirect addressing through registers. This is shown pictorially in Figure 3-7 for the instruction

```
CLRW    @PABC
```

where we assume that the address of the symbolic location ABC is held in a memory longword labelled PABC.

Indirect addressing is used in the following program segment to clear the contents of the longword at location TARGET:

```
POINTER: .ADDRESS TARGET    ; contains address of TARGET
TARGET:  .LONG    1234       ; contents of TARGET
         .
         .
         .
         CLRL     @POINTER    ; clear operand indirectly
         .
         .
         .
```

Using a register to hold the address of the item to be cleared, we can use the following sequence:

```
POINTER: .ADDRESS TARGET    ; contains address of TARGET
TARGET:  .LONG    1234       ; contents of TARGET
         .
         .
         .
         MOVL     POINTER,R2  ; load address of TARGET in R2
         CLRL     (R2)        ; clear longword at TARGET
```

The MOVL instruction loads R2 with the address of the operand to be cleared. The notation (R2) indicates that R2 contains the operand address.

Since the loading of addresses occurs frequently, the VAX-11 has a Move Address instruction that loads the address of a specified element into a longword. Using the Move Address of Longword (MOVAL) instruction below, we no longer need the POINTER longword.

```
TARGET: .LONG  1234          ; contents of TARGET
        .
        .
        .
        MOVAL   TARGET,R2    ; load address of TARGET in R2
        CLRL    (R2)         ; clear longword at TARGET
```

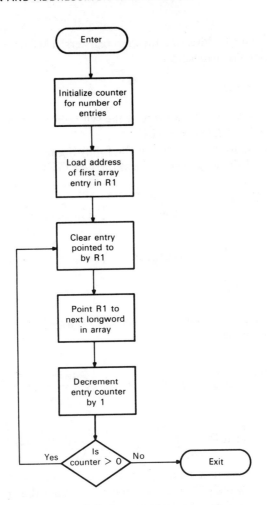

```
;
; Program to zero array of N longwords.
;

        N = 50                  ; define array size
A:      .BLKL   N               ; define array
        •
        •
        •
START:  MOVL    #N,R0           ; initialize loop count
        MOVAL   A,R1            ; load array A base address
LOOP:   CLRL    (R1)            ; clear entry pointed to by R1
        ADDL    #4,R1           ; point to next longword
        DECL    R0              ; decrement loop count
        BGTR    LOOP            ; continue while R0 > 0
```

Figure 3-8.   Indirect addressing example.

The operation of clearing a memory location can be applied to clearing an array of memory locations. The logical flow of operations to be performed is shown by the program segment in Figure 3-8. In this example, the MOVAL instruction is used to initialize R1 to the address of the first item in array A. R1 is advanced each time to point to the next element in the array.

It is possible for some computers to utilize multi-level indirect addressing if the location indirectly addressed is itself the address of another location to be indirectly referenced. Multi-level indirect addressing requires that each location referenced has a bit that specifies whether this location is an address to be used directly or indirectly.

The choice between multi-level and single-level indirect addressing is based on user convenience and cost. On a typical machine, every bit must be utilized efficiently, and multi-level indirect addressing is not provided. The reason is an economic one: multi-level indirection reduces the size of the address space by a factor of two.

Autoincrement and Autodecrement Modes

In Figure 3-8, the constant 4 was added to R1 during each loop iteration to advance it to the next longword in the array. Indexing forward or backward through an array occurs so frequently that some machines have built-in hardware to increment or decrement the contents of registers automatically.

The *autoincrement* and *autodecrement* addressing modes of VAX-11 provide for automatically stepping a register through the sequential elements of a table or array. This mode assumes the contents of the selected general register to be the address of, or pointer to, the operand. Thus, the pointer is stepped through a series of addresses so that it always points to the next sequential element of a table. And since the VAX-11 recognizes the data-type being addressed, it knows whether to increment the register by 1, 2, 4, or 8 for byte, word, longword, or quadword operands.

In autodecrement mode, written as –(R), the contents of the register are decremented *before* being used as the address of the operand. In autoincrement mode, written as (R)+, the contents of the register are incremented *after* being used as the address of the operand.

With this addressing mode, Figure 3-8 can be recoded as shown in Figure 3-9. Following each CLRL instruction at LOOP, the contents of R1 are automatically incremented by four. If the instruction were

```
CLRW    (R1)+
```

```
            .
            .
            .
START:  MOVL    #N,R0       ; initialize loop count
        MOVAL   A,R1        ; load array base address
LOOP:   CLRL    (R1)+       ; clear entry and advance
                            ; ...pointer to next entry
        DECL    R0          ; decrement loop counter
        BGTR    LOOP        ; continue until done
```

Figure 3-9.   Use of autoincrement addressing.

then the value of R1 would be incremented by two since this instruction operates on word-sized data elements. If the instruction were

```
CLRB    (R1)+
```

then the value of R1 would be incremented by one.

Figure 3-10 shows symbolically how autoincrement addressing is performed. In this figure we assume that register 8 contains the operand address ABC.

These addressing modes can be illustrated with the following example. Suppose that the contents of the registers and memory are as shown below. The table shows the contents of the longword beginning at each memory location.

Memory Address	Memory Contents	Register	Contents
200	1 3 0 F F 0 1 D	R0	200
400	0 0 1 3 7 0 1 3	R1	400
600	9 1 E B 0 8 1 0	R2	602
800	0 0 1 1 2 3 4 5	R3	802

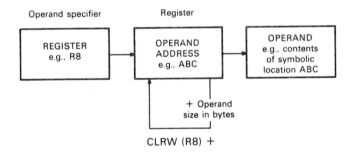

CLRW (R8) +

Figure 3-10.   Autoincrement addressing.

Following execution of the two instructions

```
ADDB    (R0)+,(R1)+
ADDW    (R2)+,-(R3)
```

the contents of the registers and memory will be:

Memory Address	Memory Contents	Register	Contents
200	1 3 0 F F 0 1 D	R0	201
400	0 0 1 3 7 0 3 0	R1	401
600	9 1 E B 0 8 1 0	R2	604
800	0 0 1 1 B 5 3 0	R3	800

Now suppose we wish to rewrite Figure 3-9 using autodecrement addressing. We begin by loading R1 with the address of the longword *following* array A since the decrement is done before the operation is performed:

```
BEGIN:   MOVL    #N,R0           ; initialize loop count
         MOVAL   A+<4*N>, R7     ; load address of longword
                                 ; ...following array A
LOOP:    CLRL    -(R1)           ; clear previous entry
         DECL    R0              ; decrement loop counter
         BGTR    LOOP            ; continue until done
```

In the previous autoincrement example, following each execution of the CLRL instruction at loop, R1 points to the *next* element to be cleared. Following the execution of the CLRL instruction in this autodecrement example, R1 points to the *last* element cleared.

Using autoincrement addressing, Figure 3-2 from an earlier section can now be rewritten using a loop:

```
START:   MOVL    #N,R0                  ; initialize loop count
         MOVAL   A,R1                   ; get address of array A
         MOVAL   B,R2                   ; get address of array B
         MOVAL   C,R3                   ; get address of array C
LOOP:    ADDL3   (R1)+,(R2)+,(R3)+      ; form C := A+B
         SOBGTR  R0,LOOP                ; loop until done
```

Here we have also introduced an instruction provided specifically for loops such as this. The Subtract One and Branch on Greater Than Zero instruction (SOBGTR) subtracts one from the loop counter (R0) and branches to the supplied address (LOOP) if the counter is still greater than zero. Otherwise, control continues at the next instruction. The SOBGTR implements a Pascal "for i := N downto 1" loop. It replaces the DECL and BGTR instructions in previous examples. A companion instruction, Subtract One and Branch on Greater Than or Equal to Zero (SOBGEQ), implements a "for i := N downto 0" loop, replacing a DECL and BGEQ pair. More loop instructions appear in a forthcoming section.

Operand Context

Each operand in a VAX instruction has an implied *context* that defines the type of data element on which it operates. For the more sophisticated addressing modes such as autoincrement and indexed (yet to be discussed), it is important to understand the context to be certain how the registers will be used or modified. In the examples in the previous section, we saw that the context of the operand (R1)+ was determined by the instruction; R1 was handled differently for CLRL than for CLRW.

It is sometimes possible for different operands of an instruction to have different contexts. For example, the Move Address instruction, used to store the address of a data element in a specified longword, has two operands:

1. The first or *source operand,* which provides the address specification of the data element. Its context is specified by the instruction, e.g., MOVAB, MOVAW, and MOVAL respectively for byte, word, and longword elements.

2. The second or *destination operand,* which provides the address of a longword to receive the calculated 32-bit effective address. Its context is always longword, since effective addresses are always 32 bits.

For the instruction

```
MOVAW   TEMP,R0           ; R0 <- address of TEMP
```

the context is unimportant because there is no ambiguity about how to determine the address of TEMP, and there are no side effects on registers (for example, autoincrementing). The address of TEMP is the same regardless of its length; hence, whether a MOVAL or MOVAB instruction is used, the outcome is not affected. The programmer can choose one form rather than another to enhance readability and to indicate the size of the operand.

In contrast, for the instruction

```
MOVAW   (R0)+,(R1)+
```

the difference is critical. In this instruction, the address of a word pointed to by R0 is moved into a longword pointed to by the contents of R1. Following the execution of this instruction, R0 will be incremented by two (a word increment), while R1 will be incremented by four (a longword increment).

Displacement Mode

Another common addressing requirement is to be able to address data elements in a data structure as offsets from the base of the structure. *Displacement mode,* whose format is

```
displacement(R)
```

is provided for this purpose. The displacement is a signed integer offset; that is, it may be positive or negative. As shown below, displacement mode is similar to indirect register mode except that the effective address is computed by adding an integer displacement to the contents of the register. In Figure 3-11, we assume that R2 contains the address of LIST in the instruction CLRW 4(R2). In the figure, two components of the operand specifier are shown: the register and the displacement.

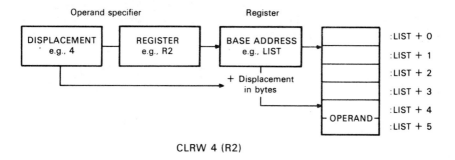

CLRW 4 (R2)

Figure 3-11.   Displacement addressing mode.

An example to help us better understand the use of displacements is contained in the following data structure:

```
USRDATA:
         .BLKQ   1              ; user's first name
         .BLKQ   1              ; user's last name
         .BLKB   1              ; user's age
         .BLKB   1              ; user's height
         .BLKW   1              ; user's weight
         .BLKL   1              ; user's social security number
```

which can be pictured in memory as

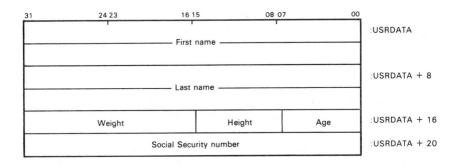

This could be the format of one entry in a large table of entries for many users of a system. To access any field for a particular table entry, we load the base address of the entry into a register and address each element by its *offset in bytes* from the base. For example, we can define symbolic offsets into the data structure shown as

```
Q_FIRSTNAME=0
Q_LASTNAME=8
B_AGE=16
B_HEIGHT=17
W_WEIGHT=18
L_SOC_SEC=20
```

(Note that the offset names have been chosen to in-dicate the element size as well as the contents)

where each symbol is the offset in bytes from the start of the structure to the given field. Then we could use displacement mode to access the needed field:

```
        .
        .
        .
MOVAL   USERDATA,R1            ; load table address
MOVL    L_SOC_SEC(R1),TEMP1    ; get SS number
MOVB    B_AGE(R1),TEMP2        ; get user's age
MOVQ    Q_LASTNAME(R1),TEMP3   ; get user's name
        .
        .
        .
```

In this example notice the advantage of displacement mode for addressing variable-length data elements from a fixed base address.

VAX also supports a *deferred displacement* addressing mode. In this mode, specified as

```
@displacement(R)
```

the displacement is added to the contents of the register to form the address of the operand address. A graphical representation of this addressing mode would be similar to that for displacement addressing (Figure 3-11) except that the operand now contains the address of the operand, instead of the operand itself.

This mode is useful for accessing a data element whose address is stored in a data structure being accessed with displacement mode addressing. For example, if the contents of R6 and the memory locations are as shown:

Memory Address	Memory Contents	Register	Contents
208	0 0 1 F D A 1 0	R6	208
20C	1 3 A B F 0 1 0		
210	0 0 0 0 0 8 1 0		
810	0 F 1 D 0 2 3 4		

Then, following execution of the instruction,

```
CLRW    @8(R6)
```

the contents of the register and memory will be:

Memory Address	Memory Contents	Register	Contents
208	0 0 1 F D A 1 0	R6	208
20C	1 3 A B F 0 1 0		
210	0 0 0 0 0 8 1 0		
810	0 F 1 D 0 0 0 0		

Index Mode

One of the most powerful addressing features of the VAX-11 is the ability to use an *index register* to specify the index of an array entry. The index register specifies which element of the array (e.g., the first, second, or third) is being addressed.

The format for index mode addressing is

```
base_address[R]
```

where base_address is a general address specification for the first element in the array and register R contains the index of the desired element. Because the array may be composed of byte, word, longword, or quadword entries, the index value must be multiplied by the appropriate size—one, two, four, or eight—before being added to the base address. The VAX-11 CPU selects the multiplier based on the context of the operand. The specification of the base address can use any addressing mode encountered so far, forming instructions such as

```
MOVL    ARRAY[R1],R2        ; displacement indexed
MOVAW   (R0)[R1],R2         ; register deferred indexed
MOVB    -(R0)[R1],R2        ; autodecrement indexed
```

The effective address of the operand is calculated by first computing the address of the base of the array or table. Then the value of the index register is multiplied by one, two, four, or eight, depending on the data-type of the operand, and added to the base address. As with autoincrement or autodecrement, the context of the operand affects the value of the register. In

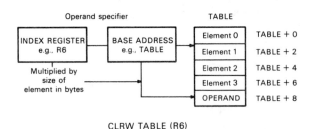

CLRW TABLE (R6)

Figure 3-12.   Indexed addressing mode.

Figure 3-12, we index into element four of the array called TABLE using the instruction CLRW TABLE[R6] (i.e., the contents of R6 is 4). Each element in the array TABLE is two bytes long.

We may illustrate this indexing technique further by considering the instruction

```
MOVW    2(R1)[R2],2(R1)[R3]
```

Suppose that the initial values of the registers and memory are

Memory Address	Memory Contents	Register	Contents
452:	F7	R1	450
453:	24	R2	2
454:	6C	R3	3
455:	10		
456:	56		
457:	0D		
458:	98		
459:	73		

ARRAY |0|	2	4	F	7	:452
ARRAY |1|	1	0	6	C	:454
ARRAY |2|	0	D	5	6	:456
ARRAY |3|	7	3	9	8	:458

This instruction moves the contents of the third element to the location of the fourth element of a word array (remember that the first index is zero). First, we must compute the address of the base of the array, which is specified by 2(R1). This means that the array base address is two bytes past the address contained in register R1, or at address 452. Next, because this is a word-sized array, we compute the offset to the element by multiplying the value in the index register R2 by two. Thus, the element is four bytes (2 × 2) past the array base, or at address 452 + 4 = 456. The destination address is evaluated in the same manner, giving effective address 458 for the operand (this is the adjacent word in the array since the array indices were 2 and 3). Following the execution of this instruction, the registers and memory look like this:

Memory Address	Memory Contents	Register	Contents
452:	F7	R1	450
453:	24	R2	2
454:	6C	R3	3
455:	10		
456:	56		
457:	0D		
458:	56		
459:	0D		

Returning to the Pascal example shown in Figure 3-2,

```
for i := 1 to 50 do
    C[i] := A[i] + B[i] ;
```

we can now "compile" this higher level code into VAX-11 assembly code using index mode addressing:

```
        CLRL    R0                      ; start at index 0
LOOP:   ADDL3   A[R0],B[R0],C[R0]       ; add elements
        AOBLSS  #50,R0,LOOP             ; loop while R0 < 50
```

Few machines could translate this Pascal loop into so few machine instructions. Note that another looping instruction has been introduced, called Add One and Branch Less Than (AOBLSS). On each execution, one is added to the index operand, R0 in this case, and the incremented index is compared with the limit operand, which is 50 in this instruction. If the index is less than the limit operand, a branch is taken to LOOP, the destination. Otherwise, execution continues at the next instruction.

INSTRUCTION FORMATS

Two features of the VAX architecture make the VAX-11 an efficient programming machine. First is the variety of instructions and addressing modes, which allow the programmer to express complicated constructs in only a few machine language instructions. Second is the instruction encoding, which allows these instructions to be represented efficiently in memory. This section discusses what an instruction looks like when assembled and stored in the memory of the computer.

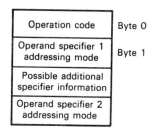

Figure 3-13.   VAX-11 instruction format.

General Instruction Format

In some machines, instructions are encoded as a series of words, where each word is divided into a number of fields. These fields are used to describe the operation code and the operand specifiers. Word-based instructions often consume more space than needed because they must be represented as an integral number of words.

The VAX-11 instruction set was designed to be both general and highly memory-efficient. The result is a variable-length instruction format in which instructions are represented as a series of bytes. The first byte of each instruction is the opcode (although the architecture allows future expansion to two-byte opcodes). Following the opcode are from zero to six operand specifiers. Each operand specifier can be from one to nine bytes long, with the first byte describing the addressing mode. Figure 3-13 shows this general format.

In the execution of an instruction, the CPU examines the first byte of the instruction, which contains the opcode. The opcode determines how many operand specifiers follow. For each operand specifier, the CPU examines the first byte to determine the addressing mode for that specifier. Depending on the addressing mode used, the CPU may need to examine more bytes to compute the effective address of the operand. This process continues until all the specifiers have been evaluated. The operands are then fetched, and the operation is performed.

Encoding an Instruction

Every instruction consists of an opcode and from zero to six operand specifiers. The first byte of each operand specifier always indicates the addressing mode. Usually, this byte is broken into halves, one specifying the addressing mode, the other specifying the register to be used for addressing.

For example, in *register mode,* in which the operand is contained in a general register, the format of the operand specifier is

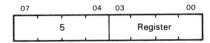

where the high order four bits specify that this is register mode (5) and the low four bits specify which register is to be used.

Let us consider the instruction

```
ADDL    R0,R1
```

which adds the contents of register 0 to register 1. The opcode for the ADDL instruction is C0 hex. The operand specifiers for R0 and R1 are 50 and 51 hex, respectively, where the 5 indicates register mode. Each one-byte specifier would appear as:

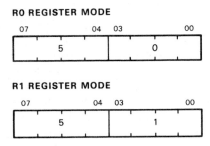

Stored at address 200, this instruction appears in memory as follows:

Memory Address	Memory Contents	Interpretation
200:	C0	ADDL opcode
201:	50	R0 register mode
202:	51	R1 register mode

Suppose that one operand is autoincrement mode, such as

```
ADDL    R3,(R8)+
```

The operand specifier format for autoincrement mode is:

AUTOINCREMENT MODE

07	04	03	00
8		Register	

The instruction thus appears in memory as:

Memory Address	Memory Contents	Interpretation
200:	C0	ADDL opcode
201:	53	R3 register mode
202:	88	(R8)+ autoincrement mode

Now let us examine a slightly more complex addressing mode, displacement addressing. In displacement addressing, the register contains a base address to which a byte, word, or longword displacement is added to determine the operand address. The displacement follows the addressing mode in the instruction. Thus, depending on the size of the displacement, there are really three displacement addressing modes. Their representations are shown in Figure 3-14.

The displacements in the figure are signed integers. As a result, byte and word displacements are sign-extended and then added to the base register. If the operand is within ±127 bytes from the base register address, byte

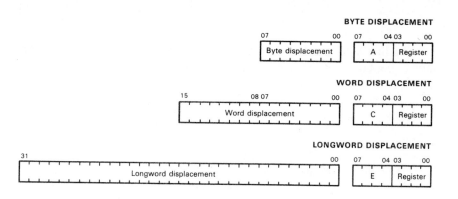

Figure 3-14. Displacement address encoding.

displacement is used. If the operand is within ±32,767 bytes from the base register address, word displacement is used. The assembler chooses the most efficient addressing mode whenever possible. Because displacements are often small, byte displacement is frequently used, saving up to three bytes in instruction length. As an example, look at the following three-operand Add instruction:

```
ADDL3   8(R6),(R7)+,R8
```

This instruction would be assembled in memory as follows:

Memory Address	Memory Contents	Interpretation
200:	C1	ADDL3 opcode
201:	A6	byte displacement (R6)
202:	08	8 (byte displacement)
203:	87	(R7)+
204:	58	R8

Finally, we will examine an indexed mode example, in which two registers are required to specify the addressing mode. In index mode, both the index register and the base address specification must be included. Therefore, an index mode (mode 4) specifier must be at least two bytes long:

INDEX MODE

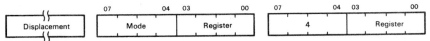

The first byte specifies that this is index mode, with the index register number contained in the low four bits. The following byte or bytes specify the base address. For instance, the instruction

```
INCB    8(R2)[R3]
```

would be assembled as

Memory Address	Memory Contents	Interpretation
200:	96	INCB opcode
201:	43	[R3] index mode
202:	A2	byte displacement (R2)
203:	08	8 (byte displacement)

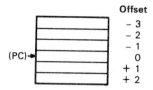

Figure 3-15. PC relative addressing.

Program Counter Relative Addressing

We have yet to discuss how simple direct addresses are represented. Addressing memory in this way is actually quite similar to displacement mode addressing, but it involves a unique feature of the PDP-11 family architecture—the use of the PC as a general register. Although we described the symbolic name as a representation for the 32-bit operand address, the assembler actually uses a more compact encoding. Called *relative addressing,* this mode represents the data element by its displacement or position relative to the program counter value, as shown in Figure 3-15.

Like displacement mode, in relative addressing a signed byte, word, or longword offset is added to a register to form the operand address. In this case, however, the register used is the program counter (R15 or PC). The effective address of the operand is formed by adding a byte, word, or longword displacement to the value of the program counter when the instruction is being decoded. Memory is addressed by its distance from the instruction referencing it. The format of relative mode is shown in Figure 3-16.

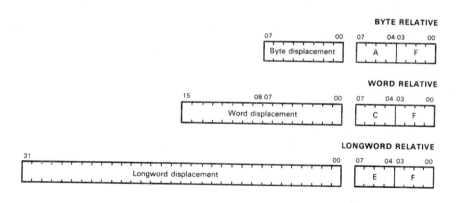

Figure 3-16. PC relative address encoding.

This style of addressing is useful for two reasons. First, it is efficient because most operands are relatively close to the instructions that reference them, and the offset can be specified in 8 or 16 bits. Second and more important is the fact that relative mode addressing is *position-independent*. As long as the distance relationship between the instruction and the operand remains fixed, the program can be loaded anywhere in memory and will still execute correctly without modification. If the instruction contained an actual 32-bit address instead of a relative address, the data item would always have to be loaded at the same base address. Position independence becomes important in a multiprogramming system, in which several programs share a single routine. If the routine is position-independent, it can be loaded any place within each user's memory space, giving the system more flexibility in arranging routines.

As an example of relative addressing, we will now consider how the instruction

```
MOVW    MYDATA,R1
```

would be assembled. Suppose that the instruction is located at address 600 in memory and that the word MYDATA is stored at address 804. Memory would appear as follows:

Memory Address	Memory Contents	Interpretation
600:	B0	MOVW opcode
601:	CF	word relative mode
602:	00	16-bit displacement
603:	02	. . . is 200 hex
604:	51	R1, register mode
.		
.		
804:	05	MYDATA first byte
805:	14	MYDATA second byte

Effective
operand address =   604 (program counter)
                +   200 (word displacement)
                ─────
                     804

To understand how the effective address of the operand is calculated, consider the following. As the opcode and operand specifiers are fetched and evaluated, the PC is advanced over them to the next operand specifier or instruction. When the first operand specifier is fetched, the PC is incremented to the next operand specifier at address 604. The relative displacement, 200 hex, is added to the updated PC, giving address 804 for the operand MYDATA. The second operand is then evaluated, and the word at MYDATA is moved into R1.

If this routine were moved so that it was loaded at address 1024 instead of 600, the contents of memory would be

Memory Address	Memory Contents	Interpretation
1024:	B0	MOVW opcode
1025:	CF	word relative mode
1026:	00	16-bit displacement
1027:	02	. . . is 200 hex
1028:	51	R1, register mode
.		
.		
.		
1228:	05	MYDATA first byte
1229:	14	MYDATA second byte

Effective
operand address =   1028 (program counter)
                  + 200 (word displacement)
                    1228

Notice that even though the instruction and datum have been moved, the instruction still executes properly without change because the relative distance between the instruction and operand remains constant.

When an operand is addressed using an indirect memory reference, as in

```
MOVW    @MYDATA,R1
```

relative deferred mode addressing is used. This is similar to relative mode except that the effective address calculated is the address of a longword containing the operand address rather than the operand itself.

Immediate Addressing

When an immediate operand is specified in an instruction, such as

```
MOVW    #^X200,R3
```

immediate mode addressing is used. It is similar to autoincrement mode except that once more the PC is used as the general register. In other words, as the operand is decoded, the PC points to the literal (constant value) in the instruction stream. The PC is incremented over the operand as the operand is fetched. The size of the operand is determined by the context of the instruction. The format for immediate mode is:

IMMEDIATE MODE

For the preceding Move Word instruction, the memory format would be:

Memory Address	Memory Contents	Interpretation
. . . . .	B0	MOVW opcode
. . . . .	8F	immediate mode
. . . . .	00	word
. . . . .	02	. . . constant
. . . . .	53	R3 register mode

When the first byte of the operand specifier is fetched, the PC points to the 16-bit constant. The constant is then fetched and the PC incremented by the size of the constant.

Since many literals used in programs are small, the VAX-11 has a special addressing mode called *short literal*. In this mode, the constant is held in the operand specifier itself. The format of a short literal specifier is:

LITERAL MODE

In other words, any operand specifier in which the high two bits are zeros contains a literal constant in the low six bits. Because the literal is unsigned, integer values from 0 through 63 can be represented, avoiding the need for immediate mode addressing. For example, the instruction

MOVL   #8,R5

would be assembled as:

Memory Address	Memory Contents	Interpretation
. . . . .	DO	MOVL opcode
. . . . .	08	short literal (8)
. . . . .	55	R5

This is four bytes shorter than immediate mode.

Absolute Addressing

On occasion, instructions must reference an *absolute address*, that is, a location fixed in the address space. This is usually a location defined by the operating system to be constant for all processes in the system. For absolute mode addressing, the actual 32-bit address is contained in the instruction stream. This mode is the same as autoincrement deferred, but again the PC is specified as the general register. The format for absolute mode is:

ABSOLUTE MODE

31	00	07	04	03	00
Address			9		F

The assembler syntax for absolute addressing is @#address. An example of such an instruction might be:

```
TSTL    @#^X1234
```

This instruction tests the longword at address 00001234 regardless of where the instruction is located in memory. The instruction would be assembled as:

Memory Address	Memory Contents	Interpretation
. . . . .	D5	TSTL opcode
. . . . .	9F	absolute mode
. . . . .	34	32-bit
. . . . .	12	. . . operand
. . . . .	00	. . . address
. . . . .	00	. . . is 00001234

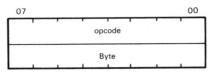

Figure 3-17. Conditional branch encoding.

Branch Addressing

The last addressing mode we will examine is *branch addressing*. The coding of a conditional branch instruction, shown in Figure 3-17, differs from the modes previously discussed in that there is no operand specifier. Each conditional branch consists of a one-byte opcode followed by a one-byte signed displacement. The signed displacement is used in a fashion similar to relative addressing and is added to the program counter to form the branch destination address. This different addressing choice was made because most conditional branch instructions specify a destination within a short distance. Also, very few branches require advanced addressing modes.

For example, the instruction sequence

```
        TSTL    R0          ; check for R0 zero
        BEQL    NILL        ; branch if so
        INCL    R0          ; else add one
NILL:     .
          .
          .
```

would appear in memory as:

Memory Address	Memory Contents	Interpretation
200:	D5	TSTL opcode
201:	50	R0 register mode
202:	13	BEQL opcode
203:	02	byte displacement
204:	D6	INCL opcode
205:	50	R0 register mode
206:		NILL: label

$$
\begin{array}{ll}
\text{Branch} & 204 \text{ (program counter)} \\
\text{destination} & \underline{+\ 02} \text{ (byte displacement)} \\
\text{address} = & 206
\end{array}
$$

Because of this addressing mode, a conditional branch can be used only if the branch target is within ±127 bytes from the instruction. If the branch target is farther away, the code sequence must be changed. Suppose that the location NILL in the preceding example was actually at address 600 so that the conditional branch instruction BEQL would not reach. We would then recode the instruction as follows:

```
                TSTL    R0              ; check for R0 zero
                BNEQ    NOTNILL         ; branch if not zero
                BRW     NILL            ; branch to NILL if zero
        NOTNILL:INCL    R0              ; add one
                .
                .
                .
```

Here the condition of the branch has been reversed, and an unconditional Branch with Word Displacement (BRW) instruction has been inserted. As one might expect, the BRW instruction consists of a one-byte opcode followed by a 16-bit signed displacement. This technique is used often when the target of a conditional branch is more than 127 bytes away. For short distance unconditional branches, there is also a Branch with Byte Displacement (BRB) instruction.

SUMMARY

In this chapter, we have focused on the addressing modes available to the VAX-11 programmer and on how instructions and operand specifiers are encoded in memory. All the VAX-11 addressing modes, except for short literal and branch addressing, use at least one register to specify the operand address. This register may be specified explicitly by the programmer, as in the register deferred example, INCL (R5). Or the assembler may use a register to encode the effective address of an operand or a literal. For example, in the instructions

```
        TSTL    VAR1
```

and

```
        MOVL    #100,R6
```

the assembler uses the program counter as a general register to point to the operand address displacement or the operand itself within the instruction. In this way, almost all references on the VAX-11 are position-independent.

The indexed addressing modes use two registers, one for the index register and one for the specification of the base address of the array. The base address of the array can be specified using any mode except for literal, indexed, and register.

Tables 3-3, 3-4, and 3-5 contain descriptions of all the VAX-11 addressing modes. The notations B^, W^, and L^ are used to indicate byte, word, and longword values respectively. Notice the variety of addressing that is provided using only four bits of encoding within an operand specifier. The flexibility comes from the indexed addressing mode and from the use of the program counter as a general register.

Table 3-3.   VAX-11 General Addressing Modes

Name of Mode	Assembler Notation	Hex	Description
Short Literal	#literal	0–3	The literal value is contained in bits 0 through 5 of the operand specifier.
Index	base[Rx]	4	The effective address of the operand is formed by first calculating the effective address of the array base, and then adding the value of the index register multiplied by the size in bytes of each array element.
Register	Rn	5	The register contains the operand.
Register Deferred	(Rn)	6	The register contains the address of the operand.
Autodecrement	–(Rn)	7	Register is decremented by the size of the operand in bytes and then used as the address of the operand.
Autoincrement	(Rn)+	8	Register is used as the address of the operand and then incremented by the size of the operand in bytes.

Table 3-3.   VAX-11 General Addressing Modes (Cont.)

Name of Mode	Assembler Notation	Hex	Description
Autoincrement Deferred	@(Rn)+	9	Address in register is a pointer to the effective address of the operand. Register is incremented by 4 after being used to access the effective address.
Byte Displacement	B ^ D(Rn)	A	Displacement is sign-extended to 32 bits and added to the register to form the effective address.
Byte Displacement Deferred	@B ^ D(Rn)	B	Displacement is sign-extended to 32 bits and added to the register to form a pointer to the effective address.
Word Displacement	W ^ D(Rn)	C	Displacement is sign-extended to 32 bits and added to the register to form the effective address.
Word Displacement Deferred	@W ^ D(Rn)	D	Displacement is sign-extended to 32 bits and added to the register to form a pointer to the effective address.
Long Displacement	L ^ D(Rn)	E	Displacement is added to the register to form the effective address.
Long Displacement Deferred	@L ^ D(Rn)	F	Displacement is added to the register to form a pointer to the effective address.

Table 3-4. VAX-11 Program Counter Addressing Modes

Name of Mode	Assembler Notation	Hex	Description
Immediate	#literal	8	Literal operand follows in the operand specifier in the instruction stream. Assembled addressing mode is (PC)+.
Absolute	@#address	9	The address of the operand follows the operand specifier in the instruction stream. Assembled addressing mode is @(PC)+.
Relative	address	A,B,C	Operand is located at specified address. The effective address is formed by adding the contents of the updated PC to the byte, word, or longword offset that follows the operand specifier in the instruction stream. The assembled addressing mode is Displacement(PC).
Relative Deferred	@address	E,F,G	The effective address of the operand is located at specified address. The effective address of the pointer is formed by adding the updated PC to the byte, word, or longword offset that follows the operand specifier in the instruction stream. The assembled addressing mode is @Displacement(PC).

Table 3-5. VAX-11 Indexed Addressing Modes

Name of Mode	Assembler Notation	Description
Register Deferred Indexed	(Rn)[Rx]	The index register is multiplied by the size in bytes of the operand, forming the adjusted index. The result is added to the contents of Rn to form the operand address.
Autoincrement Indexed	(Rn)+[Rx]	Same as register deferred indexed except that Rn is incremented after the operand address is calculated.
Autodecrement Indexed	–(Rn)[Rx]	Same as register deferred indexed except that Rn is decremented before the operand address is calculated.
Displacement Indexed	D(Rn)[Rx]	The base address, formed by adding the byte, word, or longword displacement to the contents of the register, is added to the adjusted index to form the operand address.
Displacement Deferred Indexed	@D(Rn)[Rx]	The displacement is added to Rn to form the address of a pointer to the base address. The base address is then fetched and added to the adjusted index to form the operand address.
Autoincrement Deferred	@(Rn)+[Rx]	Rn contains the address of a pointer to the base address. The base address is fetched and added to the adjusted index to form the operand address. Rn is then incremented by 4.

REFERENCES

The material in this chapter is rather specific to the VAX-11. Since there are no other books than the manufacturer's literature, these are the best sources for more details. The ones to look at are the *VAX-11 Architecture Handbook* and the *VAX-11 Technical Summary*. In addition, the manufacturer has several self-paced courses (1978) which cover some of the material discussed here.

EXERCISES FOR CHAPTER 3

1. Describe the operation of the condition codes.

2. What are the contents of A and B following the execution of the instructions below?

    ```
    A:      .LONG   5
    B:      .LONG   -5
    ```

    Assume for each case that the same initial contents of A and B apply (i.e., A is 5 and B is –5).

    ```
    a.              CMPL    A,B
                    BLSS    NEXT
                    INCL    A
            NEXT:   INCL    A
    b.              CMPL    A,B
                    BLSSU   NEXT
                    INCL    A
            NEXT:   INCL    A
    c.              SUBL    B,A
                    BGTR    NEXT
                    INCL    A
            NEXT:   INCL    A
    ```

3. Suppose you wished to hand translate the FORTRAN arithmetic IF into VAX-11 code, i.e.,

    ```
    IF (K) 10,20,30
    ```

    what would you write? Assume K is stored as a 32-bit integer.

4. Generally speaking, which do you imagine requires more memory space, immediate or simple addressing?

5. What are the contents of Y, Z, R0, and R1 following the execution of
    the instructions below? As before, assume the same initial contents for
    the variable for each instruction.

Address	Assembly Statement			Register	Contents
532	Y:	.LONG	12	R0	532
536	Z:	.LONG	532	R1	536

    a. MOVL   Z,Y
    b. MOVAL   Z,Y
    c. MOVL   @Z,Y
    d. MOVAL   @Z,Y
    e. MOVAL   @Z,@Z
    f. MOVL   R0,R1
    g. MOVL   (R0),R1
    h. MOVAL   (R0),R1
    i. MOVAL   (R0),(R1)
    j. MOVL   (R0),(R1)

6. Rewrite the program of Figure 3-6, which forms the sum of the first 50
    integers, to count upwards from one to fifty.

7. For the VAX-11, is it correct to say that it is a multi-accumulator
    machine as well as a general purpose register one?

8. What is the difference between one level of indirect addressing and the
    use of general purpose registers for addressing?

9. Using autoincrement addressing, code the instructions to initialize the
    10-element longword array A to the values 0 through 9. Perform the
    same task using autodecrement addressing.

10. For each instruction below, what is the operand context for R1, and
    by what value will R1 be incremented following the execution of the
    instruction?

    a. CLRB   (R1)+
    b. MOVW   ABC,(R1)+
    c. MOVW   #1,(R1)+
    d. MOVAW   ABC,(R1)+
    e. MOVAW   (R1)+,ABC
    f. MOVW   (R1)+,(R1)+

11. What is the effect on R2 and R3 after the execution of the instruction:

```
MOVAB   -(R3),(R2)+
```

12. By what value will R1 be multiplied to compute the array index in the instructions below?

   a.   `CRLB     ARRAY[R1]`
   b.   `MOVAW    TEST,(R0)[R1]`
   c.   `MOVAW    (R0)[R1],TEST`

13. Explain the uses of the following addressing modes and write a short code segment to demonstrate the use of each.

   a.   Register deferred mode
   b.   Displacement mode
   c.   Index mode

14. "Reassemble" the following machine instructions into the symbolic assembly instructions from which they were generated. (Bytes are shown right to left. Use the programmers card in the appendix to find the opcodes and addressing modes.)

| | **Byte** | | | | |
	4	3	2	1	0
a.			50	D4
b.			56	65	D0
c.		57	65	45	DE
d.	82	43	51	60	C1
e.			50	05	D0

15. Write an assembly language program segment to compute

```
for i := 2 to 49 do
    A[i] := A[i-1] + A[i+1]
```

16. Translate the above assembly language program solution into its hexadecimal equivalent VAX-11 machine code.

17. Explain the difference between PC-relative and absolute addressing. Why is is PC-relative preferable in most addressing applications?

18. In a machine such as the VAX-11, with both indirect and immediate addressing, what is the meaning of an indirect immediate operand?

19. Write a program to inclusively sum all of the positive longwords between the addresses held in the longwords FIRST and LAST. For example, the beginning and ending of the program might look like:

```
FIRST:   .ADDRESS   THIRD
SECOND:  .LONG      1123
THIRD:   .LONG      -54A3
FOURTH:  .LONG      177D
FIFTH:   .LONG      -1122
SIXTH:   .LONG      9A9
LAST:    .ADDRESS   FIFTH
START:     .
           .
           .
```

Chapter 4

More Advanced Programming Techniques

Chapter 3 presented the basics of VAX-11 programming. There are, however, other techniques that facilitate good programming in assembly language. These advanced techniques demand additional VAX-11 instructions. This chapter will introduce new VAX-11 instructions along with Case and subroutine facilities. Equally important are macro facilities, which allow the programmer to literally write his or her own instruction set.

THE JUMP INSTRUCTION

Elementary branching and looping were illustrated in Chapter 3. Two types of conditional branches were given, signed and unsigned, along with the two unconditional branches, Branch Byte (BRB) and Branch Word (BRW), which transfer to locations within 8-bit or 16-bit offsets, respectively. Although the unconditional branches are very efficiently encoded, they do not allow the use of sophisticated addressing modes and are incapable of transferring control outside of the range of a 16-bit offset. For requirements such as these, the Jump instruction (JMP) is provided. Unlike Branch instructions, in which the destination is a displacement to be added to or subtracted from the PC, the destination of a JMP instruction can be specified by any of the legal addressing modes. The target location may be any location within the address space of the user's program. What follows are some examples of legal JMP instructions:

```
JMP     CONTINUE         ; transfer to location CONTINUE
JMP     @NEXTADDR        ; NEXTADDR contains target
                         ; ...address
JMP     (R1)             ; R1 contains target address
JMP     @(R4)+           ; R4 points to a longword
                         ; ...containing the target
                         ; ...address. Fetch the target
                         ; ...address, increment R4 by
                         ; ...4 and jump to the
                         ; ...destination.
```

A common use of the generalized addressing capability of the JMP instruction occurs when one has to take a specified action based on a numeric code. The computed GO TO of FORTRAN is one example in which transfer of control is made to one of several labelled statements, based on the value of the variable INDEX, as in

```
GO TO (100,200,300,400,...),INDEX
```

Another example might be found in writing a machine simulator, in which transfer of control is made to the Add, Subtract, Multiply, or Divide routines based on the value of the variable CODE. If the addresses of these routines are placed in a table, an indirect jump could be used to transfer control to the appropriate arithmetic routine. For instance, suppose codes of 0 through 3 indicate ADD, SUB, MUL, and DIV, respectively. The dispatching code might appear as in Figure 4-1.

This example again illustrates the use of indexing on the VAX-11. If the value of CODE is 3, for instance, the MOVL instruction will load the longword at TABLE+12 (the address of the DIV routine) into R1. The JMP then transfers control to that routine.

```
           .
           .
           .
TABLE:  .ADDRESS  ADD,SUB,MUL,DIV ; addresses of simulated ops
           .
           .
DISPATCH:
        MOVL      CODE,R1         ; load routine indicator
        MOVL      TABLE[R1],R1    ; get routine address
        JMP       (R1)            ; jump to routine
HERE:   .                         ; return here when done
           .
           .
```

Figure 4-1. Jump table problem.

CASE STATEMENTS

The problem of dispatching to a routine based on the value of a variable occurs frequently enough that some high level languages include special constructs to handle it, such as the computed GO TO in FORTRAN and the Case statement in Pascal. Because of this, the VAX-11 instruction set includes a Case instruction so that such control structures can be represented efficiently. Not only does Case handle the transfer of control, but it also handles the initialization and bounds checking for the INDEX variable.

The general form of the VAX-11 Case statement is

```
          CASE    SELECTOR,BASE,LIMIT
TABLE:    displacement₀
          displacement₁
             .
             .
             .
          displacementₙ₋₁
OUTOFBOUNDS:
             .
             .
             .
```

The objective of the Case statement is to transfer control to one of n locations based on the value of the integer SELECTOR operand. The BASE operand specifies the lower bound for SELECTOR. Following the Case instruction is a table of word displacements for the n branch locations. Just as the displacements in branch instructions are added to the PC to give the branch destination, these word displacements are added to the address of the first displacement (TABLE in this example) to form the Case branch destinations.

The instruction subtracts BASE from SELECTOR, producing a zero-origin index into the table of branch locations. This index is compared with LIMIT to check that it is in the table range. Therefore, the LIMIT operand specifies the largest legal value of SELECTOR – BASE, and is one less than the number of branch displacements.

Although the explanation of this statement is somewhat complex, we can represent the instruction with the following description:

```
if SELECTOR = BASE+0    then GO TO (TABLE+displacement₀)
if SELECTOR = BASE+1    then GO TO (TABLE+displacement₁)
if SELECTOR = BASE+2    then GO TO (TABLE+displacement₂)
   .
   .
   .
if SELECTOR = BASE+LIMIT    then GO TO (TABLE+displacementₙ₋₁)
otherwise
     GO TO OUTOFBOUNDS
```

In other words, if the SELECTOR operand is between BASE and BASE + LIMIT, then the value of SELECTOR – BASE is used to select a table entry with which the branch destination is computed. If the SELECTOR is not between BASE and BASE + LIMIT, control continues at the instruction following the Case table.

A simple example of the use of the Case statement is the computed FORTRAN GO TO of the last section

```
GO TO (100,200,300,400,500),INDEX
```

where we would expect to branch to one of the statement labels based on the value of INDEX. We can also represent this example using the Pascal Case statement

```
case INDEX of
  1: <statement for INDEX=1>;
  2: <statement for INDEX=2>;
  3: <statement for INDEX=3>;
                        .
 _ 4:                   .
                        .
  5:
end;
```

In VAX-11 MACRO, we would code this as

```
            CASEL   INDEX,#1,#4          ; range is from 1 to 5
CASETABLE:
            .WORD   L100-CASETABLE       ; if INDEX = 1, go to L100
            .WORD   L200-CASETABLE       ; if INDEX = 2, go to L200
            .WORD   L300-CASETABLE       ; if INDEX = 3, go to L300
            .WORD   L400-CASETABLE       ; if INDEX = 4, go to L400
            .WORD   L500-CASETABLE       ; if INDEX = 5, go to L500
            BRW     ERROR                ; if INDEX > 5 or < 1,
                                         ; ...go to ERROR
```

It is important to observe that displacements are used rather than actual addresses. Thus, to form the displacement, the difference between the branch address and the base address of the Case table is computed and stored. Since the branch table elements are differences, the Case instruction is position independent. In addition, notice that the Case instruction specifies the data-type of the SELECTOR operand, so there are three forms: CASEB, CASEW, and CASEL.

Similarly, the Jump table example in the previous section can be recoded to use the Case statement. This is left as an exercise for the reader.

One problem with these techniques for transferring control is that there is no automated way for the code at the destination to return to the main line following the dispatch. In subsequent sections, we will consider more generalized subroutine facilities possible on the VAX-11. However, before looking at these advanced programming techniques, let us examine additional methods of constructing loops for the VAX-11.

LOOPS

Chapter 3 introduced several looping examples in the context of sample programs, including the Subtract One and Branch and Add One and Branch instructions. There are two versions of each instruction, depending on the desired end conditions. Thus, these instructions implement the following high level language equivalents:

```
SOBGEQ   INDEX,LOOP      ; for index = initial down to 0 do
SOBGTR   INDEX,LOOP      ; for index = initial down to 1 do
AOBLEQ   LIMIT,INDEX,LOOP ; for index = initial to limit do
AOBLSS   LIMIT,INDEX,LOOP ; for index = initial to limit-1 do
```

The flow of control for these instructions is similar. We can demonstrate it with the flowchart below when the conditions are replaced by the appropriate operation for each instruction.

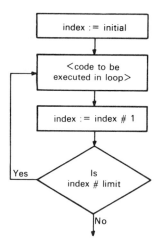

Step

① Initialize   index

② LOOP:

③ # is – for SOBGEQ and SOBGTR
  # is + for AOBLEQ and AOBLSS

④ Limit is 0 for SOBGEQ and SOBGTR
  # is ≥ for SOBGEQ
      > for SOBGTR
      ≤ for AOBLEQ
      < for AOBLSS

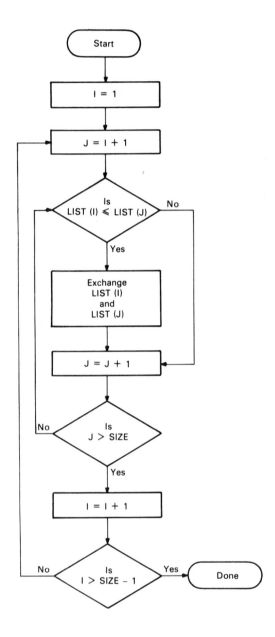

Figure 4-2.   Bubble sort flowchart and routine.

The use of the AOB instructions is exemplified in the construction of a typical Bubble Sort routine. If LIST is the array of values to be sorted and SIZE is the number of elements in the array, then the Sort algorithm in Pascal could be expressed as:

```
for i := 0 to SIZE-1 do
begin
     for j := i+1 to SIZE do
     if LIST[i] < LIST[j] then
     begin
          TEMP := LIST[i] ;
          LIST[i] := LIST[j] ;
          LIST[j] := TEMP ;
     end ;
end ;
```

In VAX-11 Macro, we can code this routine as shown in Figure 4-2. Notice that the VAX-11 Macro and Pascal routines are not equivalent if size ≤ 1.

Even more interesting are the Add Compare and Branch (ACB) generic instructions that efficiently implement the general FOR or DO loops found in all higher level languages. The ACB—which uses a word branch displacement and can be used with byte, word, longword, floating, and double floating operands—allows the programmer to construct loops with increasing or decreasing index values.

The execution of the instruction

```
ACBL   LIMIT,INCR,INDEX,LOOP
```

results in the increment value, INCR, being added to index value INDEX; a test to see whether the LIMIT has been reached; and if it has not, then a

```
           MOVL    SIZE,R0           ; get number of elements
           DECL    R0                ; form index of last entry
           MOVAL   LIST,R1           ; get array base address
           CLRL    R2                ; initialize I to first index
OUTER:     ADDL3   #1,R2,R3          ; initialize J to I+1
INNER:     CMPL    (R1)[R2],(R1)[R3] ; test for order
           BLEQ    CONTINUE          ; branch if first LEQ second
           MOVL    (R1)[R2],TEMP     ; save LIST(I)
           MOVL    (R1)[R3],(R1)[R2] ; exchange LIST(I)
           MOVL    TEMP,(R1)[R3]     ; ...and LIST(J)
CONTINUE:
           AOBLEQ  R0,R3,INNER       ; update J
           AOBLSS  R0,R2,OUTER       ; update I
```

Figure 4-2.   Bubble sort flowchart and routine (cont.).

branch to the branch address LOOP. If INCR is negative, the loop continues while INDEX $\geqslant$ LIMIT, and if INCR is positive, the loop continues while INDEX $\leqslant$ LIMIT. For example, to implement the FORTRAN DO-loop

```
        DO 30 LCV=10,0,-2
          .
          .
          .
30          CONTINUE
```

which loops six times while LCV takes on the values 10,8,6,4,2, and 0, the ACBL equivalent instruction would be

```
        MOVL    #10,LCV            ; initialize loop control value
DO_LOOP: .
         .
         .
        ACBL    #0,#-2,LCV,DO_LOOP ; increment and test LCV
```

THE STACK

Before proceeding to more advanced control structures, we will examine one of the most important data structures in both systems and applications programming, the stack. A *stack* is an area of memory, that is, an array of contiguous data cells, used to store temporary data, and procedure and subroutine invocation information. Data items are dynamically added to or removed from a stack in *last-in, first-out* (LIFO) fashion. When we remove or *pop* an entry from the stack, it is always the last item that was added or *pushed* onto the stack.

Imagine a stack to be like a spring-loaded cafeteria tray holder in a school cafeteria, where the trays are the data items to be saved. If we wish to save several items, we place (push) them onto the stack (of trays). To get them back, we simply pick them up in reverse order, remembering that the last we placed onto the stack is the first one we get back.

For the VAX machine, a variable called the *stack pointer* always points to the last entry pushed on the stack, as shown in Figure 4-3. This last entry is referred to as the top of the stack.

On the VAX-11, a register can be used as a stack pointer. The auto-increment and autodecrement addressing modes are convenient for pushing entries on or popping them off a stack. By convention on the VAX-11, stacks grow in the negative direction, toward memory location zero. To

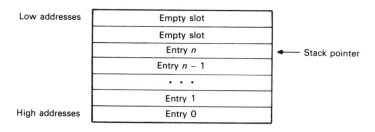

Figure 4-3.   Stack pointer.

push a new entry onto the stack, we use the autodecrement addressing mode, subtracting the element size from the stack pointer and moving the element to memory. An example of a stack (containing longwords) is shown:

Address (hex)	Memory	Stack Pointer
100	?	
104	?	
108	?	
10C	?	
110	20	←R6

R6 is being used as a stack pointer for a stack that has one entry. The current top of the stack is location 110, which contains the value 20. We use a question mark (?) to show that we do not know or care about the values above the stack pointer. Suppose the location at ITEM contains the value 65. The instruction

```
MOVL    ITEM,-(R6)          ; save ITEM on R6 stack
```

moves the stack pointer to the next location and inserts the value of ITEM there, leaving the stack as follows:

Address (hex)	Memory	Stack Pointer
100	?	
104	?	
108	?	
10C	65	←R6
110	20	

We remove an item from the stack using the autoincrement addressing mode. Executing the instruction

```
MOVL    (R6)+,R8            ; pop stack to R8
```

moves the top entry in the stack to R8 and changes the stack pointer to point to the previous top of stack. The stack now appears as follows:

Address (hex)	Memory	Stack Pointer
100	?	
104	?	
108	?	
10C	?	
110	20	←R6

The stack pointer now points at the first entry, exactly where it was before the push and pop operations. Of course, we know that there is a 65 at location 10C, but it will be overwritten by the next Push instruction.

On the VAX-11, register 14 is reserved for a stack pointer. R14 is usually denoted as SP, for stack pointer, by the assembler. When a program is loaded, the operating system automatically allocates a block of memory in the user's address space and loads SP with the address of the block. Some instructions implicitly use SP and the user's stack. For example, the instruction

```
PUSHL  R5
```

pushes the contents of R5 onto the stack pointed to by SP. This instruction is equivalent to

```
MOVL  R5,-(SP)
```

but is shorter since the –(SP) is implied. Likewise, we can write

```
POPL   R3
```

to remove the top entry from the stack and store it in R3. (The VAX-11 does not actually have a POPL instruction because, as we shall see, there are a number of mechanisms for removing items from the stack automatically. However, the assembler recognizes "POPL Destination" and generates "MOVL (SP)+,Destination" instead.)

As an example of how the stack may be used to store temporary variables, we will use the three-instruction exchange in the sorting routine from the previous section:

```
        .
        .
        .
MOVL    (R1)[R2],TEMP        ; save LIST(I)
MOVL    (R1)[R3],(R1)[R2]    ; exchange LIST(I)
MOVL    TEMP,(R1)[R3]        ; ...and LIST(J)
        .
        .
        .
```

Instead of using the variable TEMP to hold LIST(I) during the exchange, we could have easily used the stack and written:

```
PUSHL   (R1)[R2]            ; save LIST(I) on stack
MOVL    (R1)[R3],(R1)[R2]   ; replace LIST(I)
POPL    (R1)[R3]            ; replace LIST(J)
```

This is shorter because we need not represent the address of TEMP in the instruction stream. It also allows the use of "reusable storage space," that is, stack space that any routine can use. The destination of the push and the source of the pop are implied by the register SP.

The stack is also commonly used to save registers. Often we need to use registers for a section of code, but we want to save their current values for later use. In the following section of code, registers 4, 5, and 6 are saved and then restored from the stack:

```
PUSHL   R6          ; save R6
PUSHL   R5          ; save R5
PUSHL   R4          ; save R4
    . (instructions that
    .   modify R4-R6)
    .
POPL    R4          ; restore R4
POPL    R5          ; restore R5
POPL    R6          ; restore R6
```

Notice that the registers are restored in opposite order since the stack is last-in, first-out.

Registers are saved and restored so frequently that the VAX-11 has special Push and Pop Registers instructions to store and retrieve multiple registers from the stack. The operand to these instructions is a 16-bit mask

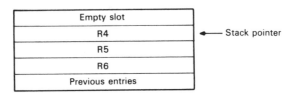

Figure 4-4.   Stack following PUSHR # ^ M<R4,R5,R6>.

with one bit corresponding to each register in the VAX-11 register set. The assembler syntax ^ <R$_a$,R$_b$,...,R$_n$ > automatically generates the mask with the proper bits set for the registers to be saved or restored. For example, the preceding example can be replaced with the following sequence:

```
PUSHR   #^M<R4,R5,R6>        ; save three registers
  .
  . (instructions that
  .    modify R4-R6)
  .
POPR    #^M<R4,R5,R6>        ; restore three registers
```

The Push Registers instruction pushes the registers in high-register to low-register order, while the Pop Registers instruction restores them in low to high order. This is done so that contiguous registers will be stored in increasing memory addresses on the stack. Registers are pushed and popped in this order regardless of the order in which they are specified in the list. Thus the Push Registers instruction, as well as the three Push Long instructions in the previous example, will copy the registers as shown in Figure 4-4.

As we shall see, the stack is often used to contain arguments for a subroutine being called. Since addresses as well as values are passed to subroutines, the VAX-11 also has Push Address instructions to store addresses on the stack. The instruction

```
PUSHAL ITEM
```

pushes the *address* of ITEM onto the stack. This is the same as writing

```
MOVAL   ITEM,-(SP)
```

but shorter. There are four Push Address instructions, PUSHAB,

PUSHAW, PUSHAL, and **PUSHAQ.** Each instruction pushes a 32-bit address onto the stack. The data-type indication is used to evaluate context-dependent addresses, as in the instruction

```
PUSHAW ARRAY[R3]
```

in which the word context indication is needed to evaluate the effective address.

We conclude this section with a short routine that uses the stack. This code, shown in Figure 4-5, takes an integer number and uses routine OUT-

```
;
; Output an integer in ASCII representation.
;
; Input:
;
;        NUMBER contains value to be evaluated
;
; Output:
;
;        ASCII value output by OUTCHAR macro
;
; Register Usage:
;
;        R2 = number to be evaluated
;        R3 = upper 32 bits of quadword (64-bit) number
;        R4 = number of digits to be output
;

OUTASC:
        PUSHR   #^M<R2,R3,R4>       ; save registers to be modified
        CLRQ    R3                  ; clear R3 (upper dividend
                                    ; ...bits) and R4 (digit
        MOVL    NUMBER,R2           ; ...counter)
LOOP1:  EDIV    #10,R2,R2,-(SP)     ; get number to be evaluated
                                    ; push low order decimal digit
                                    ; ...on stack, R2 gets quotient
        BEQL    LOOP2               ; branch if zero quotient
        INCL    R4                  ; count one more digit
        BRB     LOOP1               ; continue for next digit

;
; The digits have been pushed on the stack in reverse order.
; Now pop them off, converting to ASCII, and write them out.
;

LOOP2:  ADDL3   #^A/0/,(SP)+,R0     ; R0 <- ASCII digit
        OUTCHAR R0                  ; OUTCHAR writes a digit
        SOBGEQ  R4, LOOP2           ; continue until done
        POPR    #^M<R2,R3,R4>       ; restore registers
```

Figure 4-5.   Integer to ASCII conversion routine.

CHAR to output the number in ASCII. The stack is used because the algorithm extracts the digits from least significant to most significant, although we read numbers in the opposite order. When a digit is extracted in binary, the ASCII equivalent is computed by adding the value of ASCII zero to the number. This example also introduces a new instruction, Extended Divide (EDIV), which divides a 64-bit dividend by a 32-bit divisor, producing a quotient and remainder of 32 bits each. The format of EDIV is

```
EDIV    divisor,dividend,quotient,remainder
```

Because we are using all longword values, the upper half of the quadword dividend is cleared before the loop begins. In addition, the CLRQ instruction, when given a register operand, clears two consecutive registers.

For example, suppose NUMBER contains the value 35. Following the execution of the EDIV instruction at LOOP1, the stack appears as:

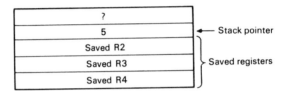

The second time through the loop, the stack appears as:

3	◄—Stack pointer
5	
Saved R2	
Saved R3	
Saved R4	

In LOOP2, the characters are popped off the stack and are converted to ASCII.

SUBROUTINES AND PROCEDURES

The best way to write a program to solve a problem is to subdivide the problem into manageable pieces. Experience has shown that large, monolithic programs are difficult both to debug and to maintain. Building programs in small units that can be debugged independently allows productivity, reliability, and maintainability to be substantially increased. (Of course, dividing a program into small pieces does not in itself guarantee that the program will be productive, reliable, or maintainable.)

In addition to making programs easier to maintain, subroutines save on program space. When a single function must be performed several times within a program, the function is made into a subroutine so that the same code is not duplicated at each point where it is needed. However, it is not required that a routine be called more than once from a program. An instruction sequence should be made into a subroutine whenever doing so simplifies coding or comprehension of the program.

One of the more important aspects of dividing a program into subprograms is defining the routine interfaces and the standards followed for transferring control. A good subroutine facility must include the following properties:

1.   The subroutine must be able to be invoked from many different places in the program. This is known as "calling" the subroutine.

2.   The subroutine must be able to return to the caller without knowing explicitly where it was called from.

3.   There must be a simple and unambiguous mechanism for transmitting arguments between the calling routine and the called procedure.

4.   The subroutine must be able to operate without knowledge of the environment in which it is called or the state of the variables in the outside program, except for the information passed explicitly in the calling sequence.

If a subroutine is specified in such a way that it receives its input arguments and output arguments explicitly and has no knowledge of the outside world, then it will be able to be debugged independently. A special test program may easily be written that simply passes arguments to the subroutine and examines the results. Both input arguments and results are passed via the calling mechanism—neither party has global knowledge. Subroutines written in this way can be used without change as part of other programs that need the same function. This reusability reduces work tremendously because commonplace functions need be written only once. A well-defined interface also makes the calling program independent of the implementation of the function provided by the subroutine. If a sorting procedure is too slow, for example, the algorithm can be changed without requiring any modification to the calling program.

Invoking routines and transmitting arguments are so important in programming that the VAX-11 instruction set contains some high-level mechanisms to deal with them. Indeed, the VAX-11 has two forms of the subprogram call: the procedure call and the subroutine call. The significant difference between these two forms is in the linkage mechanism. The procedure call, to be discussed first, is much more powerful in its handling of the arguments. As we shall see, several of the 16 general purpose registers have been reserved for the procedure calling facility, and the stack is heavily used to automate the transfer of control and the passing of arguments. On the other hand, the subroutine call, while still using some of the registers, is simpler and faster.

The VAX-11 general *procedure* calling facility is provided by the Call instruction. The Call mechanism provides the following features:

1. Arguments are transmitted uniformly and consistently. The called routine can determine the number of arguments passed and can address them as offsets from a fixed pointer called the *argument pointer* (AP).

2. Registers are saved so that the called procedure can use registers without modifying values left there by the caller.

3. The called procedure can allocate local storage on the stack and address local variables as offsets from a fixed pointer called the *frame pointer* (FP).

4. Returning is done uniformly and consistently. The called procedure may return at any time. Any values pushed on the stack will be popped off, the saved registers will be restored, and control will be returned to the instruction following the Call, all automatically.

The following sections examine how these features are implemented.

Argument Lists and Call Instructions

For the VAX-11, arguments are transmitted to a called procedure in an argument list. A VAX-11 argument list is an array of longwords in which the first longword contains a count (in the first byte) of the number of arguments to follow. The general format is shown in Figure 4-6.

Each entry in the list can be a value or an address. Passing data to a

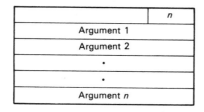

	n
Argument 1	
Argument 2	
•	
•	
Argument n	

Figure 4-6.   VAX-11 call argument list.

procedure by address is known as *call by reference,* while passing immediate values in the argument list is known as *call by value.* The argument list can be allocated in static memory or can be pushed on the stack prior to the call. Consequently, there are two forms of the Call instruction.

The General form, CALLG, takes as operands the address of an argument list anywhere in memory and the address of the procedure to call. For example, suppose we wish to invoke routine **MYPROC** and pass it two arguments whose values are 600 and 84. The following code shows the allocation of the argument list and the Call instruction:

```
            <data section>
ARGLST: .LONG   2                    ; argument count
        .LONG   600                  ; first argument
        .LONG   84                   ; second argument
            .
            .
BEGIN:      .
            <code section>
            .
            .
        CALLG   ARGLST,MYPROC        ; call procedure MYPROC with
            .                        ; ...argument list ARGLST
            .
            .
```

If a second call to **MYPROC** is needed with different values for the arguments, the main procedure could use a different argument list or dynamically move the values into the list starting at label **ARGLST**.

The second form of the call instruction is the Stack form, CALLS, in which the argument list is pushed onto the stack. The following example shows the invocation of MYPROC using the CALLS instruction:

```
        .
        .
        .
    PUSHL   #84             ; push second argument
    PUSHL   #600            ; push first argument
    CALLS   #2.MYPROC       ; call procedure MYPROC
        .
        .
        .
```

Notice two important details about the use of CALLS. First, the arguments are pushed in *reverse order* because the stack grows toward lower addresses. Second, the CALLS instruction itself pushes the argument count on the stack before transferring control. When the called procedure terminates by executing a Return (RET) instruction, the argument list is automatically removed from the stack if a CALLS instruction was used. Execution of a RET instruction by the procedure returns control to the instruction following the Call that invoked it. Thus, following the return from the call, the calling routine does not have to remove its arguments from the stack.

There are a number of tradeoffs between the use of CALLS and CALLG. CALLG makes sense where the number of arguments and the value of each argument are fixed. CALLG is usually faster because the argument list is allocated at the time the calling routine is written. No instructions need to be executed to push arguments on the stack. Depending on the number of calls used in the program, either form could be more efficient of storage space. On the VAX-11, the instruction to push a value on the stack is often shorter than the storage required for the value itself because of short literal addressing. For example, the instruction to push the integer 1 on the stack takes 2 bytes, while a longword argument containing 1 takes 4 bytes. Still more important, the stack form of the call allows for nested routine invocations and permits recursion and re-entrancy (to be discussed later).

The Argument Pointer

Before transferring control to the procedure, the Call instruction loads register 12, the argument pointer (AP), with the address of the argument list in memory or on the stack. The procedure can access arguments as fixed offsets from AP. The first longword that AP points to always contains the number of arguments to follow. For instance, procedure MYPROC could access its calling arguments with the following code:

```
MYPROC:     .
            .
            .
       MOVL    (AP),R0          ; get argument count
       MOVL    4(AP),R1         ; get first argument
       MOVL    8(AP),R2         ; get second argument
            .
            .
            .
       RET                      ; return to caller
```

Saving Registers

The CALLS and CALLG instructions transfer control to the procedure at the address specified by the second operand. To make it simple to save registers, the first word of the called procedure always contains a save mask similar to the one used in the PUSHR and POPR instructions. The Call instruction examines the mask and saves on the stack the registers corresponding to the bits set in the mask. By convention on the VAX-11, all registers used in a procedure must be preserved by that procedure with the exception of R0 and R1, which are used to return values to the caller. The calling routine, then, does not have to worry about saving or restoring registers across procedure calls. The execution of a RET instruction restores the saved registers before returning control.

Each procedure that is called has the same basic format:

```
PROC:   .WORD   ^M<R_a,...,R_n>      ; registers to save
            .
            .
            .
        <routine code>
            .
            .
            .
        RET                          ; return to caller
```

Because one of the most common mistakes in VAX-11 programming is omitting the register save mask at the start of a routine, it is important to remember this format.

Sample Procedure

Now that we have seen how arguments are transmitted, how registers are saved, how control is transferred with the Call instruction, and how control is returned with RET, we will use the sorting example from our discussion of loops to build a callable procedure. The Sort procedure will be called with an argument list containing two arguments: the address of an array of longwords to be sorted and the address of the number of elements in the array. This example also shows the style we will use for documentation within the program. Normally, procedure values are returned in R0 and R1; therefore, these registers are usually not saved and restored by the called procedure.

```
          .SBTTL SORT - Procedure to Sort a Longword Array
;++
;
; FUNCTIONAL DESCRIPTION:
;
;         This procedure arranges an array of signed longword
;         integers into increasing numerical order.
;
; CALLING SEQUENCE:
;
;         Called with CALLS or CALLG to Sort.
;
; INPUT PARAMETERS:
;
;         ARRAY(AP) - the address of the array of longwords to be
;                     sorted
;         ARRAYSIZE(AP) - the address of the number of longwords
;                         in ARRAY
;
; OUTPUT PARAMETERS:
;
;         None
;
; COMPLETION CODES:
;
;         None
;
; SIDE EFFECTS:
;
;         All registers except R0 and R1 are preserved.
;--

          ARRAY=4                   ; offset to array address
          ARRAYSIZE=8               ; offset to array length

;
; The following implements a bubble-up sort, where the smallest
; values are "bubbled" up to the top of the list.
;
```

```
SORT:
        .WORD   ^M<R2,R3>            ; registers to save
        SUBL3   #1,@ARRAYSIZE(AP),R0 ; subtract 1 from array size
                                     ; ...to form last entry index
        MOVL    ARRAY(AP),R1         ; get array base address
        CLRL    R2                   ; I is index of first entry
10$:    ADDL3   #1,R2,R3             ; initialize J to I+1
20$:    CMPL    (R1)[R2],(R1)[R3]    ; is first LEQ second?
        BLEQ    30$                  ; branch if so

;
; Found larger number before smaller one, exchange them.
;

        PUSHL   (R1)[R2]             ; save LIST(I)
        MOVL    (R1)[R3],(R1)[R2]    ; exchange LIST(I)
        POPL    (R1)[R3]             ; ...and LIST(J)
30$:
        AOBLEQ  R0,R3,20$            ; update J
        AOBLSS  R0,R2,10$            ; update I
        RET                          ; return to caller
```

One of the changes made to this code sequence is the introduction of *local labels.* A local label is a symbol of the form Integer$ used to replace alphanumeric labels. A local label is defined only within the *local symbol block* in which it appears. The definition of another alphanumeric symbol begins a new local symbol block in which local symbols using the same number can be defined. In other words, a routine following Sort could also use local symbols 10$, 20$, and 30$. Since another routine cannot transfer to Sort at any place except at its entry point, local symbols enforce the isolation of routines.

The Call Frame

On execution of a RET instruction by a procedure, the following functions are performed automatically:

1. Anything pushed on the stack by the procedure is removed.

2. The registers saved on entry are restored.

3. If the procedure was invoked by a CALLS, the argument list is removed from the stack.

4. Control is returned to the instruction following the Call statement.

In other words, the state of the main routine is restored except for any output results that may have been written within the procedure (or values returned in registers R0 or R1).

The RET instruction can perform these functions and remember all the work to be done because, once more, the stack is a convenient mechanism for maintaining information. When a Call instruction is executed, a data structure known as a *call frame* is built on the user's stack. The call frame contains the state information needed by the RET instruction to restore the registers, restore the stack, and return control. Register 13, the frame pointer (FP), is loaded with the address of the call frame. Therefore, the RET instruction simply uses FP to locate the call frame and restore the previous state.

The structure of the call frame is shown in Figure 4-7. The components of the call frame are:

1. A longword condition handler address. Here, the calling routine may store the address of an error-handling routine to be called if an exceptional error condition arises in the procedure.

2. The saved Processor Status Word (PSW) of the calling routine. The PSW contains enable bits indicating how to handle arithmetic error conditions. The condition codes, also part of the PSW, are stored as zero and are not preserved over the call.

3. A copy of the register save mask found at the call site. This mask is saved so that the RET instruction knows which registers are to be restored from the call frame.

4. A single bit indicating whether this call was the result of a CALLS or a CALLG. If a CALLS was used, RET removes the argument list from the stack, examining the argument count in the first longword of the list to determine the number of arguments.

5. A two-bit field called Stack Pointer Alignment (SPA). The Call instruction always aligns the call frame on a longword boundary. Therefore, if the stack is not aligned at the time of the call, up to three spare bytes may be skipped before the first entry in the frame (the highest numbered register saved) is pushed. SPA is used to remember how many bytes were skipped so that the stack can be restored when the call frame is removed.

6. All registers specified by the save mask, saved highest numbered register first as in the PUSHR instruction.

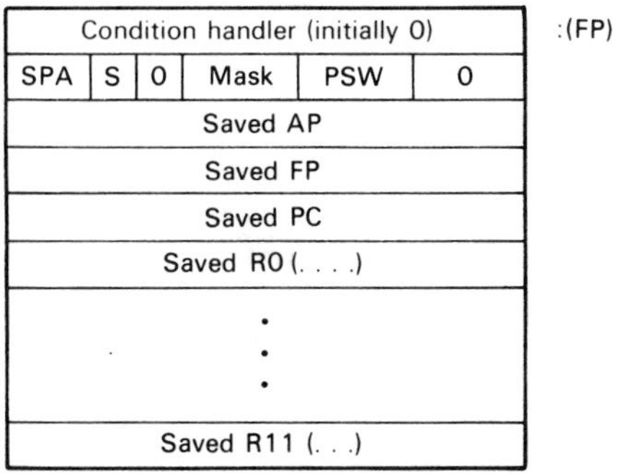

(0 to 3 bytes specified by SPA)
S = Set if CALLS; clear if CALLG

Figure 4-7.   VAX-11 call frame.

To see what might happen to the stack on a procedure call, consider the following example. Suppose that the code below is used to call the procedure Sort:

```
LISTSIZE:
        .LONG  20              ; size of array
AGELST:
        .BLKL  20              ; array of 20 elements
        .
        .
        .
MAIN:   <code sequence>
        .
10$:    PUSHAL LISTSIZE        ; push address of array length
        PUSHAL AGELST          ; push address of array
        CALLS  #2,SORT         ; call Sort routine
20$:    .
        .
        .
```

Assuming that the stack is aligned on a longword before the PUSHAL instruction at location 10$, the state of the stack following the call is shown in Figure 4-8. Although the called procedure may use the stack and the value of SP changes accordingly, FP remains fixed. The call frame can thus always be found.

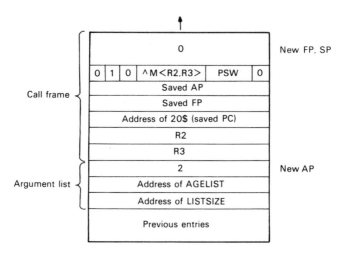

Figure 4-8.   Stack following CALLS to Sort routine.

Local Variables

Another advantage of fixing FP is that the procedure can allocate local variables on the stack and address them as fixed offsets from FP. The following procedure has two local variables, A and B, which are allocated on the stack. The example shows the allocation and addressing of these locals:

```
          A=-4                    ; offset to local A
          B=-8                    ; offset to local B
            .
            .
            .
PROC:   .WORD  ^M<R2,R3,R8,R10>   ; registers to save
        SUBL   #8,SP              ; make room for 2 longwords
                                  ; ...on the stack
            .
            .
        MOVL   R0,A(FP)           ; store R0 in A
        MOVL   R1,B(FP)           ; store R1 in B
            .
            .
        RET                       ; return to caller
```

The advantage of this method is that once the local storage is allocated, the stack can still be used for temporary storage without affecting the addressing of the locals. If the start of the procedure stack is not fixed at FP, we must manually keep track of the changing offset between SP and local storage. This can become a problem when one procedure calls another. Another advantage of fixing FP, illustrated previously, is that the RET instruction automatically deallocates the temporary storage for A and B.

FAST LINKAGES

The procedure call is used as the standard interface between routines written in all languages. Consequently, it is possible for a FORTRAN routine, for instance, to call a Pascal or assembly language routine.

However, in assembly language it is sometimes desirable to call a short procedure, known as a *subroutine* in VAX-11 terminology, without invoking the overhead of the general Call facility. In this quick linkage, input and output arguments are usually transmitted in general registers. There is no automatic saving of registers or restoring of the stack. The called subroutine must take care of these tasks explicitly.

Branch Subroutine Byte and Branch Subroutine Word (BSBB and BSBW) instructions are used to invoke such short subroutines. Just like Branch instructions BRB and BRW, these instructions transfer to subroutines within byte or word offsets from the current location. When a BSBB or BSBW is executed, it simply pushes the PC (the address of the instruction to return to) on the stack and branches to the subroutine. To return, the subroutine executes a Return from Subroutine (RSB) instruction, which merely pops the return address from the stack and returns. Because BSB instructions do not use a frame pointer, the subroutine must be sure to save and restore registers and to restore the stack to its original condition before an RSB is executed.

In the following code sequence using the BSB instruction, the problem is to compute the value of

$$ARRAY[0]^0 + ARRAY[1]^1 + ARRAY[2]^2 + \ldots + ARRAY[n]^n$$

given the address of ARRAY and the number of elements, n. A subroutine is used to raise each entry to the necessary power.

```
        .SBTTL COMPUTE - Calculate Sum of Array(i)^i
;++
;
; FUNCTIONAL DESCRIPTION:
;
;       This routine computes the value of
;
;           ARRAY[0]^0 + ARRAY[1]^1 + ARRAY[2]^2 + ... + ARRAY[n]^n
```

```
;
; CALLING SEQUENCE:
;
;       CALLS or CALLG
;
; INPUT PARAMETERS:
;
;       ARRAY(AP) - address of the array
;       SIZE(AP) - number of elements in array
;       RESULT(AP) - address of longword to receive computed
;                    result
;
; OUTPUT PARAMETERS:
;
;       RESULT(AP) - longword pointed to receives computed value
;
; SIDE EFFECTS:
;
;       None
;--

        ARRAY = 4               ; offset to array address
        SIZE = 8                ; offset to array size
        RESULT = 12             ; offset to address of result
                                ; longword
;
; Register Usage:
;
;       R1 = value of current array entry
;       R2 = address of next array entry
;       R3 = power to raise value to
;       R4 = sum accumulator
;

COMPUTE:
        .WORD   ^M<R2,R3,R4>    ; registers to save
        MOVL    ARRAY(AP),R2    ; get first element address
        CLRQ    R3              ; zero R3 (first power)
                                ; ...and R4 (accumulator)
10$:    MOVL    (R2)+,R1        ; get next array entry
        BSBB    POWER           ; compute to proper exponent
        ADDL    R0,R4           ; add this element to sum
        AOBLSS  SIZE(AP),R3,10$ ; continue with next entry
                                ; ...and power
        MOVL    R4,@RESULT(AP)  ; store result
        RET                     ; return to caller


;
; Subroutine to raise element to a given power.
;
; INPUT PARAMETERS:
;
;       R1 = value
;       R3 = power to raise value to
;
; OUTPUT PARAMETERS:
```

```
;
;          RO = (R1)^R3
;

POWER:
           MOVL    #1,RO          ; assume result is 1
           PUSHL   R3             ; save register
           BLEQ    30$            ; branch if power LEQ 0
           MOVL    R1,RO          ; copy value for first power
           BRB     20$            ; begin loop at end
10$:       MULL    R1,RO          ; compute next power
20$:       SOBGTR  R3,10$         ; continue until done
30$:       POPL    R3             ; restore saved register
           RSB                    ; return to main routine
```

The BSB instructions, like the BR instructions, allow only for branch addressing or transfers to locations within the reach of an 8- or 16-bit offset from the current location. The Jump to Subroutine (JSB) instruction, like the JMP instruction, accepts any general addressing mode as the routine address operand. Routines invoked by JSB still return with the RSB instruction.

RECURSION

It is often useful for a routine to be able to call itself. Such routines, known as *recursive* routines, simplify the expression of many mathematical and syntactical algorithms. For a routine to be recursive, it must have no static storage. All local variables must be allocated on the stack so that the variables from one call are not modified by another recursive call. Here we see another reason why the call frame is so useful. As Figure 4-9 shows, if we look at the stack after several levels of recursive calls, we will see the state information for each level.

The classic example of recursion is in the calculation of N factorial, denoted by $N!$. N factorial is the product of all the numbers from 1 through N inclusive:

$$N! = N \times (N-1) \times (N-2) \times \ldots \times 1$$

The value of zero factorial is defined as one, so we may write the recursive definition for $N!$ as

$$N! = \{N \times (N-1)! \qquad N > 0$$
$$= \{1 \qquad N = 0$$

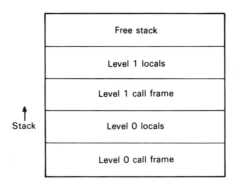

Figure 4-9.   Recursive call frames.

Because most FORTRAN compilers use static variable allocation rather than stacks and call frames, they are not capable of executing recursive routines. In Pascal, however, we could execute the recursive N! routine as follows:

```
function FACTORIAL (n: integer): integer;
begin if N < 1 then FACTORIAL :=1
    else FACTORIAL := n * FACTORIAL (n-1)
end;
```

There are two ways to represent this in VAX-11 Macro, depending on whether the CALLS or BSB instruction is used for linkage. Both work because both use the stack to store the return information. Each one uses R0 to return the value of N!. The CALLS version receives N through the call frame, while the BSB version receives N through R0 (see Figures 4-10a and 4-10b).

Although the recursive definition of N! is notationally nice, it is not a good way to implement the computer calculation. In this case, the straightforward solution shown next is much faster and shorter, as well as making better use of stack space:

```
NFACT:  MOVL   #1,R0          ; initialize factorial
        TSTL   N              ; test N
        BEQL   20$            ; N is 0, return 1
        MOVL   #1,R1          ; initialize counter
10$:    MULL   R1,R0          ; compute N*(N-1)
        AOBLEQ N,R1,10$       ; continue until done
20$:    RSB                   ; return to caller
```

```
START:  .WORD   0               ; entry mask for main routine
        PUSHL   N               ; number to compute factorial
        CALLS   #1,NFACT        ; call factorial routine
        RET                     ; return with result in R0

;
; Recursive routine to compute N!.
;

NFACT:  .WORD   ^M<>            ; save no registers
        MOVL    #1,R0           ; assume N is 0, return 1
        MOVL    4(AP),R1        ; copy N
        BEQL    10$             ; exit if N=0

;
; Build call frame with N-1 for next invocation to
; compute (N-1)!.
;

        SUBL3   #1,R1,-(SP)     ; push N-1 on stack
        CALLS   #1,NFACT        ; recursive call
        MULL    R1,R0           ; compute N*(N-1)!
10$:    RET                     ; return to caller
```

a.   CALLS.

```
START:  MOVL    N,R0            ; load factorial to compute
        BSBB    NFACT           ; compute N factorial
        RSB                     ; return to caller

;
; Recursive routine to compute N!.  N is passed to the routine
; in R0.  At each level, N is saved in R1, and N-1 is passed to
; the recursively called routine to calculate (N-1)!.
;

NFACT:  PUSHL   R1              ; save R1
        MOVL    R0,R1           ; copy N
        BNEQ    10$             ; continue if N not 0
        MOVL    #1,R0           ; N is 0, return 1
        BRB     20$             ; exit
10$:    DECL    R0              ; compute N-1
        BSBB    NFACT           ; recursive call
        MULL    R1,R0           ; compute N*(N-1)!
20$:    POPL    R1              ; restore R1
        RSB                     ; return to caller
```

b.   BSB.

Figure 4-10.   Recursive *N*! routine using CALLS and BSB.

One problem of recursive routines, then, is that they can require a tremendous amount of stack space for the nested call frames and variables. As perhaps a more sensible example of the use of a recursive routine, the following subroutine recodes the procedure to convert an integer to ASCII presented earlier in our discussion of the stack.

```
;
; Output an integer in ASCII representation.
;
; Register Usage:
;
;       R2 = number to be evaluated
;       R3 = upper 32 bits of quadword number
;       R4 = number of digits to be output
;

OUTASC:
        PUSHR   #^M<R2,R3>      ; save registers
        CLRL    R3              ; clear upper bits for EDIV
        MOVL    NUMBER,R2       ; get number to be output
        BSBB    PUTNUM          ; call routine to output it
        POPR    #^M<R2,R3>      ; restore register
        RSB                     ; return


;
; Recursive routine to output a number in ASCII.  Each level
; extracts a low order digit and makes a recursive call if the
; result is not 0.  When the last digit is reached, a return
; is made winding back through the levels and writing the
; digits in high to low order.
;

PUTNUM:
        EDIV    #10,R2,R2,-(SP) ; stack low order digit
        BEQL    10$             ; branch if done
        BSBB    PUTNUM          ; recursive call for next digit
10$:    ADDL3   #^A/0/,(SP)+,R0 ; R0 <- ASCII digit
        OUTCHAR R0              ; output digit macro
        RSB                     ; return to caller
```

RE-ENTRANT ROUTINES

With recursion, we have seen that several simultaneous invocations of a routine can exist, each in its own stage of execution. This is possible because each invocation has its own local state information maintained by the call frame and local storage. Whenever a recursive call is made, a new state is created by building a new call frame on the stack, thereby preserving the state of the calling routine.

On multiprogramming systems, it is particularly advantageous for commonly used programs to be shareable. It is desirable for several user processes to be able to execute a routine without each needing a private copy. This sharing can save memory space, allowing more users to fit in memory and thus increasing performance. The biggest gain comes from sharing utilities such as editors, compilers, and linkers. Although many people may be editing at any time, there need be only one copy of the editor code in memory.

Programs or routines that can be shared among many users are known as *re-entrant*. Several different user processes may be in some stage of execution at different places within a re-entrant routine. For a routine to be re-entrant, it must consist of pure code and data. In other words, no part of the routine can be modified by its execution. Any variables that are modified must be part of the private state information belonging to each user, such as the registers and stacks. Since each user process has its own program counter, stack pointer, general register set, and stack, several user programs may be in the process of executing the same code section. If one user is interrupted and another begins executing the same code sequence, no problems occur because the modified data is unique in each user's private state area.

Besides the utilities already mentioned, the VAX/VMS operating system, for example, is composed of re-entrant code. All processes in the system share the operating system implicitly, and many of them can execute operating system routines at the same time.

MACROS

Subroutines and procedures are usually called *closed* routines. They consist of self-contained code that performs a specified function. Only one copy of the routine is required, and it may be invoked from many places within the program. Control is passed to the site of the routine by a Call and is returned to the instruction following the Call upon completion. In contrast, a routine embedded at the place of invocation in such a way that no linkage mechanism is required to pass values or control is an *open* routine.

Assembly language programmers often find that certain instruction sequences occur frequently within their code. The assembly language *macro* capability allows the programmer to define a sequence of statements to be substituted for the macro name wherever it is used within the program. A macro defines an open routine in that the source statements are placed in line at each site where the macro is used.

For example, if we frequently need to zero the registers R0 through R5, defining the macro CLRREGS lets us simply write CLRREGS in the program as if it were a machine instruction:

```
.MACRO  CLRREGS
CLRQ    R0              ; clear R0 and R1
CLRQ    R2              ; clear R2 and R3
CLRQ    R4              ; clear R4 and R5
.ENDM   CLRREGS
```

Macros such as this give us a shorthand notation. At each occurrence of CLRREGS within the program, the assembler substitutes the three instructions contained in the macro. Called *macro expansion,* this is a simple character-string substitution process allowing the programmer to specify one set of character strings (the macro body) to be substituted for another character string (the macro name).

A macro must be defined before it is used. The pseudo-operation .MACRO begins the definition of the macro, while .ENDM informs the macro assembler that this is the end of the source text to be included in the macro expansion. When the assembler encounters a .MACRO directive, it adds the macro name to its macro name table and stores the source text for future use. Normally, macro expansions are not printed in the assembly listing unless the special .LIST directive includes the macro expansion argument (ME). (Other arguments to .LIST can be found in the *VAX-11 Macro Language Reference Manual.*)

Each time the macro CLRREGS is used, it generates exactly the same instructions. It is sometimes useful to write macros that contain parameters so that slightly different sequences can be produced. This can be done by using formal arguments with the macro definition. When the macro is expanded, any occurrences of the formals are replaced by the actual arguments specified when the macro is invoked. For instance, using a formal argument, we can write a general macro to push a quadword onto the stack:

```
.MACRO  PUSHQ   ITEM
MOVQ    ITEM,-(SP)
.ENDM   PUSHQ
```

Whenever the macro is invoked, the actual argument specified replaces the formal argument, ITEM, in the expanded macro. A code sequence containing

```
PUSHQ   ARRAY2[R4]
```

generates the instruction

```
MOVQ    ARRAY2[R4],-(SP)
```

In this way, macros are used to create an extended instruction set.
When several arguments are needed, they are separated by commas (,).
In this case, the actual arguments must be specified in the same order as the
formals. By using *keywords,* however, the arguments can be specified in any
order. A keyword is a formal argument name along with its default value.
The general format for a macro definition with keywords is

```
.MACRO macro_name keyword1=default1,keyword2=default2,...
.
.   macro body
.
.ENDM  macro_name
```

When the user codes a keyword macro, the actual argument is specified
as keyword = actual. If no actual argument is given for a formal argument,
its default value is used. For example, if the macro PUSHQ is frequently
used to push R0 and R1, it could be recoded with this default as

```
.MACRO PUSHQ  ITEM=R0
MOVQ    ITEM,-(SP)
.ENDM  PUSHQ
```

Now just coding PUSHQ without arguments produces MOVQ R0,
–(SP). Using the macro with an actual argument, we would write

```
PUSHQ  ITEM=ARRAY2[R4]
```

Of course, keywords are more useful in macros with many arguments because the arguments can be written in any order.

Creating Local Labels

Having labels in macros is often useful. Although the programmer can
specify labels in the macro definition, these labels may be unintentionally
duplicated in the source code that surrounds the macro call, thereby causing
errors. Furthermore, each invocation of the macro produces the same label.
To avoid duplication, the assembler has the ability to create unique local
labels in the macro expansion.

To illustrate this point, let us consider the macro that implements the new instruction JUMPIFZERO. The macro definition might be given as

```
        .MACRO  JUMPIFZERO  A,TARGET
        TSTL    A               ; is A 0?
        BNEQ    X               ; continue if not
        JMP     TARGET          ; else jump to target
X:
        .ENDM   JUMPIFZERO
```

(Note that macros may contain comments.) Each time the macro is expanded, the label X will be redefined, causing an error. While it is possible to make the label one of the parameters of the macro definition, a better solution is to use a created local label. Local labels created by VAX-11 Macro start at 30000$ and range up to 65535$. Each time the assembler generates a new local label, the number part of the label is incremented by one. Consequently, a unique label is generated each time that should not interfere with user-defined local labels.

Using this facility, the JUMPIFZERO macro can be rewritten as

```
        .MACRO  JUMPIFZERO  A,TARGET,?X
        TSTL    A
        BNEQ    X
        JMP     TARGET
X:
        .ENDM   JUMPIFZERO
```

Placing a question mark (?) in front of a formal argument name specifies a created local label. When the macro is expanded, the assembler creates a new local label if the corresponding actual argument is blank. If the corresponding actual argument is specified, the assembler substitutes the actual argument for the formal argument. If JUMPIFZERO is invoked twice,

```
        JUMPIFZERO  FIRST,HERE
        JUMPIFZERO  SECOND,THERE
```

the resulting code is

```
            TSTL    FIRST
            BNEQ    30000$
            JUMP    HERE
30000$:
            TSTL    SECOND
            BNEQ    30001$
            JUMP    THERE
30001$:
```

Macro Calls Within Macro Definitions

To build more complex macros, it is often convenient to use one macro within the definition of another. In other words, if a macro has been defined previously, it may be called by another macro as if it were a part of the basic instruction set. Consider the simple macros to push and pop quadwords:

```
.MACRO PUSHQ  A          .MACRO POPQ  A
MOVQ   A,-(SP)           MOVQ   (SP)+,A
.ENDM  PUSHQ            .ENDM  POPQ
```

These macros can now be used to write a more complex macro that allows us to exchange the contents of two quadwords:

```
.MACRO SWAPQ  A,B
PUSHQ  A
MOVQ   B,A
POPQ   B
.ENDM  SWAPQ
```

An interesting generalization of this "complex" macro would be to allow it to work for either longwords or quadwords. PUSHL and POPL instructions already exist in the basic VAX-11 instruction repertoire (POPL is actually an assembler-defined macro). Having defined PUSHQ and POPQ, it is a simple matter to modify the macro definition so that one of the arguments is the data-type. We do so by using argument concatenation. That is, we form the operation name by combining the string PUSH with the value of a parameter containing the type indicator L or Q. This operation of constructing a single string from two strings is *concatenation*.

Argument Concatenation

The argument concatenation operator, the apostrophe ('), concatenates a macro argument with some constant text. Apostrophes may precede or follow a formal argument name in the macro source. If a formal argument name in the macro definition is preceded (or followed) by an apostrophe, the text before (or after) the apostrophe is concatenated with the actual argument when the macro is expanded. The apostrophe itself does not appear in the macro expansion.

Turning to the SWAP macro, we generalize it by including the TYPE formal argument:

```
.MACRO SWAP  A,B,TYPE
PUSH'TYPE    A
MOV'TYPE     B,A
POP'TYPE     B
.ENDM        SWAP
```

This macro exchanges two longword or quadword arguments, using the stack for temporary storage. Coding the two lines

```
SWAP    X,Y,L
SWAP    R,S,Q
```

expands into the instructions

```
PUSHL   X
MOVL    Y,X
POPL    Y
PUSHQ   R
MOVQ    S,R
POPQ    S
```

Repeat Blocks

A programmer occasionally needs to create a table of values. While every line could be typed individually, it is far easier to write a macro to generate the entire table. The *repeat block* directive, specified by the .REPT and .ENDR pseudo-ops, provides the necessary function. For example, to build a table of ten entries, each containing a five, we can write

```
.REPT   10
.BYTE   5
.ENDR
```

A more interesting example consists of generating ten entries containing the integers 1 through 10, each of which is labelled uniquely (e.g., L1 to L10). To do this, we introduce the passing of numeric values as arguments.

When a symbol is specified as an actual argument in a macro, the name of the symbol (the character string), not its value, is passed to the macro. However, it is possible to pass a value provided that a backslash (\) precedes the symbol name. The macro assembler then passes the decimal value of the symbol.

To generate the 1 through 10 list, we first create the TABLE macro, which generates the label and storage for each integer:

```
        .MACRO TABLE    VALUE
L'VALUE:
        .BYTE   VALUE
        .ENDM   TABLE
```

To generate the 10-element labeled storage, the TABLE macro is included in the following REPEAT block:

```
COUNT=1
   .REPT   10
   TABLE   \COUNT
COUNT=COUNT+1
   .ENDR
```

The symbol COUNT is used within the assembler REPEAT loop to generate the integers from 1 through 10.

Of more general purpose use is the *indefinite repeat block*. Indefinite repeat allows a list of arguments to be specified. The block is repeated once for each argument in the list. The general format is

```
.IRP    symbol,<argument list>
  .
  .
  .
.ENDR
```

Each time the block is repeated, "symbol" is replaced by successive actual arguments. The actual argument list must be enclosed in angle brackets (<>) and separated by commas.

For example, the following indefinite repeat block pushes a number of longwords on the stack:

```
.IRP   ITEM,<VALUE,R0,FROG,SQUAREROOT>
PUSHL  ITEM
.ENDR
```

The assembler expands this repeat loop as:

```
PUSHL   VALUE
PUSHL   R0
PUSHL   FROG
PUSHL   SQUAREROOT
```

A more sophisticated example, in which the list is passed as an argument to a macro, occurs in generating a Case statement. The CASE macro automatically generates the Case table from a list of branch destinations and calculates the index limit. This macro can be coded as

```
.MACRO   CASE      SOURCE,DISPLIST,TYPE=B,BASE=#0,?TABLE,?ENDTABLE
CASE'TYPE           SOURCE,BASE,#<<ENDTABLE-TABLE>/2>-1
```

```
TABLE:
  .IRP    DESTINATION,<DISPLIST>
  .WORD   DESTINATION-TABLE
  .ENDR
ENDTABLE:
  .ENDM   CASE
```

It uses several of the techniques already described, namely,

1. Concatenation to form either a CASEB, CASEW, or CASEL instruction.

2. Use of defaults, so that the default instruction is CASEB (i.e., TYPE=B) and the default base is 0.

3. Computation of the expression

    #<<ENDTABLE-TABLE>/2>-1,

    producing the limit operand based on the number of elements in DISPLIST.

4. Use of the indefinite repeat to produce the table of offsets following the Case instruction.

5. Use of created local labels.

For example, the statements

```
            CASE    APPLE,<A,B,C>,TYPE=W
              .
              .
              .
A:          MOVL    TYPE1,R0
            BRB     HERE
B:          MOVL    TYPE2,R0
            BRB     HERE
C:          MOVL    TYPE3,R0
HERE:         .
              .
              .
```

cause the following to be generated:

```
            CASEW   APPLE,#0,#<<30001$-30000$>/2>-1
30000$:
            .WORD   A-30000$
            .WORD   B-30000$
            .WORD   C-30000$
30001$:
```

```
              .
              .
              .
A:        MOVL    TYPE1,RO
          BRB     HERE
B:        MOVL    TYPE2,RO
          BRB     HERE
C:        MOVL    TYPE3,RO
HERE:       .
            .
            .
```

Conditional Assembly

A final example of controlling the assembly process involves conditional assembly. While not strictly a function of a macro assembler, conditional directives are usually used within macro definitions.

The value of conditional code lies in its use in the modification, and hence "customizing," of the assembly code generated. Different final code can be produced depending on symbol values or environment conditions in the program. For example, some smaller versions of the PDP-11 did not have hardware Multiply and Divide instructions. Conditional assembly was often used to generate either Multiply and Divide instructions or calls to routines to simulate these instructions, depending on a symbol in the program specifying the machine version.

However, conditional assembly should be used with caution. Many programs with large amounts of conditional assembly are never fully debugged because so many possible versions can be generated.

The format for the conditional assembly block directive is

```
.IF    condition argument(s)
  .
  .  <conditional statements>
  .
.ENDC
```

If the specified condition is met, the assembler generates statements contained within the block. If the condition is not met, the statements are not generated. The conditon codes are shown in Table 4-1.

The blank and identical tests can be used only within the body of a macro. All others can be used anywhere within the assembly program. There are other forms of conditional code, but we will not examine them here.

Table 4-1. **Condition Tests for Conditional Assembly Directives**

Condition Tests*

Positive	Complement	Format	Condition that Assembles Block
EQ	NE	.IF EQ expression	Expression is equal to 0 (or not equal to 0).
GT	LE	.IF GT expression	Expression is greater than 0 (or less than or equal to 0).
LT	GE	.IF LT expression	Expression is less than 0 (or greater than or equal to 0).
DF	NDF	.IF DF symbol	Symbol is defined (or not).
B	NB	.IF B macro—argument	Argument is blank (or not).
IDN	DIF	.IF IDN argument 1, argument 2	Arguments are identical (or different).

*VAX-11 Macro also allows long forms for these condition tests such as EQUAL for EQ and NOT—BLANK for NB.

As an example of the use of conditional assembly, the following macro implements a general procedure call. Arguments to the macro consist of the procedure to call and as many as 10 longword parameters for the procedure. The parameters are pushed on the stack in reverse order. Since the macro can have a variable number of arguments, the not blank operator (NB) is used to avoid pushing arguments that are not specified.

```
.MACRO CALL   ROUTINE,P1,P2,P3,P4,P5,P6,P7,P8,P9,P10
ARGCOUNT=0                   ; no arguments pushed yet
.IRP   NEXTARG,<P10,P9,P8,P7,P6,P5,P4,P3,P2,P1>
.IF NB NEXTARG               ; if argument is there, then
PUSHL  NEXTARG               ; ...push longword argument
ARGCOUNT=ARGCOUNT+1          ; count argument pushed
.ENDC                        ; end of conditional
.ENDR                        ; end of indefinite repeat
CALLS  #ARGCOUNT,ROUTINE     ; call ROUTINE
.ENDM  CALL                  ; end of macro
```

The symbol ARGCOUNT is used to keep track of the number of arguments pushed for the CALLS instruction. Arguments are checked in reverse order by the .IRP loop and pushed if they are supplied. For example, the statement

```
CALL    FIZZ,R0,ARRAY2[R3],PEANUT,#5,@INDIR
```

generates the following code sequence:

```
PUSHL   @INDIR                  ; push longword argument
PUSHL   #5                      ; push longword argument
PUSHL   PEANUT                  ; push longword argument
PUSHL   ARRAY2[R3]              ; push longword argument
PUSHL   R0                      ; push longword argument
CALLS   #ARGCOUNT,FIZZ          ; call FIZZ
```

When the CALLS is assembled, the symbol ARGCOUNT will have the value five.

SUMMARY

This chapter has covered many important concepts in program control. We saw how the Loop and Case instructions provide capabilities similar to those available with high level languages. We also examined the procedure calling mechanisms. Although somewhat complex, the existence of these mechanisms helps achieve better program structuring. Even more important, the implementation of a procedure call in the architecture creates a standard for VAX-11 language compilers. Therefore, a program can call procedures written in several different languages.

We also examined the stack and the useful properties that come with using a stack for linkage. In the next chapter, we will examine other data structures and their manipulation by the VAX-11.

REFERENCES

Again, the details of the VAX-11 architecture can be found in the manufacturer's literature. The *VAX-11 Macro Language Reference Guide* contains the specifics of VAX macro programming. A more general coverage of this material can be found in Barron (1968) and Kent (1969). Subprograms are discussed, as they apply to high level languages, in Ralston (1971), and Eckhouse and Morris (1979), as they apply to assembly language. Maurer (1977) is another good reference.

EXERCISES FOR CHAPTER 4

1. Recode the Jump Table problem of Figure 4-1 to use the Case statement.

2. Rewrite the sort example of Figure 4-2 to arrange the list in decreasing order.

3. Rewrite the sort example of Figure 4-2, but this time replace the AOB instructions with SOB instructions. Next, replace the AOB instructions with ACB instructions.

4. The VAX-11 macro routine of Figure 4-2 to sort numbers is not equivalent to the Pascal bubble sort. How can the macro routine be rewritten to be equivalent?

5. Code a routine to sum all of the numbers between 0 and 100 that are divisible by three.

6. Suppose that the code segment shown in Figure 4-5 to convert an integer to ASCII begins with (R2) = 1578. Show the state of the stack at each execution of the statements at LOOP1 and LOOP2.

7. In the program of Figure 4-5, show the stack and R2 contents within the loop labelled LOOP1 where the value contained in NUMBER is 412.

8. Code a routine to convert a numeric ASCII string to binary. Assume that the routine receives three input parameters: the number of digits in the string, the address of the string, and the address of a longword in which to return the binary value. For example, the calling sequence could be as follows:

```
SIZE:   .LONG  3              ; number of digits in string
STRING: .ASCII /154/          ; the string to be converted
VALUE:  .BLKL  1              ; place to hold returned value
        .
        .
        .
        PUSHAL VALUE          ; address of returned value
        PUSHAB STRING         ; address of string
        PUSHL  SIZE           ; size of string
        CALLS  #3,CVT_TO_BINARY ; call convert procedure
```

9. Suppose we have an application that requires the use of two stacks that grow at different rates. To make the maximum use of our memory of size N longwords, we wish to implement both stacks so that if one has less than $N/2$ elements, the other can have more than $N/2$ elements. The stacks can be built so that they grow from opposite ends of the memory block towards the middle, as shown below:

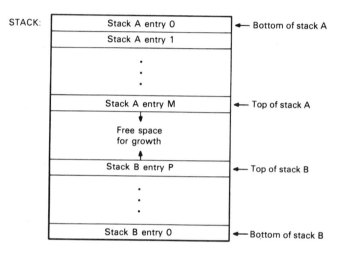

Write routines PUSHA, POPA, PUSHB, and POPB to push and pop longwords from the stacks A and B. Also write routine INITSTACKS to initialize the stack pointers. Assume the stacks use the array at address STACK that contains N longwords.

10. Write the procedure call for the procedure of Figure 4-5. Show what the call frame would look like after the procedure is invoked.

11. What is the advantage of reserving one register as a frame pointer? What is the advantage of a reserved argument pointer?

12. What are the advantages and disadvantages of using the CALL instruction as opposed to the BSB instruction? When would you choose one over the other?

13. Write a multiply subroutine that computes the product of two 32-bit values held in registers R0 and R1. The 64-bit result should be left in R2 and R3.

14. Show the contents of the stack at each execution of the statement at NFACT for both recursive factorial routines of Figure 4-10 when the value of N is 4.

15. What is the difference between a MACRO and a subroutine?

16. Code a macro to initialize a table of longwords to the values 0 through 9. Modify the macro to accept the table size, lower bound, and upper bound as parameters.

17. Write a macro to copy N words from the array A to the array B (e.g., COPY A,B,N). Next write a macro using COPY that switches the contents of the arrays A and B using the stack (e.g., SWITCH A,B,N).

Chapter 5

Data-Types and
Data Structures

An important aspect of program design is the definition of the data structures to be manipulated. Proper data structuring can make the difference between simple and difficult implementation or between superior and mediocre performance. For many applications, writing code is nearly automatic once the data structures are defined, because the instructions merely move data between the structures. The ease of coding depends on the thought given to the data design. This is especially true for operating systems, for which an examination of the data structures often tells more about the system than the code itself.

Among the benefits of high level languages is the ability to define abstract data structures. These languages allow us to describe complex structures and data-types. The compilers for these languages can also check to see that we use the data-types properly. To simplify the generation of code by such languages, new computers have begun to include more complex data-types and data structures in their basic instruction sets.

In this chapter, we will examine the manipulation of simple data-types such as bits, bit strings, and byte strings on the VAX-11. We will look at various representations for numeric values, such as decimal and floating-point, used for different applications. We will also see how the VAX-11 instruction set is used to manipulate more complex structures such as records, arrays, lists, queues, and trees.

BITS AND BIT FIELDS

Bit manipulation instructions were more meaningful in earlier mini-computers, in which memory size and instruction sets were limited. Under these conditions, it was often necessary to manipulate individual bits within a word or byte (hence the designation of such a programmer as a "bit hacker") to conserve space, or to mask out individual bytes within a word for computers without byte manipulation instructions. With the large address space of the VAX-11, it is not necessary for programmers to be as concerned with such bit efficiency. However, because of the VAX-11 I/O architecture inherited from the PDP-11, these instructions are still needed to test and set individual bits contained within I/O device registers.

Bit manipulation instructions can be divided into three classes. The first includes instructions that perform logical functions on bits contained within a byte, word, or longword. The second class covers instructions that test a single bit within a longword to determine if a branch is to be taken. The final class consists of instructions that deal with arbitrary bit strings.

Logical Bit Instructions

Bit Set (BIS), Bit Clear (BIC), Bit Test (BIT), and EXCLUSIVE OR (XOR) are the generic set of logical operations that manipulate byte, word, or longword data. These instructions are defined in Table 5-1.

When using these instructions, we usually think of the first operand as being a mask whose bits are applied to the second operand according to the instruction. A *mask* is a sequence of bits used in a logical operation to test, set, or clear the corresponding bits of an operand in a bit manipulation instruction. For example, the instruction

```
BICB    #3,R4
```

masks, or clears, bits 0 and 1 in R4. These are the bits set in the mask operand, or the binary equivalent of 3 decimal. The Bit Set instruction

```
BISB    #3,R4
```

sets bits 0 and 1 in R4 to 1. The Bit Test instruction tests to see if any of the bits set in the mask are also set in the destination operand. Neither operand is changed, but the condition codes are set based on the result of the logical AND of the two operands.

Table 5-1.   VAX-11 Logical Bit Instructions

Operation	Mnemonic	Data-Types	Number of Operands
Bit Set (logical OR). Set all bits in the second operand corresponding to bits set in the first operand.	BIS	B,W,L	2,3
Bit Clear. Clear all bits in the second operand corresponding to bits set in the first operand.	BIC	B,W,L	2,3
Bit Test. Test the condition of the bits in the second operand to determine if they correspond to the bits set in the first operand.	BIT	B,W,L	2
EXCLUSIVE OR. Form the EX-CLUSIVE OR of the two operands.	XOR	B,W,L	2,3

Single-Bit Instructions

The VAX-11 has a number of instructions that test the condition of one bit or test and modify the bit in a single operation. As we shall see, this second form is particularly useful for synchronizing several processes. Both types of instructions are listed in Table 5-2.

A special case of the Bit Test instructions is covered by the Branch on Low Bit (BLB) pair of instructions. BLBC and BLBS test the least significant bit, bit 0, of a longword and branch if it is clear or set, respectively. Together with the TSTL instruction, BLBC and BLBS enable the programmer to test either the most significant bit (MSB) or the least significant bit (LSB) of any longword. These instructions were provided specifically for examining values returned from subroutines. In the VAX/VMS operating system, for example, all system routines return a code in R0 giving an indication of the final status of the routine. The values of these codes are defined such that all error codes are even (bit 0 is 0) and all success codes are odd (bit 0 is 1). The programmer can easily test for the success or failure of a routine with the BLBC and BLBS instructions.

The Branch on Bit instructions and the Branch on Bit and Modify instructions allow the programmer to test and set a bit within an arbitrary bit field. In each case, the single bit specified by the position and base operands

Table 5-2. VAX-11 Single-Bit Instructions

Operation	Mnemonic	Operands
Branch if Low Bit Clear	BLBC	source,branch_ destination
Branch if Low Bit Set	BLBS	source,branch_ destination
Branch if Bit Set	BBS	position,base,branch_destination
Branch if Bit Clear	BBC	position,base,branch_destination
Branch if Bit Set and Set Bit	BBSS	position,base,branch_destination
Branch if Bit Set and Clear Bit	BBSC	position,base,branch_destination
Branch if Bit Clear and Set Bit	BBCS	position,base,branch_ destination
Branch if Bit Clear and Clear Bit	BBCC	position,base,branch_ destination

is tested. If it is in the state tested for, a branch is taken to the destination. If the instruction so specifies, the tested field is set or cleared regardless of the initial state of the bit. The bit is located by specifying the address of a byte (base operand) and the offset to the bit to be tested (position operand). For example, the following two sequences are equivalent:

```
BBC     #3,R0,NOTSET        BITB    #8,R0
                            BEQL    NOTSET
```

Both test to see if the fourth bit in R0 (bit 3) is zero and branch if so. Note that the BBC instruction takes a bit position while the BITB instruction takes a mask.

Two more instructions not included in Table 5-2, BBSSI and BBCCI, are identical to BBSS and BBCC except that the memory location under examination is interlocked. These instructions are provided so that if more than one VAX processor or I/O device is cooperatively accessing memory, only one at a time will be able to test and modify the given bit.

Designers of operating systems will recognize these instructions as useful for implementing Dijkstra's *P* and *V* operations. For those unfamiliar with them, a simple example will demonstrate how two bit fields can be used to coordinate or synchronize two processes within a computer.

We might suppose that two processes share a resource that only one process may access at a time. The Bit Test and Set instructions can be used to ensure unique access. First, we define a flag bit in memory shared between the processes. When this flag is set, the resource is free. Before accessing the shared resource, each process tests the bit and branches to its code if the flag is set. If the flag is not set, the process continues to loop until the bit becomes set. When a process finds the bit set, it clears the bit until it is finished with the resource. This coordination is coded as follows:

```
FLAGS:  .LONG   1                       ; flag initially 1 (free)
        .
        .
        .
;
; Code for first process
;
;
; Start of unique access code for first process
;
WAIT1:  BBCC    #0,FLAGS,WAIT1          ; loop until bit is set
                .
GO_ON1: .
        <access shared resource>
                .
                .
        BISL    #1,FLAGS               ; restore flag bit
                .                      ; continue processing
                .
                .
;
; Code for second Process
;
;
; Start of unique access code for second process
;
WAIT2:  BBCC    #0,FLAGS,WAIT2          ; loop until bit is set
                .
GO_ON2: .
        <access shared resource>
                .
                .
        BISL    #1,FLAGS               ; restore flag bit
                .                      ; continue processing
                .
                .
```

Both processes wait for the flag bit. The first process to find the flag bit set is allowed to fall into its main body of code. The other process continues to clear the already clear flag bit until it is (re)set to 1. Of course, a coordination mechanism like this should be used only when the code section to be used exclusively is extremely short. On most systems, a process requesting an unavailable shared resource is forced to wait until the resource becomes available. In a later chapter we will discuss event flags that implement this coordination between processes as a part of the operating system.

It is important to note that on all VAX-11 single-bit and variable-length bit field instructions, the bit position operand is interpreted as a signed longword offset from the base address. That is, the selected bit can be in the range of -2^{31} to $2^{31} - 1$ bits from the base address. Therefore, the upper 29 bits of the position operand contain a signed byte offset from the base address to the byte containing the selected bit. The low three bits of the position operand contain the bit number within the selected byte.

A good demonstration of the use of this feature is shown below in the Sieve of Eratosthenes program for producing prime numbers. The program uses a string of N bits to represent the integers from 0 through $N - 1$, where the bit position of each bit represents an integer (e.g., bit 6 in the string represents the integer 6). The program begins with the prime number 2, and marks off all multiples of 2 by setting the bits whose position number is a multiple of 2. These can not be prime, since they are evenly divisible by 2. The program then searches for the next zero bit in the string. This bit represents a prime number since it is not a multiple of any lower number. As each prime is found, all of its multiples are marked off, and a search is made for the next zero bit.

```
;
; Sieve of Eratosthenes routine for producing prime numbers.
;

              SIEVESIZE = 10000        ; find all primes < 10000
SIEVE:  .BLKB   SIEVESIZE/8            ; produce initial table of
                                       ; ...SIEVESIZE bits (zeroed)

PRIMES:                                ; routine entry point
         .WORD   ^M<>                  ; save no registers
         MOVL    #2,R0                 ; start with prime 2
10$:     OUTASC  R0                    ; output prime number
         MOVL    R0,R1                 ; use R1 to form multiples

;
; Set all bits that are multiples of the prime just found.
;

20$:     BBCS    R1,SIEVE,30$        ; eliminate next multiple
30$:     ACBL    #SIEVESIZE-1,R0,R1,20$ ; form next multiple
```

```
;
; Search for the next zero bit in the string.
;
40$:     BBC     R0,SIEVE,10$        ; check for next prime
         AOBLSS  #SIEVESIZE,R0,40$   ; continue looking for bit
         RET                         ; return to caller
```

Having considered instructions operating on single bits, we next consider instructions that operate on bit strings.

Variable-Length Bit Fields

The VAX-11 also has instructions to extract, insert, or compare bit strings up to 32 bits long. The bit string is described by three arguments: its base address, the position of the first bit relative to the base, and the size in bits of the string. When extracting a bit field, the bit string, specified by the position, size, and base operands, is moved right-justified into the longword destination operand. The upper bits of the destination may be sign-extended from the field or zeroed, depending on the instruction. The bit field instructions are listed in Table 5-3.

An example of the use of the Extract Zero-Extended Field (EXTZV) instruction to print the ASCII hexadecimal value of a 32-bit longword follows. The field instruction is used within a loop to extract the eight 4-bit digits from left to right. We assume that the OUTCHAR statement calls a routine to print the digit contained in R2. On each execution of the EXTZV, a 4-bit field is extracted from R0 and placed, right-justified and zero-extended, into R2. R1 specifies the starting bit position for the string.

```
;
; Print hexadecimal ASCII representation of a longword.
;
;       R0 - contains longword to be evaluated
;       R1 - position of the 4-bit field to be extracted
;
HEXDIGITS:                           ; ASCII names for hex digits
        .ASCII /0123456789ABCDEF/
          .
          .
          .
PRINTHEX:
        MOVL    NUMBER,R0            ; get binary number to output
        MOVL    #<<4*8>-4>,R1        ; begin with last hex digit
10$:    EXTZV   R1,#4,R0,R2          ; R2 <- next binary digit
        MOVB    HEXDIGITS[R2],R2     ; R2 <- ASCII representation
        OUTCHAR R2                   ; output ASCII hex digit
        ACBL    #0,#-4,R1,10$        ; continue left to right
```

Table 5-3.   VAX-11 Bit Field Instructions

Operation	Mnemonic	Operands
Extract Field. Move the specified field into the destination, right-justified and sign-extended to 32 bits.	EXTV	position,size,base,destination
Extract Zero-Extended Field. Move the specified field into the destination, zero-extended to 32 bits.	EXTZV	position,size,base,destination
Compare Field. Compare the sign-extended field with the source operand, setting the condition codes.	CMPV	position,size,base,source
Compare Zero-Extended Field. Compare the zero-extended field to the source operand, setting condition codes.	CMPZV	position,size,base,source
Insert Field. This size operand specifies the number of low order bits to be moved from the source to the field described by position, size, and base.	INSV	source,position,size,base
Find First Set. Locates the first 1 bit in the specified field.	FFS	position,size,base,findposition
Find First Clear. Locates the first zero bit in the specified field. If a zero bit is found, findposition is replaced by the position of the bit and the Z condition code is cleared. Otherwise, Z is set and findposition is replaced by the position (relative to the base) of the bit one position past the specified field.	FFC	position,size,base,findposition

The Find First Set and Find First Clear bit instructions are included in Table 5-3 because they also deal with bit fields. However, these instructions are used to locate the first 0 or 1 bit in a string of from 0 to 32 bits. The instruction returns the position of the first bit found in the specified state and clears the Z condition code. If a bit is not found in the specified state, the instruction returns the position of the bit following the field and sets the Z condition code. For example, the instruction

```
FFS     #0,#32,ENTRY,R0
```

will cause R0 and Z to be set to the following values:

Contents of ENTRY	R0	Z
1	0	0
4	2	0
8	3	0
9	0	0
0	32	1

As noted in the previous section, the starting position argument can be greater than 32 bits from the base address. This is useful for searching long bit strings. The string can be searched 32 bits at a time, and, if the specified bit is not found, the findposition argument will contain the position of the next 32-bit field to search. The use of this feature is left as an exercise at the end of the chapter.

CONVERTING INTEGER DATA-TYPES

It is often necessary to convert an item of one data size into another, whether to be stored in a field of a different size, loaded into a register, or used in an arithmetic operation. The VAX-11 makes data conversion simple with two instructions, Convert and Move Zero-Extended.

The Convert instructions allow us to move a signed byte, word, or long-word datum to a field of a different size. The six signed-integer Convert instructions are shown in Table 5-4.

When a shorter data-type is converted to a longer data-type, a sign extension is performed. That is, the high order bit, which is the sign bit, is

Table 5-4. VAX-11 Integer Convert Instructions

Operation	Mnemonic	Operands
Convert Byte to Word.	CVTBW	byte _ datum,word _ datum
Convert Byte to Longword.	CVTBL	byte _ datum,longword _ datum
Convert Word to Byte.	CVTWB	word _ datum,byte _ datum
Convert Word to Longword.	CVTWL	word _ datum,longword _ datum
Convert Longword to Byte.	CVTLB	longword _ datum,byte _ datum
Convert Longword to Word.	CVTLW	longword _ datum,word _ datum

duplicated in the high order bits of the longer destination and the low order bits are copied. Consider the following byte-to-word conversion:

```
A:      .BYTE   ^B11010011      ; byte of binary data
B:      .WORD   0               ; word to receive
                                ; sign-extended byte
        CVTBW   A,B             ; extend byte to word
```

Following execution of the Convert instruction, the contents of A and B would be

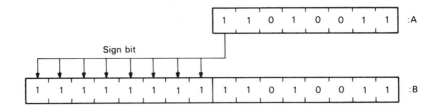

Notice that the low order seven bits of byte A, the magnitude, have been copied directly into the low order seven bits of word B. The sign bit of byte A has been extended left to fill the high byte of word B.

On a conversion from a longer to a shorter data-type, the sign bit is also copied, but the larger number is *truncated* to fit in the smaller datum. Truncation is illustrated in the following conversion:

```
A:      .BYTE   0                       ; byte to receive truncated
                                        ; ...word
B:      .WORD   ^B1111111101001111  ; binary word
        .
        .
        CVTWB   B,A                     ; convert word to byte
```

Following this instruction, the contents of B and A are

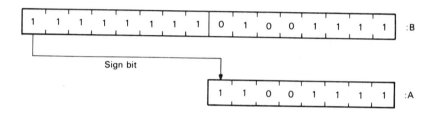

In this case, only the sign bit and the least significant seven bits of B are preserved in A. If the upper byte was not all one's as shown, integer overflow would occur. In using the convert instruction, one must be careful when the destination field is smaller than the source field. Integer overflow will occur whenever all the upper bits of the source (the bits truncated) are not the same as the resulting sign bit of the destination field.

A frequent use of these instructions, particularly smaller-to-larger conversions, is movement of a byte or word datum to a register in order to perform arithmetic. If the datum were moved to the register with a Move instruction, the high order bits of the register would retain their old values.

To extend an unsigned data-type, there are three Move Zero-Extended instructions that zero-extend bytes to words (MOVZBW), bytes to longwords (MOVZBL), and words to longwords (MOVZWL). These are also frequently used to move a short datum to a register, where we prefer the high order bits of the register to be zeroed first. Instead of coding

```
A:      .BYTE   5                       ; the data byte
        .
        .
        .
        CLRL    R0                      ; clear register
        MOVB    A,R0                    ; move byte to R0<0:7>
```

we can instead write

```
MOVZBL A,R0              ; move zero-extended
                        ; ...byte to register
```

The context of the operand is always determined by the data-type of the operand. Thus, in the instruction Move Zero-Extended Byte to Longword (MOVZBL), the first operand has byte context and the second has longword context. Following the execution of the instruction

```
MOVZBL (R0)+,(R1)+
```

the value of R0 is incremented by one, while R1 is incremented by four.

CHARACTER STRINGS

As we have seen, bytes can be used to hold 256 different numerical values (00 to FF hex). We can assign representations to these numbers to allow us to manipulate characters, decimal numbers, special symbols, and so on. Although we could choose any representation we like for the characters, we use the ASCII code to allow the connection of computers and peripherals made by different manufacturers.

On some machines that are not byte addressable, handling characters is a complex task because several characters may be packed into the smallest unit. On the VAX-11, character handling is aided by the fact that each character is uniquely addressable and by the existence of a full set of instructions that manipulate strings of characters. These instructions move, compare, and search strings of characters up to 65,536 (65K) bytes in length. In descriptions of these instructions, the terms "byte" and "character" are equivalent because the instructions deal with strings of bytes independent of the representation used. However, the instructions are called *character string* instructions because they are usually used with character text strings.

A character string on the VAX-11 is specified by the length of the string in bytes (the length is contained in a word, hence the 65K maximum string length) and the address of the first character of the string. The character string instructions use from two to six of the general registers, R0 through R5, to hold temporary values and to return updated string pointers. In other words, regardless of what registers may be specified as operands to the instructions, some of the low numbered registers will be modified to contain values returned by the instructions. It is important for the programmer to set up the registers carefully, when using string instructions or to save and restore low numbered registers that contain useful information. Therefore, the PUSHR and POPR instructions can be used effectively to preserve registers that are modified by the character string instructions.

As an example, look at one of the string instructions, MOVC3. This instruction moves a byte string from one location to another; that is, it copies a block of memory. The three operands are the length of the string to be moved, the address of the source string to move, and the address of the destination to receive the string. Thus, the format of the instruction is

```
MOVC3   length,srcaddress,dstaddress
```

Following the execution of MOVC3, the registers have the following values:

R0, R2, R4, and R5 = 0
R1 = The address one byte beyond the source string
R3 = The address one byte beyond the destination string

Let us consider the following example in which there are three message strings, including one that will be moved to the block of memory at OUT-BUFFER depending on the value contained in R6. Each of the three strings is stored as a counted ASCII (.ASCIC) string; in other words, the first byte contains the length of the string, not including the count byte. If R6 contains a zero, the first message will be moved; if it contains a one, the second message will be moved; and so on.

```
            MAXMSG = 2              ; maximum message number
MSGADDRS:                          ; addresses of the messages
            .ADDRESS MSG1
            .ADDRESS MSG2
            .ADDRESS MSG3
MSG1:   .ASCIC  /THIS IS THE FIRST MESSAGE/
MSG2:   .ASCIC  /THIS IS THE SECOND MESSAGE/
MSG3:   .ASCIC  /THE THIRD MESSAGE IS HERE/
OUTBUFFER:                         ; 100 byte output buffer
            .BLKB   100
            .
            .
            .
            CMPL    R6,#MAXMSG     ; validate range of msg number
            BGTRU   ERROR          ; error if too large
            MOVL    MSGADDRS[R6],R8 ; get address of ASCIC
                                   ; ...string to be moved
            MOVZBL  (R8)+,R7       ; R7 <- length of string
                                   ; R8 now points to first char.
            MOVC3   R7,(R8),OUTBUFFER ; move string to output buffer
            .
            .
            .
```

The MOVC5 instruction copies a block of memory in which the source and destination strings may differ in length. If the source is longer than the destination, only the number of characters specified by the destination length is copied (i.e., the string is truncated). If the source is shorter than the destination, the remainder of the destination is filled with copies of a "fill" character specified as one of the operands. The format for MOVC5 is

```
MOVC5   srclength,srcaddress,fillchar,dstlength,dstaddress
```

Following MOVC5, the registers are the same as for MOVC3 except that R0 contains the number of characters not moved if the source was longer than the destination. In addition, the condition codes are set based on the comparison of the source length and destination length. MOVC5 is the preferred way to fill a block of memory with any one character because a source length of zero causes the entire destination to be filled with the fill character. For instance, the instruction

```
MOVC5   #0,(R0),#0,#512,OUTBUF
```

causes the 512-byte buffer OUTBUF to be zeroed. Note that the source operand pointed to by R0 is never referenced, therefore R0 need not contain a valid address.

Table 5-5 describes some of the other string instructions. More can be found in the *VAX-11/780 Architecture Handbook.*

As a final example, the routine of Figure 5-1 checks an input buffer to see whether it contains the name of a chess piece. Leading blanks are first removed from the input buffer, and the string is then checked against the names of chess pieces stored at NAMES. If a match is found, a variable is returned indicating which piece it was. On return, R0 indicates whether a match was found.

PACKED DECIMAL STRING INSTRUCTIONS

For some languages such as COBOL, it is often more convenient to treat the computer as a decimal machine than a binary machine. Consequently, many machines have implemented decimal arithmetic as well as binary. The internal representation of a number for decimal arithmetic is the packed decimal string. This string is a contiguous sequence of 4-bit digits, each representing a decimal digit from 0 to 9, with the low digit representing the sign. A decimal string is described by its length in digits (not bytes) and

Table 5-5. VAX-11 String Instructions

Operation	Mnemonic	Operands
Compare two strings. These instructions do a byte-by-byte comparison, setting the condition codes based on a comparison of the first bytes, if any, that do not match.	CMPC3 CMPC5	length,src1address,src2address src1length,src1address,fillchar, src2length,src2address
Locate a character in a given string. Following this instruction, R1 contains the address of the located character or one byte past the string if the character was not found. R0 contains the number of bytes left in the string.	LOCC	character,srclength,srcaddress
Skip over all consecutive occurrences of a character in a given string. This is like LOCC except the test is for inequality instead of equality. The registers are set in a manner similar to LOCC.	SKPC	character,srclength,srcaddress
Find a substring within a string. The string specified by src1length and src1address is searched for a substring matching the one specified by src2length and src2address. Following execution, if a match was found, R0 contains the number of bytes remaining in string one including the substring; R1 contains the address of the located substring. On no match, R0 contains zero and R1 points one byte past string one.	MATCHC	src1length,src1address,src2length, src2address

```
              .SBTTL VALIDATE - Validate Name of Chess Piece
;++
; FUNCTIONAL DESCRIPTION:
;
;      This routine locates the next string in a buffer and
;      checks to see if it is the name of a chess piece.
;
; CALLING SEQUENCE:
;
;      CALLS or CALLG
;
; INPUT PARAMETERS:
;
;      BUFLEN(AP) - length of the buffer to be checked
;      BUFADR(AP) - address of the buffer
;      RETKEY(AP) - address of a longword to receive the piece
;                   number
;
; OUTPUT PARAMETERS:
;
;      RETKEY(AP) = if name is valid, address pointed to receive
;                   the piece number with the encoding
;                   0 = king, 1 = queen, 2 = bishop, 3 = knight,
;                   4 = rook, 5 = pawn
;
; RETURN VALUE:
;
;      R0 = 0 if no match, 1 if valid name is found
;
;--

              BUFLEN = 4              ; offset to length argument
              BUFADR = 8              ; offset to address argument
              RETKEY = 12             ; offset to return address

;
; List of counted string names for pieces.  Zero length
; terminates the list.
;
NAMES:
              .ASCIC /KING/
              .ASCIC /QUEEN/
```

Figure 5-1.   Validate name of chess piece subroutine.

the address of the low order byte. The assembler directive .PACKED is used
to store one packed decimal string of variable length up to 31 digits in multiple consecutive bytes.

Corresponding to the set of binary arithmetic instructions, the packed
decimal instruction set includes Move Packed (MOVP), Compare Packed
(COMP), Add Packed (ADDP), Subtract Packed (SUBP), Multiply Packed

```
                .ASCIC  /BISHOP/
                .ASCIC  /KNIGHT/
                .ASCIC  /ROOK/
                .ASCIC  /PAWN/
                .BYTE   0                       ; terminate list

VALIDATE:
                .WORD   ^M<R2,R3,R4,R5,R6>  ; registers to save
                SKPC    #^A/ /,BUFLEN(AP),@BUFADR(AP) ; skip leading
                                                ; ... blanks
                BEQL    30$                     ; exit if nothing there
                MOVQ    R0,R4                   ; save input length and
                                                ; ...address in R4 and R5
                CLRL    R6                      ; zero piece indicator
                MOVAL   NAMES,R1                ; get address of piece list
10$:
                MOVZBL  (R1)+,R0                ; R0 <- length of piece name
                                                ; R1 <- address of first char.
                BEQL    30$                     ; exit if table exhausted
                CMPC5   R0,(R1),#^A/ /,R4,(R5) ; strings match?
                BEQL    20$                     ; exit if strings match
                ADDL    R0,R1                   ; form address of next ASCIC
                                                ; ...string to check
                INCL    R6                      ; note next piece number
                BRB     10$                     ; continue loop

;
; Piece was located, return success and piece number.
;

20$:
                MOVZBL  #1,R0                   ; success return code
                MOVL    R6,@RETKEY(AP)          ; return piece number
                RET
;
; Valid name not found, return error code.
;

30$:
                CLRL    R0                      ; error code
                RET
```

Figure 5-1.   Validate name of chess piece subroutine (cont.).

(MULP), and Divide Packed (DIVP). The decimal string instructions always treat the decimal strings as integers, with the decimal point immediately to the right of the least significant digit of the string. If the result of a
decimal instruction is to be stored in a string that is larger than the result,
the most significant digits are filled with zeros. Thus, the only difference
between these instructions and the binary arithmetic instructions is that a
length operand is required, since packed decimal strings may be of varying
length. The formats for these instructions are presented in Table 5-6.

Table 5-6.   VAX-11 Packed Decimal String Instructions

Operation	Mnemonic	Operands
Move source string to destination.	MOVP	length,srcaddress,dstaddress
Compare source string to destination string.	COMP	length,srcaddress,dstaddress
Add source string of length ADDLENGTH to destination string of length SUMLENGTH.	ADDP	addlength,addaddress,sumlength, sumaddress
Subtract source string from destination string.	SUBP	sublength,subaddress,diflength, difaddress
Multiply multiplier by multiplicand and place result in product.	MULP	mulrlength,mulraddress,muldlength, muldaddress,prodlength,prodaddress
Divide dividend by divisor and store result in quotient.	DIVP	divrlength,divraddress,divdlength, divdaddress,quolength,quoaddress
Convert packed decimal string to longword integer.	CVTPL	srclength,srcaddress,dstaddress
Convert longword integer to packed decimal.	CVTLP	srcaddress,dstlength,dstaddress

The setting of the condition codes for packed decimal arithmetic is similar to that for binary arithmetic instructions, with decimal overflow resulting when the destination string is too short to contain all the non-zero digits of the result. If overflow occurs, the destination string is replaced by the correctly signed least significant digits of the result.

The VAX-11 instruction set includes instructions for converting from packed decimal to other formats. Thus, the representation of a number can be chosen for a particular application and converted, as necessary, to a different internal representation for manipulation. In general, however, the decimal string instructions are used by language compilers and are rarely used at the assembly level.

MULTIPLE PRECISION INTEGER ARITHMETIC

Handling large numbers in earlier 12- and 16-bit minicomputers required the programmer to use multiple precision arithmetic. With the advent of minicomputers having longer word lengths such as the VAX-11, multiple precision is not used as frequently. Still, a corollary to Murphy's Law holds that whatever the available precision, some programmers want more.

For VAX-11 double precision arithmetic, several adjacent longwords are used to hold an arithmetic value. With 32-bit arithmetic on the VAX-11, the range of signed integers is from $-2,147,483,648$ to $2,147,483,647$; for 64-bit arithmetic, the range is extended from -2^{63} to $2^{63} - 1$, almost beyond imagination.

Multiple precision addition and subtraction are performed using the Carry bit, along with the instructions Add with Carry (ADWC) and Subtract with Carry (SBWC). To add two 64-bit numbers takes two instructions, one to add the low order 32 bits and another to add the high order 32 bits and any carry from the first addition.

For instance, if we have two longwords containing the double precision operand A and two containing the double precision operand B, we perform a double precision Add as follows:

```
A:      .LONG   4321        ; least significant bits of A
        .LONG   8765        ; most significant bits of A
B:      .LONG   1212        ; least significant bits of B
        .LONG   7878        ; most significant bits of B
        .
        .
        .
        ADDL    A,B         ; adds least significant bits
                            ; ...of A and B together
        ADWC    A+4,B+4     ; adds most significant bits of
                            ; ...A and B with Carry bit
                            ; ...from previous instruction
```

For greater precision, additional ADWCs can be appended.

Another improvement of the VAX-11 over its predecessors is in fixed-point multiplication and division. Earlier minicomputers either did not offer multiply and divide instructions or made them optional components of the CPU. The VAX-11 offers not only Multiply (MUL) and Divide (DIV) instructions in two- and three-operand formats, but also extended forms of multiply and divide. Extended Multiply (EMUL) multiplies two 32-bit values, producing a 64-bit product, and also adds another 32-bit value to the result. The format of EMUL is

```
EMUL    multiplier,multiplicand,addend,product
```

Extended Divide (EDIV) divides a 64-bit number by a 32-bit number, producing a 32-bit quotient and a 32-bit remainder. The format of EDIV is

```
EDIV    divisor,dividend,quotient,remainder
```

This instruction is often used when the remainder of a division is required because the integer divide instructions produce only the quotient.

Finally, there are shift instructions for moving bits within longwords and quadwords as shown in Table 5-7. These complementary instructions allow the programmer to shift the bits within longwords and quadwords using the Arithmetic Shift (ASH) and to rotate bits within longwords using the Rotate Long (ROTL).

Table 5-7.   VAX-11 Shift Instructions

Operation	Mnemonic	Operands
Arithmetically shift the source operand into the destination field. The number of bits shifted is given by the count field. A positive count is a left shift; a negative count is a right shift, with the sign bit replicated. Destination value sets N and Z bits.	ASHL ASHQ	count,source,destination
Rotate logically the source operand into the destination field. A positive count rotates to the left, a negative count to the right. Destination value sets N and Z bits.	ROTL	count,source,destination

FLOATING-POINT ARITHMETIC

Early minicomputers did not include any real floating-point hardware. Rather, software was used to manipulate the signs, exponents, and fractions as well as any required normalization associated with floating-point values. As hardware became cheaper and instruction sets were expanded, floating-point instructions were added, but were often incompatible with existing instruction sets. The PDP-11 series, for example, had several different instruction sets using two-word and four-word formats to manipulate the same floating-point values. The problem of compatibility arose in part because floating-point was added after the basic architecture was frozen; as a result, the set of unassigned opcodes was not large enough to implement this new set of instructions gracefully.

Fortunately, the VAX-11 was planned to allow for orderly growth of instructions, and floating-point instructions were a part of the base instruction set. Table 5-8 lists the floating-point instructions. Note that floating-point, in both single and double precision formats, simply adds two more data-type qualifiers to the standard instruction set. The F and D data-types are appended to the generic arithmetic instructions to provide for handling of floating-point values. There is also a complete set of conversion instructions to convert between floating-point and integer representations, which makes handling of floating-point significantly easier. The assembly programmer can thus use floating-point without knowing the details of the floating-point format.

A particularly interesting VAX-11 instruction is POLY, the polynomial evaluation. This instruction is used in the calculation of math functions such as SINE and COSINE. Given a table of floating point coefficients $C(0)$ through $C(n)$, and a floating-point argument, X, POLY computes the value of the function:

$$C(0) + C(1) \times X + C(2) \times X^2 + \ldots + C(n) \times X^n$$

There are two forms of POLY, POLYF for single precision and POLYD for double precision floating-point values.

MULTI-ELEMENT STRUCTURES AND RECORDS

Collections of data items that must be manipulated as a group occur frequently in programming. Arrays, lists, queues, and trees are typical multi-element data structures commonly used in both high level and assembly language programming. These data structures are alike in that they are homogeneous collections of data elements.

Table 5-8. VAX-11 Floating Instructions

Operation	Mnemonic	Operands
Move source operand to destination field (floating and double precision). Set condition codes N and Z.	MOVF MOVD	source,destination
Clear destination field. Clear N bit and set Z bit.	CLRF CLRD	destination
Move negated source to destination, setting N and Z bits.	MNEGF MNEGD	source,destination
Convert single to double precision floating format.	CVTFD	source,destination
Convert between integer and floating-point data-types.	CVTBF CVTBD CVTWF CVTWD CVTLF CVTLD	source,destination
Convert from floating to integer by truncating the fraction.	CVTFB CVTDB CVTFW CVTDW CVTFL CVTDL	source,destination
Convert and round to nearest integer.	CVTRFL CVTRDL	source,destination
Compare floating operands.	CMPF CMPD	source,destination
Test floating operand.	TSTF TSTD	source
Add floating operands.	ADDF ADDF3 ADDD2 ADDD3	addend,sum addend1,addend2,sum

Table 5-8.   VAX-11 Floating Instructions (Cont.)

Operation	Mnemonic	Operands
Subtract operands.	SUBF2 SUBF3 SUBD2 SUBD3	subtrahend,result subtrahend,difference,result
Multiply operands.	MULF2 MULF3 MULD2 MULD3	multiplier,product multiplicand,multiplier,product
Divide operands.	DIVF2 DIVF3 DIVD2 DIVD3	divisor,quotient divisor,dividend,quotient
Extended multiply and integerize.	EMODF EMODD	
Move address of floating operand.	MOVAF MOVAD PUSHAF PUSHAD	source, destination source
Evaluate polynomial.	POLYF POLYD	argument,degree,tableaddress

Other multi-element data structures are not homogeneous. Collections of data items are called *records,* and the collection of records is called a *file* in COBOL, a *structure* in PL/I, and a *record structure* in Pascal. Each record is actually a logical data item, with its own characteristics of size, type, and initial value, conveniently grouped to form a composite data structure.

Records and files are logical entities that must be manipulated based on a knowledge of their structure. Therefore, different sequences of instructions, offsets, and pointers may be needed to access the elements of different records. For example, we found in the discussion of displacement mode in Chapter 3 that it is necessary to provide the offsets for the different elements that make up the structure. In contrast, we saw when dealing with arrays that the indexed form of addressing is sufficient to step through the elements of the array sequentially.

Arrays

The simplest implementation of an *array* is nothing more than contiguous collection of identical memory elements. In this form, accessing any individual element is performed by computing an address based on the size of the element—byte, word, longword, etc.—and the relative position (index) of the element in the array. For example, the assembly language code to perform the FORTRAN statement:

```
J = A*K+B(I)
```

in VAX-11 Macro would be

```
MOVL    I,R1            ; place subscript in register
CVTLF   K,R0            ; convert integer K to floating
MULF2   A,R0            ; form A*K as floating value
ADDF2   B[R1],R0        ; add in B to form A*K+B(I)
CVTFL   R0,J            ; store integer result in J
```

When multi-dimensional arrays are used, the problem of accessing a particular element becomes one of the mapping of a multi-dimensional array into the linear or one-dimensional form of the computer's memory. For instance, arrays in FORTRAN are stored by column. The two-dimensional array

1   2

3   4

is stored in memory by the compiler as

1

3

2

4

To access an element $A(I,J)$, we must compute the index to the column and then to the element within the column. This requires a knowledge of the bounds of the array indices.

To make it easier for compilers to address arrays, the VAX-11 instruction set contains an Index instruction. This instruction calculates an index for an array of fixed-length data-types, both integer and floating, and even for arrays of bit fields, character strings, and decimal strings. It also checks upper and lower bounds for high level language compilers. To compute indices for multi-dimensional arrays, several Index instructions are used. We will not examine this instruction in more detail because it is used almost exclusively by compilers. However, the instruction format is

```
INDEX   subscript,lower_limit,upper_limit,size,index_in,index_out
```

Circular Lists

One common application of a list is in the implementation of a circular queue or ring buffer. A *circular list,* illustrated in Figure 5-2a, is used to pass information between two or more routines or programs. One routine is usually a producer, the other a consumer. The first feeds information to the list, while the other removes and processes information.

Two pointers, TOP and BOTTOM (see Figure 5-2b), point to the next element to remove and the next slot to insert data, respectively. When the producer has data, it places the data in the array slot pointed to by BOTTOM and updates BOTTOM to point to the next slot. When the consumer wants to process data, it removes the entry pointed to by TOP and updates TOP to point to the next entry. Since the circular buffer is implemented in linear memory, the routines check for the end of the list when updating pointers. If a pointer is updated past the end of the list, it is reset to point to the first list entry, producing the circular effect.

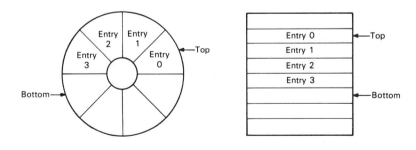

a.   Logical structure.   b.   Physical structure in memory.

Figure 5-2.   Circular list.

The only restriction is that the producer must not insert faster than the consumer is able to remove. Otherwise, the buffer overflows and data is lost. What follows are routines for inserting and removing characters from a character ring buffer. Such routines might be used by a terminal handler that is to accept complete lines from a remote terminal and pass the lines to the operating system command interpreter for processing.

```
        .SBTTL  Circular Buffer Management Routines

;
; Storage for the buffer and pointer variables.
; The variable COUNT keeps the number of entries in the buffer
; so that it is easy to check for empty or full conditions.
;

        BUFSIZE = 100              ; define size of buffer
BUFFER: .BLKB  BUFSIZE            ; define character ring buffer
COUNT:  .LONG  0                  ; initial count is 0

;
; The pointers TOP and BOTTOM contain indices to the current
; first and last data items in the list.
;

BOTTOM: .LONG  0                  ; start bottom at 0
TOP:    .LONG  0                  ; start top at 0


        .SBTTL  INSBUF - Routine To Insert In Circular Buffer

;++
; ROUTINE DESCRIPTION:
;
;       This routine inserts a byte into the circular buffer.
;
; CALLING SEQUENCE:
;
;       CALLS or CALLG
;
; INPUT PARAMETERS:
;
;       CHAR(AP) - the low byte of the first argument contains
;                  the character to be inserted
;
; OUTPUT PARAMETERS:
;
;       None
;
; RETURN VALUES:
;
;       R0 =
;               0 -> buffer is full
;               1 -> character successfully inserted
;
;--
```

```
        CHAR = 4                        ; offset to first argument
INSBUF:
        .WORD   ^M<>                    ; save no registers
        CLRQ    R0                      ; assume full buffer error
                                        ; ...and zero R1 for EDIV
                                        ; ...instruction
        CMPL    #BUFSIZE,COUNT          ; is buffer full?
        BEQL    10$                     ; exit with error if so
        MOVL    BOTTOM,R0               ; get last entry index
        MOVB    CHAR(AP),BUFFER[R0]     ; insert char. in buffer
        INCL    COUNT                   ; note one more in buffer
        INCL    R0                      ; update bottom pointer
        EDIV    #BUFSIZE,R0,R1,BOTTOM   ; wrap pointer by using
                                        ; ...MOD(pointer, bufsize)
                                        ; ...and restore it to
                                        ; ...memory
        MOVZBL  #1,R0                   ; insert success code
10$:    RET                             ; return to caller



        .SBTTL REMBUF - Routine to Remove from Circular Buffer
;++
; ROUTINE DESCRIPTION:
;
;       Remove the next character from the front of the
;       circular list.
;
; CALLING SEQUENCE:
;
;       CALLS or CALLG
;
; INPUT PARAMETERS:
;
;       CHARADR(AP) - address of byte to receive the removed
;                     character
;
; OUTPUT PARAMETERS:
;
;       Removed character is stored in address pointed to
;       by CHARADR(AP).
;
; RETURN VALUES:
;
;       R0 =
;               0 -> buffer is empty
;               1 -> character removed successfully
;--

        CHARADR = 4                     ; offset to address
                                        ; ...argument
REMBUF:
        .WORD   ^M<>                    ; save no registers
        CLRQ    R0                      ; assume buffer empty
        TSTL    COUNT                   ; is buffer empty?
```

```
            BEQL   10$                    ; exit with error if so
            MOVL   TOP,R0                 ; get top entry index
            MOVB   BUFFER[R0],@CHARADR(AP) ; return character to
                                          ; ...caller
            DECL   COUNT                  ; note one less entry
            INCL   R0                     ; point to next entry
            EDIV   #BUFSIZE,R0,R1,TOP     ; wrap pointer if needed
                                          ; ...and return to memory
            MOVZBL #1,R0                  ; insert success code
    10$:    RET                           ; return to caller
```

EDIV is used in these routines to implement a Modulus function, automatically wrapping the pointer back to the beginning of the list when it reaches the end. This occurs whenever the pointer reaches BUFSIZE, because the remainder on division is zero. Otherwise, the remainder is the same as the original index.

Linked Lists

We have already seen examples of more advanced data structures: arrays, stacks, and circular lists. Implementing these on the VAX-11 is aided by the instruction set and the addressing modes. We now turn to some more complex linked data structures.

A *linked* data structure can be conceptualized as an array in which the elements do not occupy consecutive locations in memory. To find the array element n or to move from element n to n + 1, we must have a pointer to that element, namely, its address. In the simplest scheme, in Figure 5-3,

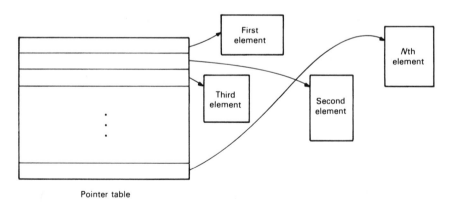

Pointer table

Figure 5-3.   Pointer table array.

there is a fixed-length table of pointers that gives the location of each element in the data structure. The elements may be of fixed or variable length. A zero in one of the pointer table entries may indicate that there is no associated data element.

By setting up such a data structure, we have simply added a level of indirection to the array addressing. This allows us to remove the restriction that the data elements be fixed in length and contiguous in memory. We can also now allocate array elements as we need them, which may be beneficial if they are large. The pointer table itself must be of fixed allocation, however, so we must know the maximum number of entries to allocate. The cost, then, is one pointer, or four bytes, per entry.

One way to remove the problem of preallocating the pointer table is to include the pointer within each data entry, as in Figure 5-4. A list *head* is needed to locate the first data element, which then points to the next, and so on. The last data entry contains a zero pointer indicating that no entries follow, i.e., that it is the end or *tail* of the list.

This structure is known as a *singly linked list*. It sacrifices the ability to directly address or locate an entry by position, or number of index, because we must search through the chain of links. However, with a singly linked list, it is easy to move from one entry to the next.

Insertion in a singly linked list is simple. We first locate the entry that the new element will follow. If the new element is to be at the head of the list, it follows the list header. Figure 5-5 shows a linked list before and after the element X is inserted following block 1. On the VAX-11, the instruction sequence is straightforward in using indirect addressing modes. The instructions of Figure 5-6a will insert a new entry in a list, assuming that R1 contains the address of the new entry and that R0 contains the address of the

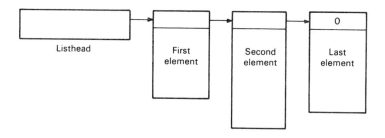

Figure 5-4.   Singly linked list.

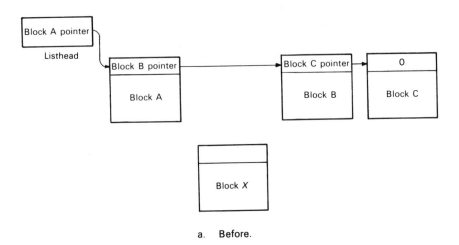

a.   Before.

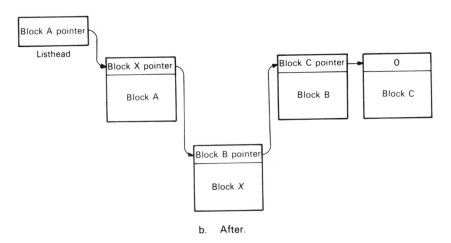

b.   After.

Figure 5-5.   Insertion in singly linked list.

entry that the new one is to follow. The removal of a block is even shorter, as shown in Figure 5-6b.

The use of a singly linked list is exemplified in the management of a dynamic memory pool. In an operating system, one large pool of memory may be shared by many programs and users. When a routine needs to allocate a block of memory for a dynamic data structure, it calls the pool manager, requesting a block of the needed size. When the program is finished

```
;
; Insert entry in singly linked list.
;

        MOVL    (R0),(R1)         ; link new entry to next one
        MOVAL   (R1),(R0)         ; link previous to new entry
```

a. Insert instructions.

```
;
; Remove entry (address in R1) from previous entry (address in
; R0).
;

        MOVL    (R1),(R0)         ; link previous to following
```

b. Remove instructions.

Figure 5-6. Inserting/removing an entry in a singly linked list.

with the block, it is returned to the pool manager. Dynamic allocation saves memory space on the system, because it is not necessary for each routine to preallocate storage that is only occasionally used.

The scheme shown in Figure 5-7 is used within the VMS operating system. The free memory pool is maintained as a list of memory blocks. The first two longwords of each block contain the size of the block and a pointer to the next block. When the system is initialized, there is only one large block. But as users begin to allocate and return memory, the pool becomes fragmented and contains many discontiguous pieces of different sizes, as shown in Figure 5-8. If memory returned to the pool is adjacent to a block already there, the two are joined to form one larger block. If all the blocks

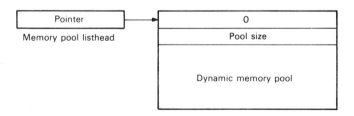

Figure 5-7. Initial dynamic list.

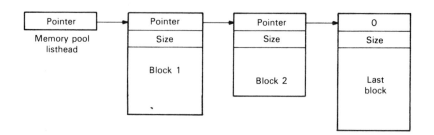

Figure 5-8.   Fragmented memory list.

were returned, the list would revert to the state shown in Figure 5-7. To make the consolidation of blocks easier, the list is kept in memory address order.

The routine in Figure 5-9, which is also flowcharted in Figure 5-10, allocates a block of memory of variable size from the pool. It scans the list for a block of sufficient size. If it finds a block of exactly the right size, that block is removed from the chain and returned to the caller. If it finds a larger block, that block is split into two pieces, one the size requested and one the remainder of the larger block. The requested block is returned to the caller, and the remainder is linked into the list with its new size.

This routine makes good use of the indirect, autoincrement, and auto-decrement addressing modes to manipulate the list and associated pointers. The memory deallocation is left as an exercise at the end of the chapter.

Doubly Linked Lists

Although singly linked lists are convenient for many applications, there are some applications in which such lists are not efficient. These applications require scanning both backward and forward in the list, or inserting at the tail of the list. Inserting at the tail can be made more efficient simply by keeping a pointer to the last entry as well as the first. For efficiently scanning backward, however, a *doubly linked list* is needed.

A doubly linked list has both backward and forward pointers in each list element, as shown in Figure 5-11. Such a doubly linked list is often used to implement a queue; a *queue* is a linear list in which elements are usually added to the end of the list and removed from the beginning of the list. On the VAX-11, each queue element is linked through a pair of longwords; the first longword is the forward link, the second the backward link. A queue is described by a queue header, which is simply a pair of longwords. A *queue header* for an empty queue appears in Figure 5-12.

Note that both the forward and backward links point to the head at location H. Figure 5-13 shows the structure of the queue following the insertion of queue elements at locations N and P. The forward pointer of the last entry always points back to the queue header.

Inserting and removing entries from a queue requires a little more work than from a singly linked list because three elements with pointers must be modified: the element to be inserted or removed, its predecessor, and its successor. The steps for inserting an entry are:

1. Store the address of the successor in the new entry forward link field.

2. Store the address of the predecessor in the new entry backward link field.

3. Store the address of the new entry in the predecessor's forward link field.

4. Store the address of the new entry in the successor's backward link field.

The steps for removal of an entry are:

1. Store the forward link of the entry to be removed in the forward link field of its predecessor.

2. Store the backward link of the entry to be removed in the backward link field of its successor.

Note that an element can be removed from a doubly linked list given only the address of the element. However, a removal from a singly linked list requires the address of the previous element.

Queue operations are used so frequently that the VAX architecture contains the instructions INSQUE and REMQUE to insert and remove entries from doubly linked lists. These are provided mainly for the operating system, which maintains almost all its dynamic data structures as queues. The formats of these instructions are:

```
INSQUE entry,predecessor
REMQUE entry,destination
```

```
                   .SBTTL ALLOCATE - Routine to Allocate Dynamic Memory
;++
;
; FUNCTIONAL DESCRIPTION:
;
;        Allocate a block of memory from the dynamic pool list.
;        (Blocks requested must be at least 8 bytes long.)
;
; CALLING SEQUENCE:
;
;        CALLS or CALLG
;
; INPUT PARAMETERS:
;
;        SIZE(AP) - size of block requested
;
; OUTPUT PARAMETERS:
;
;        RETADR(AP) - address of longword to receive address of
;                     allocated block
;
; RETURN VALUES:
;
;        R0 = 0 if no block found, 1 if block returned
;--

                   SIZE = 4                   ; offset to size argument
                   RETADR = 8                 ; offset to return address

ALLOCATE:
                   .WORD   ^M<R2,R3>          ; registers to save
                   MOVAL   LISTHEAD,R0        ; get memory listhead address
                   MOVL    SIZE(AP),R1        ; get size of requested block
10$:               MOVL    R0,R2              ; save previous block address
                   MOVL    (R2),R0            ; get next block address
                   BEQL    30$                ; exit with error if zero
                   CMPL    R1,4(R0)           ; this block large enough?
                   BGTRU   10$                ; if not, try next block
                   BEQL    20$                ; if EQL, exact size found

;
; Block of memory was found which is larger than amount needed.
; Return size requested and form new block from remainder.
;

                   ADDL3   R0,R1,R3           ; compute address of new piece
                   MOVL    (R0)+,(R3)+        ; copy forward link from old
                                              ; ...piece to new piece
                   SUBL3   R1,(R0),(R3)       ; store size of new piece in
                                              ; ...second longword
                   MOVAL   -(R3),-(R0)        ; move address of new piece to
                                              ; ...top of old block
20$:
                   MOVL    (R0),(R2)          ; link new piece to previous
                                              ; ...block
                   MOVL    R0,@RETADR(AP)     ; return allocated block addr.
                   MOVL    #1,R0              ; note success
                   RET
30$:
                   CLRL    R0                 ; error exit, note error
                   RET                        ; return to caller
```

Figure 5-9.   Allocate dynamic memory procedure.

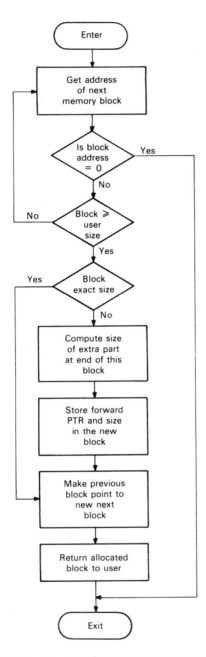

Figure 5-10.   Flowchart for dynamic memory pool allocation.

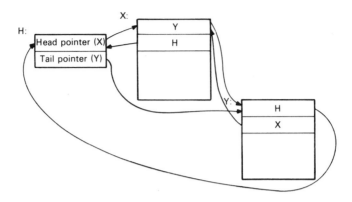

Figure 5-11.   Doubly linked list.

INSQUE inserts the element specified by "entry" into the queue following the element "predecessor." Both entry and predecessor are addresses of the two-longword queue headers within the specified elements. REMQUE removes the entry from the queue and places its address in the operand specified by destination.

To illustrate this, we return to the insertions pictured in Figure 5-13. To insert the entry N at the head of the list, we use the instruction

```
INSQUE N,H                  ; insert element N following
                            ; ...header, i.e., at head of
                            ; ...queue
```

Then, to insert element P at the tail of the list, we write

```
INSQUE P,@H+4               ; insert element P following
                            ; ...last entry, i.e., at tail
                            ; ...of queue
```

The specification @H+4 uses the tail pointer in the queue header to reference the address of the last element as the predecessor for the insertion. Had we known that the last element was at N, we could have written

```
  H:   [          H          ]  Forward link
H+4:   [          H          ]  Backward link
```

Figure 5-12.   Empty queue header.

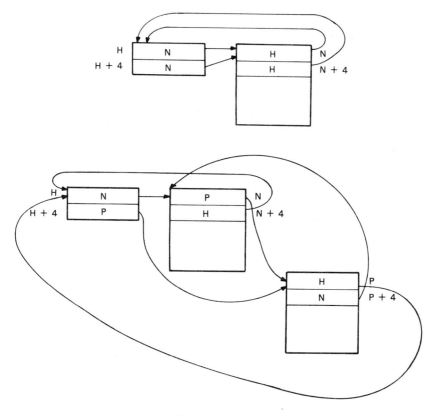

Figure 5-13.   Queue insertion.

```
INSQUE P,N                    ; insert element P following
                              ; ...element N
```

with the same effect. However, insertions at the tail of a queue normally use the pointer in the queue header.

For removing entries, the instruction

```
REMQUE @H,TEMP                ; remove element at head
```

removes the first entry in the queue, loading its address into the longword TEMP. The instruction

```
REMQUE @H+4,TEMP              ; remove element at tail
```

removes the tail entry, also loading its address into TEMP.

INSQUE sets the Z condition code if the entry inserted was the first in the queue. REMQUE sets the Z condition code if the entry removed was the last one, and the V bit if there was no entry to remove. The programmer can thus easily test for special queue conditions.

One important property of queue instructions is that they cannot be interrupted. Queues are often used for communication or synchronization among several processes. If several steps were required to insert and remove entries, it would be possible for a process to be interrupted before the operation was completed, leaving queue pointers in an inconsistent state. Because queue manipulation is done with single, uninterruptable instructions, cooperating processes do not have to worry about interrupts.

The routine that follows is an example of the use of queues by two cooperating processes. The first process collects experimental data and inserts it into a buffer. Because the data arrives quickly, the process does not want to take time to write the buffer to disk. Consequently, it queues the buffer for a second process that writes the data to the disk. There is also a queue of free buffers. When the collection process fills a buffer, it takes a new buffer from the free queue. When the writing process empties a buffer, it puts it back on the free queue for the use of the collection process.

The writing process dequeues buffers and writes them to disk. When the process finds the queue empty, it suspends, or goes to sleep. The collection process wakes it up when a new buffer is placed on the full queue. These processes must share the memory that contains the queue headers and the data buffers.

Three routines are shown: (1) an initialization routine that sets up the queues, queue headers, and associated variables, (2) the data collection routine, and (3) the writing routine from the second process.

```
        .SBTTL - Common Data Shared by Both Processes


;
; The data buffers   are initially allocated from a shared pool.
; Assume that a routine (ALLOCBUF) can be used to allocate them.
; The variables below describe the number and size of the
; buffers.
;           Note that the double == and :: are used to define
;           variables that are global, i.e., known outside of
;           a particular module.

        BUFSIZ == 512           ; size of buffers to allocate
        NUMBUFS == 10           ; number of buffers to get


;
; These are the shared variables.  The three current pointers
; describe the buffer currently being filled with data.
;
```

```
CURBUF::
        .BLKL   1                   ; address of current buffer
CUREND::
        .BLKL   1                   ; address of end of buffer
CURPTR::
        .BLKL   1                   ; address to put next data item
                                    ; ...in buffer


;
; Following are the queue headers for the free and full buffer
; queues.
;

FREELST::
        .BLKQ   1                   ; free list head
FULLST::
        .BLKQ   1                   ; full list queue

        .END



        .TITLE - Collection and Initialization Module
        .SBTTL - Initialization Routine
;++
;
; FUNCTIONAL DESCRIPTION:
;
;       This routine allocates buffers and initializes the
;       queues, queue headers, and pointers.
;
; CALLING SEQUENCE:
;
;       CALLS or CALLG
;
; INPUT PARAMETERS:
;
;       None
;
; IMPLICIT INPUTS:
;
;       FREELST, FULLST, CURBUF, CURPTR, CUREND, BUFSIZ, NUMBUFS
;
; OUTPUT PARAMETERS:
;
;       None
;
;--

INIT:   .WORD   ^M<R2>              ; register to save

;
; Initialize queue headers.
;

        MOVAL   FREELST,FREELST     ; initialize empty free queue
        MOVAL   FREELST,FREELST+4   ; ...header
        MOVAL   FULLST,FULLST       ; initialize empty full queue
```

```
          MOVAL   FULLST,FULLST+4    ; ...header

;
; Allocate buffers and place them on free queue.
; Assume that routine ALLOCATE allocates a buffer of the given
; size and returns its address in the longword passed.
;

          MOVL    #NUMBUFS,R2        ; number of buffers to get
10$:      PUSHAL  -(SP)              ; save space for buffer addr.
          PUSHL   #BUFSIZ            ; parameter for routine to
          CALLS   #2,ALLOCATE        ; ...allocate a buffer
          BLBC    R0,ERROR           ; check error status
          INSQUE  @(SP)+,FREELST     ; insert buffer on free queue
          SOBGTR  R2,10$             ; continue until done

;
; Pull one buffer off the queue and set up pointers for data
; collection.  The first data item is stored at 8 bytes past the
; start of the buffer since the first two longwords are used as
; the queue pointer links.
;
          REMQUE  @FREELST,CURBUF    ; take one for current buffer
          ADDL3   #8,CURBUF,CURPTR   ; compute address to store
                                     ; ...first data item
          ADDL3   #512,CURBUF,CUREND ; remember buffer end addr.
          RET                        ; return to caller


          .SBTTL COLLECT - Data Collection Routine
;++
;
; FUNCTIONAL DESCRIPTION:
;
;         This routine collects 32-bit data items and stores them
;         in a buffer.  When the buffer is full, it is queued for
;         another process to write.
;
; CALLING SEQUENCE:
;
;         CALLS or CALLG
;
; INPUT PARAMETERS:
;
;         None
;
; IMPLICIT INPUTS:
;
;         FREELST, FULLST, CURPTR, CURBUF, CUREND
;
; OUTPUT PARAMETERS:
;
;         None
;--
```

```
COLLECT:
        .WORD   ^M<>                    ; save no registers

;
; Assume that GETDATA returns the 32-bit data item in R0.
;

        CALLS   #0,GETDATA          ; get 32-bit datum
        MOVL    CURPTR,R1           ; place to store value
        MOVL    R0,(R1)+            ; store datum in buffer
        CMPL    R1,CUREND           ; is buffer full?
        BLSSU   10$                 ; branch if not full
;
; Buffer is full.  Queue on the end of the full queue, and
; pull off another buffer for data collection.
;

        INSQUE  CURBUF,@FULLST+4    ; queue at end of full queue
        CALLS   #0,WAKEPROCESS      ; wake buffer writing process
        REMQUE  @FREELST,R1         ; get next free buffer
        BVS     NOBUFFER            ; error if no buffer
        MOVL    R1,CURBUF           ; save current buffer address
        MOVAB   BUFSIZ(R1),CUREND   ; store buffer end address
        MOVAB   8(R1),R1            ; address for next datum

10$:
        MOVL    R1,CURPTR           ; save new data pointer
        RET                         ; return to caller

        .SBTTL OUTPUT - Routine to Write Buffer

;++
;
; FUNCTIONAL DESCRIPTION:
;
;       This routine removes buffers from a queue and
;       outputs them to disk.  It then sleeps until
;       awoken by the collection process.
;
; CALLING SEQUENCE:
;
;       CALLS or CALLG
;
; INPUT PARAMETERS:
;
;       None
;
; IMPLICIT INPUTS:
;
;       FREELST, FULLST
;
; OUTPUT PARAMETERS:
;
;       None
;--
```

```
OUTPUT:
        .WORD   ^M<R2>                  ; register to save
;
; Following is an infinite loop to remove and process entries.
;
10$:    REMQUE  @FULLST,R2              ; remove from full queue head
        BVC     20$                     ; continue if we got one
        CALLS   #0,SLEEP                ; else go to sleep
        BRB     10$                     ; try again when wakened
20$:

;
; Assume routine OUTPUT writes a buffer to disk with call
;
;       OUTPUT (BUFFERADDRESS, LENGTH)
;
;

        PUSHL   #BUFSIZ                 ; push length argument
        PUSHAL  (R2)                    ; push buffer address
        CALLS   #2,OUTPUT               ; write to disk
        INSQUE  (R2),@FREELST+4         ; insert on free queue
        BRB     10$                     ; look for more buffers

        .END
```

Trees

The final linked data structure we will examine is the tree. A *tree* is simply a linked structure in which there is one special element called the root, whose function is analogous to the queue header in a linked list. The root points to from zero to n elements, each of which is itself a tree. Figure 5-14 shows a simple tree structure.

The relationships between elements or *nodes* of a tree are often described using family tree terminology—parent, sibling, offspring, and so on. The terminal nodes are known as *leaves*. Although the tree in Figure 5-14 is drawn with the root at the top, this is not the only possible graphic representation. Since relationships such as left and right, up and down are used to describe tree elements, one must be careful to draw trees in a consistent manner.

Trees are often useful for storing representations of alternatives, particularly in game playing, where each path represents the possible moves or actions. For instance, following each move in a tic-tac-toe game, one subtree describes the remaining possible moves. Searching down the tree, we can examine the possible moves and choose one that results in a win or draw. Of course, for more complicated games, it is almost impossible to enumerate or search the entire tree.

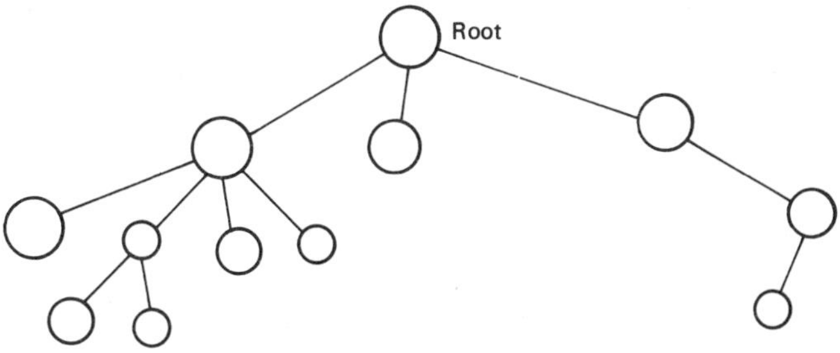

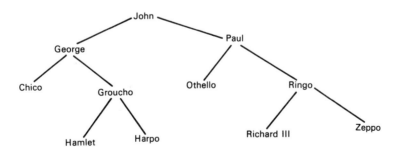

Figure 5-14.   Simple tree.

One common tree species is the *binary tree,* in which each node may have from zero to two offspring. A binary tree is usually ordered. For example, the tree can be maintained so that for the value (N) stored at each node all descendant nodes with values less than N are to the left in the tree, and all nodes with values greater than N are to the right. Binary trees are often used to maintain tables of names because the ordering allows for easy searching and alphabetical listing.

Suppose we wish to build a binary tree to store the following names: John, Paul, George, Ringo, Groucho, Chico, Harpo, Zeppo, Othello, Hamlet, Richard III. If we begin with John at the root and insert each subsequent name so as to maintain the right or left alphabetical relationship, the tree will appear as shown in Figure 5-15.

The following routine inserts an element in a binary tree. Each element is a 5-longword block in which the first two longwords are used to point to

Figure 5-15.   Alphabetical binary tree.

the two offspring, left and right, and in which the last three longwords contain a 12-byte name string. The routine searches down the tree until it finds a terminal node after which the new entry can be inserted. A zero pointer indicates that there is no offspring.

```
        .SBTTL INSTREE - Routine to Insert Element in Binary Tree
;++
;
; FUNCTIONAL DESCRIPTION:
;
;       This routine inserts a 5-longword block containing an
;       ASCII name string into a binary tree.  The longword ROOT
;       contains the address of the root node.
;
; CALLING SEQUENCE:
;
;       CALLS or CALLG
;
; INPUT PARAMETERS:
;
;       BLOCK(AP) contains the address of the 5-longword node to
;                 be inserted, structured as follows:
;
;               +---------------+
;               |    LEFT LINK  |
;               +---------------+
;               |   RIGHT LINK  |
;               +---------------+
;               | 12-byte       |
;               +               +
;               |    name       |
;               +               +
;               |     string    |
;               +---------------+
;
; OUTPUT PARAMETERS:
;
;       None
;
; RETURN VALUES:
;
;       R0 = 1 if node inserted successfully
;       R0 = 0 if name already exists in tree, duplication error
;--

        BLOCK = 4                       ; offset to argument

;
; Offsets into tree element.
;

        LEFT = 0                        ; define left link offset
```

```
          RIGHT = 4                    ; define right link offset
          NAME = 8                     ; define name string offset


INSTREE:
          .WORD  ^M<R2>                ; save R2
          PUSHL  #0                    ; push error code, assume
                                       ; ...duplicate
          MOVL   BLOCK(AP),R0          ; get input block address
          MOVAL  ROOT,R2               ; get address of root element
          BRB    20$                   ; check if root exists



;
; Check if new entry is <, >, or = to current block.  If < or >,
; then continue scanning tree or insert new entry if no successor
; to current node.  If =, then return error indication. As tree
; is scanned, R0 contains the address of the new entry to insert,
; R1 contains the address of the node in the tree being examined.
;

10$:      MOVAL  LEFT(R1),R2           ; get pointer to < (left) side
          CMPC3  #12,NAME(R0),NAME(R1) ; compare new name to node
                                       ; ...value
          BEQL   40$                   ; branch if same, return error
          BLSS   20$                   ; continue if < current node
          MOVAL  RIGHT(R1),R2          ; else get pointer to >
                                       ; ...(right) side


;
; R2 now contains address of the left or right pointer in
; the current node, depending on whether the new name is < or >
; than the name in this node.
;

20$:      TSTL   (R2)                  ; any offspring to this node?
          BEQL   30$                   ; insert new entry here if not
          MOVL   (R2),R1               ; else get offspring address
          BRB    10$                   ; ...and continue tree scan


;
; Found the place to insert new node.  R2 contains address of
; pointer in new parent.
;

30$:      CLRQ   (R0)                  ; zero both pointers in new
                                       ; ...entry
          MOVL   R0,(R2)               ; link new node to parent node
          PUSHL  #1                    ; push success code
40$:
          POPL   R0                    ; get return code from stack
          RET                          ; return to caller
```

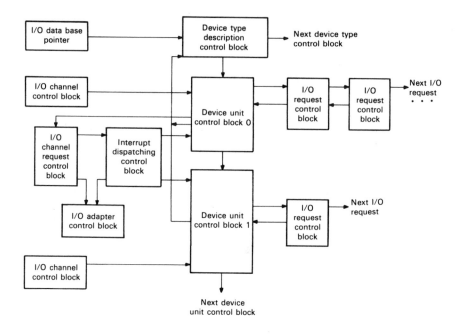

Figure 5-16.   Sample data base organization.

SUMMARY

In this chapter, we have examined a number of data structures and the way the VAX-11 instruction set is used to manage them. We can see how the instruction and addressing techniques have evolved to efficiently support the needs of compilers and operating systems.

In one way or another, most operating systems use all the data structures and manipulation techniques described here. In fact, most of the code in an operating system is there to manipulate queues, lists, records, and other data structures. The manipulated data elements are usually called control blocks. A *control block* is a data structure composed of a number of elements of different sizes that describes a resource or physical or logical entity in the system. For example, there may be control blocks to describe each device, each user program, each file, each I/O request, and so on. These control blocks are knit together to form a complex web that describes the state of the system at any point in time.

Figure 5-16 shows a small section of the VAX/VMS input and output system data base. Each box is a control block containing state information about one resource: a device unit, a device controller, a bus or data path, or an input or output request. The arrows show which control blocks contain pointers to others. Some control blocks are queued to others, while some are members of several queues at once.

With this number of components to manipulate, the design of the data structures can clearly have significant impact on the complexity and performance of a system. Careful, detailed analysis is required to ensure that data structures can be manipulated efficiently.

REFERENCES

The classic book on data structures is Knuth (1968) which discusses data structures in the context of machine and assembly language programming. Books by Gear (1974), Hayes (1978), and Stone and Siewiorek (1975) also consider data structures that can be manipultated by the assembly language programmer, but for a particular machine. Others, such as Aho et al (1976), Berztiss, Lewis and Smith (1976), and Maurer (1977) consider data structures independently of a particular machine or architecture.

EXERCISES FOR CHAPTER 5

1. Write a short sequence of instructions to test if bits 15, 12, 3, and 1 are set in a word. Write a single instruction to invert all of the bits in a longword.

2. A common data structure used in operating systems is the bit map. A bit map is a contiguous string of bits used to indicate which blocks of a fixed-size multi-block data structure are in use. For example, a disk composed of 1000 512-byte disk blocks (discussed in more detail in the next chapter) may have a 1000-bit bit map in which a 1 in bit position N indicates that block N is in use. A 0 in bit N indicates that the corresponding block is free for use.

    a. Using the Find First Bit instructions, write a routine to locate a free block from a data structure of N blocks using an N-bit bit map. The routine inputs the address of the first byte of the bit map and its size in bits, and outputs the position (number) of the first free block. The routine should set the bit for the block being allocated to note that it is in use. It should return an error code if no free block is found.

b.   Extend your routine to locate the first free collection of M contiguous blocks.

3.   One of the convert instructions, Convert Longword to Quadword, is missing from the VAX-11 instruction set. Write a macro to perform this operation.

4.   Code a macro or subroutine to duplicate the EDIV instruction using only 32-bit arithmetic.

5.   A simple encoding technique is to translate alphanumeric text into shifted text. This is done by writing the alphanumeric characters twice, one string above the other, with the second string shifted by 1 or more characters, e.g.,

```
A  B  C  D  E  F  .....  0  1  2  3  .....  !  @  $
@  $  A  B  C  D  .....  Y  Z  0  1  .....  %  &  !
```

A word is encoded then by replacing its representation on the first line by the second, e.g.,

```
CAFE   becomes    A@DC
```

Write a procedure to perform this encoding using all of the ASCII alphanumeric characters including space.

6.   The Move Characters instructions were described in some detail in the text. The MOVC5 instruction has 5 operands: the source length, source address, fill character, destination length, and destination address. Following the execution of MOVC5, the registers are

R2, R4, and R5 = 0
R1 = Number of unmoved bytes in the source string
R3 = Address 1 byte beyond the last byte moved in the source
R4 = Address 1 byte beyond the destination

and the condition codes are set based on the comparison of the source length and destination length, i.e.,

N ← Source length LSS destination length
Z ← Source length EQL destination length
V ← 0
C ← Source length LSSU destination length

Code a routine to emulate the MOVC5 instruction without using character string instructions.

7. Modify the routine of Figure 5-1 to validate chess piece names to allow for one-character abbreviations of the names. The routine should also accept N for Knight and K for King, but still allow KN or KI as valid abbreviations.

8. Write a subroutine to convert packed decimal strings to longwords, but do not use the convert instructions.

9. Write the Dynamic Memory Deallocation routine corresponding to the Allocate Dynamic Memory routine of Figure 5-10. When a block of memory is returned, the deallocation routine should check to see if it can be combined with any adjacent memory blocks.

10. Suppose the VAX-11 did not have queue instructions to manipulate doubly linked lists. Produce INSQUE and REMQUE macros that insert and delete entries from doubly linked lists without using the queue instructions. What are the differences between using the instructions and the macros?

11. Write a sequence of instructions to evaluate the high level language statement:

```
L[I] := K/L*3
```

in assembly language assuming 32-bit integers for I, J, K, and L.

12. Using a recursive method, write a procedure that descends through a binary rooted tree and prints the value of each leaf.

Chapter 6

Comparative Architectures

The preceding chapters have focused on the user-visible architecture of the VAX-11. In the course of these chapters, we have become familiar with addressing techniques, the instruction execution process, and the formation of instructions. However, with the knowledge of only one computer, we have little basis on which to evaluate that architecture.

In this chapter, we examine the instruction set architectures of three other computer systems: the IBM System 360/370, the CDC Cyber series, and the IBM Series 1. Each of these systems had different design goals, so different tradeoffs were made by their designers. Of course, systems evolve, and newer computers, such as the VAX-11 and Series 1, were designed with the knowledge of the successes and shortcomings of previous architectures.

It is not our intention to describe these architectures completely. Rather, we hope that this material will broaden the reader's perspective and solidify material already covered.

THE IBM SYSTEM 360/370 INSTRUCTION SET ARCHITECTURE

The IBM System 360/370 (S/370) family, introduced in the mid-1960s, is probably the most widely used computer and has enjoyed a long life in many implementations. The instruction set has been copied by vendors manufacturing S/370 plug-compatible CPUs, and has been carried forth by IBM in the 4300 series. In this section, we will briefly describe the S/370

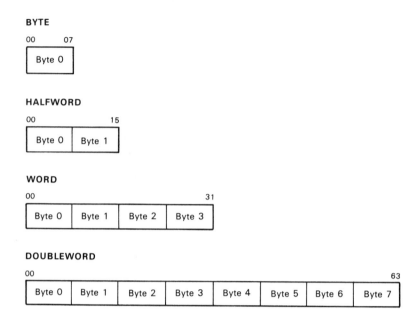

Figure 6-1. S/370 information units.

instruction set architecture and addressing. Our objective is to examine some alternatives to the addressing and instruction representation common to the VAX-11.

The S/370, like the VAX-11, is a byte-addressable computer that operates on information units that are multiples of the 8-bit byte. The main S/370 information units are the 8-bit byte, the 16-bit halfword, the 32-bit word, and the 64-bit doubleword, as shown in Figure 6-1. On the S/370, bits are numbered from left to right, making bit 0 the *most significant bit*.

The S/370 has 16 32-bit general registers, numbered from 0 to 15. The even-odd pairs may be used as double registers. For example, registers 2 and 3 may be used to contain a doubleword, but not registers 3 and 4. There are also four 64-bit floating-point registers for floating-point operations, numbered 0, 2, 4, and 6. The adjacent floating-point registers 0, 2 and 4, 6 can be used to contain extended floating-point operands.

Although the S/370 is a 32-bit system in that it operates primarily on 32-bit quantities, program addresses are 24 bits in length. When a register is used for addressing, the high order 8 bits (0–7) are ignored in the effective address calculation. Therefore, a program can address 2^{24} or 16,777,216 bytes of memory.

Address computation on the S/370 is simpler than on the VAX-11 because there are fewer options. A memory address is generally formed as the sum of the contents of a general register (known as the base register, B) and a 12-bit integer (known as the displacement, D). Only the low order 24 bits of the register are used in the computation. This is shown symbolically as D(B) and is similar to displacement addressing on VAX.

The second method of address specification uses an index register (shown as X) in addition to the base and displacement. The index register can be used to address an element of an array pointed to by the base register. The displacement is summed with the low order 24 bits of both the base and index registers, yielding the effective operand address. This is shown as D(X,B) and is similar to displacement indexed addressing on VAX-11 except that the index register is not multiplied by the array element size. Therefore, to step through an array of 32-bit entries, the index register must be incremented by 4 following each step.

These two modes provide the only method of memory address specification in an S/370 instruction. To address an item in memory, then, a base register must always be used. Since displacements are 12 bits, a base register can address a memory block of 4096 bytes. In general, then, one of the 16 general purpose registers must be reserved as a base register to address each 4096-byte segment of contiguous data or code. However, if the segments are not in use simultaneously, a single base register can be loaded with the address for a new segment whenever that segment needs to be referenced.

On the VAX-11, the instruction opcode specifies the size, type, and number of operands. In general, each operand specifier contains one byte to indicate the addressing mode used. On the S/370, the opcode specifies the addressing mode of the operand specifiers in addition to the size and type of the operands. This reduces the space required for operand specifiers, since the addressing mode is implicit. With this approach, a large number of opcodes would be required if many types of addressing are desired, but as we have stated, the S/370 has chosen to limit the number of addressing modes in favor of bit-efficient instructions.

System 370 instructions are 2, 4, or 6 bytes in length. There are 5 instruction formats, allowing for 5 forms of source and destination specification. We will examine each form briefly.

1. Register-to-Register Format (RR)
    In register-to-register format shown, both operands are contained in registers.

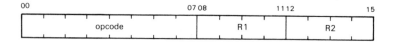

The assembler syntax for RR instructions is:

    OPCODE R1,R2

For example, the Add Register (AR) instruction to sum the contents of two registers,

    AR   4,5

adds register 5 to register 4, leaving the sum in register 4. (Note that the direction is the reverse of the VAX-11.)

2. Register-with-Indexing Format (RX)
    In register-with-indexing format, the first operand is contained in a register, the second is a memory location specified by base, index, and displacement.

The assembler syntax for an RX instruction is:

    OPCODE R1,D2(X2,B2)

The opcode determines which is the source and which is the destination. For example the memory-to-register Add instruction

    A   R,D(X,B)

adds the contents of the memory location to the register, R, leaving the result in the register, while the Store instruction

    ST   R,D(X,B)

stores the contents of the register in the specified memory location.

3. Register-to-Storage Format (RS)
The register-to-storage format shown has three operands: two registers and one memory location specified by a base register and displacement.

00	07 08	11 12	15 16	19 20	31
opcode	R1	R3	B2	D2	

The assembler syntax for RS instructions is:

```
OPCODE R1,R3,D2(B2)
```

For example, the Store Multiple (STM) instruction

```
STM    Ra,Rb,D(B)
```

stores the registers Ra through Rb at consecutive memory locations beginning with effective address base + displacement.

4. Storage Immediate Format (SI)
In this format shown below, an 8-bit immediate operand and a memory location are specified.

00	07 08	15 16	19 20	31
opcode	I2	B1	D1	

The assembler syntax for an SI instruction is:

```
OPCODE D1(B1),I2
```

For example, the Move Immediate (MVI) instruction

```
MVI    12(7),6
```

moves the immediate value 6 to the memory location specified by the sum of the contents of base register 7 and the displacement 12.

5. Storage-to-Storage Format (SS)
This storage-to-storage format is used only for string operands. The address of each operand is specified by a base register and displacement. There are two storage-to-storage formats, one

where a 4-bit length is specified for each operand, and one where a single 8-bit length is specified for both operands. The machine formats for SS instructions are shown below:

00	07	11	15	19	31	35	47
opcode	L1	L2	B1	D1	B2	D2	

00	07		15	19	31	35	47
opcode	L		B1	D1	B2	D2	

The assembler syntax for SS instructions is:

```
OPCODE D1(L1,B1),D2(L2,B2)
```

or

```
OPCODE D1(L,B1),D2(B2)
```

For example, the Move Character String instruction

```
MVC     0(64,4),16(5)
```

moves the 64-byte character string from the location specified by base register 5 and displacement 16, to the location specified by base register 4 and displacement 0.

The S/370 supports both register-to-register and memory-to-register arithmetic, but not register-to-memory or memory-to-memory. Therefore, an intermediate register must be used to add two storage locations. To add memory locations A and B, one must code:

```
L     R2,A          load A into R2
A     R2,B          add B to R2
ST    R2,B          store result in B
```

All three instructions are Register-with-Indexing (RX) format instructions. However, notice that the positions of source and destination are specified by the opcode. To specify symbolic operands such as A and B, the assembly programmer tells the assembler which register is to be used as a base register and the assembler computes the displacement.

The S/370 instruction set also does not have instructions for all of its information units. For instance, there are 5 integer add instructions:

1. Add two signed 32-bit registers (AR).

2. Add a signed 32-bit storage location to a register (A).

3. Add a signed 16-bit storage location to a signed 32-bit register (AH, for Add Halfword).

4. Add two unsigned 32-bit registers (AL, for Add Logical).

5. Add an unsigned 32-bit storage location to an unsigned 32-bit register (ALR, for Add Logical Registers).

Although our examination of the S/370 has been brief, we can make the following observations:

1. The S/370 architecture has less generality in its instruction encoding than VAX, but the equivalent addressing modes have more compact representations.

2. Memory addressing on the S/370 requires a base register that can address a block of 4096 bytes. Since a full 24-bit address can not be directly contained in an instruction, random addressing of large arrays is not as convenient as it is on the VAX-11.

3. The S/370 has index registers similar to the VAX-11, although the index register must be manually incremented by the size of each array element. However, there are S/370 instructions for incrementing index registers and testing for upper limits that simplify index register handling.

4. The S/370 general registers can not be used for floating-point operations, and only the odd-even pairs can be used as extended registers. There is no concept of autoincrement or autodecrement.

5. The S/370 does not have memory-to-memory arithmetic. The tradeoffs were made to reduce the size of instructions and to simplify instruction encoding. Thus, S/370 instructions are kept

short, from 2 to 6 bytes in length, whereas VAX instructions can be very long. It is difficult to compare this with the VAX architecture because several S/370 instructions may be required to represent a single VAX instruction.

6. Also because of the compactness of instruction representation, there is no indirection on the S/370.

THE CONTROL DATA CYBER SERIES ARCHITECTURE

The Control Data Corporation (CDC) Cyber series is the successor to the 6000 series introduced in the early 1960s. It was built initially as a scientific processor for Atomic Energy Commission installations, and, due to its speed and powerful floating-point instructions, has found wider acceptance in other computing communities as well, particularly among the academic institutions. The architecture is unusual because the Cyber is a multiprocessor system with one high-speed central processor and multiple peripheral processors. Our interest lies not in that feature of the architecture, but rather in the information units, instruction set, and addressing modes of the central processor. For, while there are several processors, only the central processor can be directly used by the programmer.

The Cyber, unlike the VAX-11 and the S/370, is not a byte addressable computer. Rather, its only information unit is the 60-bit word shown in Figure 6-2. This word can hold a 60-bit floating-point data-type or a 48-bit integer value. Indeed, the length of the word was chosen to support floating-point values that were common to the type of scientific computing expected to be performed on the Cyber.

The numbering of the bits, as shown in the figure, is like that of the VAX-11, going from right to left with bit 59 as the most significant bit. Instructions, addresses, and data are all stored within a word which is the basic addressable unit.

The central processor contains 24 operating registers. These registers are divided into three eight-register groups: the operand or X registers, the address or A registers, and the increment or B registers. They are usually referred to as the X, A, and B registers when using the assembler syntax. Figure 6-3 shows these registers and their interaction with the arithmetic unit and central memory.

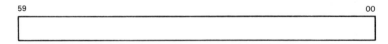

Figure 6-2. Cyber information units.

Addresses for the Cyber are 18-bit quantities. This nominally limits program addresses to 2^{18} or 262,144 words of memory. Effective address computation is even simpler for the Cyber than for either the S/370 or for the VAX-11. However, since this is basically a register machine, the style of memory addressing is rather unusual.

Figure 6-3 shows that the X register set is 60 bits wide while the A and B registers are only 18 bits wide. This is because all instructions operate on 60-bit data words, or 18-bit address or index operands. There are no special registers for floating-point values as in the S/370. Since the 60-bit floating-point value that can be stored in a word has sufficient range, there is no double precision. Double precision values, while computed (i.e., the product of two single precision floating-point values) are not normally saved. Instead, truncation is performed to save only the most significant bits of the product (or quotient).

To fetch a word from the central memory, one must load the memory address into one of the first six A registers (A0 to A5). The memory reference cycle then automatically causes the memory contents to be placed in the corresponding X register. To store a value in memory, the value is first placed in X register 6 or 7 (X6 or X7). Then, the address in memory where the value is to be stored is placed in the corresponding A register, causing the memory write to occur. Thus, the reading from and writing to memory is a side effect of loading an address into an A register. Before giving examples of Cyber instructions, we will first consider how addresses are formed.

A memory address can be contained within an instruction, just as an absolute address is held in a VAX-11 instruction. Alternatively, a memory address can be computed and/or indexed using a B register. There is no indirect addressing in the machine, no autoincrement or autodecrement, and no displacement addressing. Immediate values can be stored as address constants that are not used to reference memory. That is, any 18-bit value which is part of an instruction and is not used to load an A register can be used as an immediate value to be added to or subtracted from a B or X register.

Instructions are either 15 bits or 30 bits in length, and from two to four instructions may be stored in a word. However, if a 15-bit instruction is between two 30-bit instructions, a Pass or Loop instruction may be necessary to fill a word (see Figure 6-4). That is, 30-bit instructions can not be split over two 60-bit words.

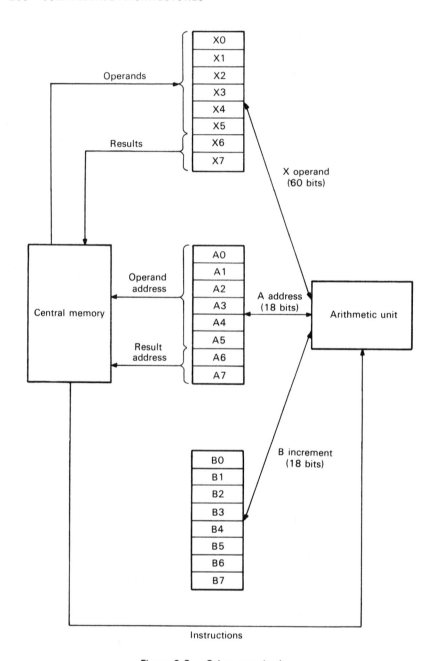

Figure 6-3.   Cyber organization.

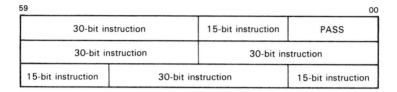

Figure 6-4.   Pass filling instruction.

Generally speaking, a 15-bit instruction contains a 6-bit opcode and three 3-bit register fields, while a 30-bit instruction contains a 6-bit opcode, two 3-bit register fields, and one 18-bit constant, as shown below.

15-BIT INSTRUCTION

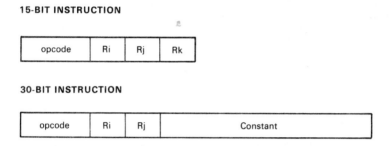

30-BIT INSTRUCTION

Symbolic opcodes specify the arithmetic, logical, floating-point, or address type of operation, along with the destination register. For example, to set X2 to 10, one would write:

        SX2   10

while the actual instruction generated is:

        SX2   B0+10

because two registers are called for in the 30-bit instruction format. Fortunately, register B0 is hard-wired to contain a zero and the assembler is smart enough to substitute the correct form for the abbreviated instruction.

To move a word from one memory location to another on the Cyber requires several instructions as it does for the S/370. On the VAX-11 one might write:

```
MOVL    HERE,THERE
```

while for the Cyber, one would be forced to write:

```
SA1     HERE
BX6     X1
SA6     THERE
```

This series of instructions causes the contents of memory location HERE to be placed in register X1 (by the Set register A1 instruction); the logical or Boolean transfer of the contents of register X1 to register X6; and the storing of the contents of register X6 into the memory address THERE which is Set into register A6. It is worthwhile repeating here that the first six A registers serve to read from memory while the last two serve for writes to memory. That is why the transfer from X1 to X6 (the BX6 instruction) is required.

The split of six A registers for reading memory and the two for writing memory relates to the number of memory fetches versus the number of memory writes. An analysis of typical programs would show that for every 10 reads from memory there is usually only one write back to memory. The 10 values read will usually be combined to form some new result which is then stored. One might then argue that there should be a 7/1 split for the Cyber series. The reason that the 6/2 split was chosen was that the earlier 6600 computer with its multiple functional units was able to perform several operations in parallel and there were occasions when even the two A registers were insufficient to allow all of the units to operate simultaneously.

Another interesting example of programming the Cyber series is illustrated with the addition of two index array elements ARRAY(i) and ARRAY(j), equivalent to the VAX-11 instruction:

```
ADDL    ARRAY[R1],ARRAY[R2]
```

which might be coded for the Cyber as:

```
SA1     B1+ARRAY
SA2     B2+ARRAY
IX6     X1+X2
SA6     A2
```

This series of instructions illustrates several new points about the Cyber. First, it shows indexing where the B registers contain the indices i and j, in the same way that the VAX-11 registers R1 and R2 contain them. However, all data words are of the same length and the index does not need to be multiplied by the number of bytes in the operand type. Second, addition can be performed as the sum of two integer values with the result stored in an X register ready for storing back into memory. Third, since the address where the resultant value is to be stored is already in an A register, it can be copied from that register into an output A register.

There are six classes of operations that can be performed on the Cyber data-types. Unlike the VAX-11 and S/370 assemblers where the opcode is distinct from the operands, the Cyber assembler format uses the first letter of the symbolic opcode to describe which hardware arithmetic unit and type of operation (e.g., floating point, logical shift, etc.) is to be performed. The actual operation, however, is given by the arithmetic operator between the two register operands. For example, a floating-point divide requires the multiply/divide unit and the first letter of the opcode is an F; the remaining part of the opcode specifies the destination register (say X5) and the actual divide operation is then given by writing X3/X1, where X3 and X1 specify the dividend and divisor operand. Symbolically, we write:

```
FX5     X3/X1
```

Some of the first letters used to specify which arithmetic or logical unit is to perform the operation are:

A   Perform arithmetic shift on an X register (the shift unit)

B   Perform logical operation on a pair of X registers (the Boolean unit)

C   Count the number of ones in an X register (the divide unit)

D   Perform double precision arithmetic operation on a floating-point value held in two X registers and truncate the result into a single precision value (the multiply and divide units)

F   Perform single precision arithmetic operation on a floating-point value held in two X registers (the multiply and divide units)

I   Integer add and subtract (add unit)

J   Jump to indexed address formed as the sum of a B register and the constant field (the branch unit)

L   Perform logical shift on an X register (the shift unit)

N,P,Z   Jump on X value being negative, positive, or zero (the branch unit)

R   Round result of floating-point operation (the multiply and divide units)

S   Set an A, B, or X register (the increment unit)

We have already seen a few of the increment and Boolean unit instructions (SA1 and BX6), and one example of the add unit (IX6). Branch instructions on the Cyber must be combined with the appropriate test, since the machine has no condition codes in which to store state information on arithmetic results. For example, the branch if negative instruction:

```
NG      X4,THERE
```

branches to symbolic location THERE if the contents of X4 are negative.

Generally there is an adequate instruction set to perform all of the functions that could be performed by the VAX-11. However, it takes careful programming to fit 15- and 30-bit instructions into an instruction stream, if one does not wish to fill memory with a lot of Pass instructions.

Earlier versions of the Cyber series (the 6000 series) did not have character manipulation instructions. Indeed, a byte on the Cyber was a 12-bit quantity, since this was the length of a peripheral processor word, although characters themselves were 6 bits which allowed for the storing of 10 characters per word. Later versions supported the ASCII character set, although not quite as gracefully as the VAX-11, and there were additional character handling instructions.

Many of the instructions of the VAX-11 used for assisting the operating system or performing I/O do not exist for the Cyber central processor. Rather, the monitor and all I/O capabilities reside with the peripheral processors. In a sense, the central processor is an attached computing engine fed by the peripheral processors.

The differences between the VAX-11 and the Cyber series are so significant that it is difficult to attempt to compare them. The Cyber was optimized for arithmetic calculations using the relatively slow core memories available at the time the architecture was designed. Once a value was fetched into an X register, a relatively slow process, it could be manipulated much more quickly using the register-to-register instructions. By providing multiple arithmetic functional units in some versions of the Cyber series, along with a fast buffer memory to hold several instruction words to be executed, it was possible to overlap operations as well as memory reads and writes. In its day, the Cyber was a very fast computing machine.

THE IBM SERIES 1 INSTRUCTION SET ARCHITECTURE

The IBM Series 1 (S/1) was introduced in 1976 as IBM's entry into the minicomputer market. In this section, we will briefly examine the instruction encoding and addressing of the S/1.

The S/1 is a 16-bit minicomputer that bears resemblance to a number of computers, including the S/370 and the PDP-11. The S/1 operates on 8-bit bytes, 16-bit words, and 32-bit doublewords. Memory is byte addressable, and word and doubleword operands must begin on word boundaries, that is, at a byte with an even address. The S/1 has eight 16-bit general registers and allows for four optional floating-point registers that can be used for floating-point arithmetic.

Memory addresses on the S/1 are 16 bits, as on the PDP-11, allowing for an address space of 65,536 bytes. Unlike the 370, many addressing modes are available for specifying the effective address of a memory location. A number of these modes are similar to those provided on the PDP-11 and VAX-11. The general memory addressing modes in symbolic S/1 assembler format are:

1. *addr*—The effective address of the operand is contained in the instruction.

2. *addr**—The instruction contains the address of a word containing the operand address (* means indirect, like @ on the VAX-11).

3. *(Reg)*—The register contains the effective address.

4. *(Reg)+*—The register is used as the effective address and then incremented by the size of the operand following the access.

5. *(Reg,waddr)*—The contents of the register are added to the 16-bit integer word address *(waddr)* to form the effective address.

6. *displ(Reg,disp2)**—This addressing mode implies two levels of indirect displacement addressing. The effective address is *((Reg)+disp2)+displ*. That is, the contents of the register are added to the 8-bit displacement, *disp2,* to form the effective address of a pointer. The 8-bit displacement, *displ,* is added to the contents of the pointer to form the effective operand address.

7. *disp(Reg)**—The effective address is formed by adding the 8-bit displacement to the contents of the word addressed by the register.

8. *(Reg)**—The register contains the address of a word that contains the effective operand address.

9. *(Reg,disp)**—The displacement is added to the contents of the register to form the address of a word containing the effective operand address. (Notice the difference between this mode and addressing mode 7.)

Like the S/370, the S/1 does not permit all possible addressing modes with all instructions. The instruction opcode specifies the addressing mode used for each operand. Also, depending on the instruction, not all of the registers can be used for memory addressing.

Instructions on the S/1 can be 2, 4, or 6 bytes in length. Bits 0 to 4 of the first word contain the instruction opcode. The simplest instruction contains the opcode, a register specifier, and an 8-bit immediate operand or word displacement, as shown:

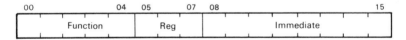

In some cases, the opcode specifies a class of instructions, and a function field located elsewhere in the first word determines which instruction is to be executed. For example, in the format:

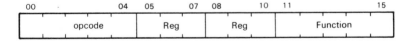

the instruction specifies two registers, and uses the additional 5-bit function field as a logical continuation of the opcode.

There are two main forms of memory addressing, known as four-bit and five-bit addressing, which are used to represent the addressing modes described above. Each of the representations uses a two-bit addressing mode (AM) field, along with a two-bit or three-bit base register (RB) field (for four-bit or five-bit addressing, respectively) as shown:

FOUR-BIT ADDRESS REPRESENTATION

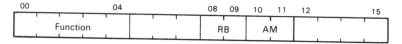

FIVE-BIT ADDRESS REPRESENTATION

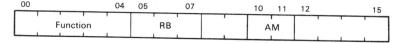

With the four-bit representation, only registers 0 through 3 can be used for memory addressing, since the RB (base register) field is only two bits in length. With the five-bit representation, any of the registers 0 through 7 can be used. The addressing mode field in these two representations has the following interpretations for the following two-bit values:

1. 00—The base register contains the effective address, i.e., *(Reg)*.

2. 01—Autoincrement register mode, i.e., *(Reg)+*.

3. 10—For this addressing mode, an additional word is appended to the instruction. The contents of this word are added to the contents of the specified register to form the effective address. However, if the specified base register is 0 (the RB field is 0), then the word contains the effective address and no register is added. Thus, register zero can not be used as a base register for this addressing mode. This addressing mode can encode the assembler formats *(Reg,waddr)* and *addr*.

4. 11—An additional word is also appended for this addressing mode. If RB is 0, then the contents of the word are used as the address of the effective address (indirect addressing, *addr**). Otherwise, the appended word is interpreted as two 8-bit unsigned displacements, and the addressing mode *displ(Reg,disp2)** is used. Therefore, register zero can also not be used for the two-displacement addressing mode.

Some instructions also contain a single-bit field that indicates whether one of the operands specifies an indirect address. If the bit is zero, the effective address is the address of the operand. Otherwise, it is the address of a pointer to the operand. On some other instructions, this bit is used to indicate the direction of the operation, for example, memory-to-register or register-to-memory.

As an example of instruction encoding, we examine the 16-bit integer Add instruction. The Add Word instruction is available in four different formats, as follows. The opcode and function fields for each form are shown in binary.

1. Add Word Register to Register

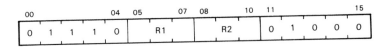

In this format, the contents of the first register are added to the second register. Any of the 8 registers can be specified.

2. Add Word Register/Memory

00				04	05		07	08	09	10	11	12	13	14	15
1	1	0	0	1	R			RB		AM		X	1	1	0

This instruction allows the addition of a 16-bit word from register to memory or memory to register. The memory address is specified in four-bit address format. Depending on the addressing mode field, an additional word may be appended to the instruction. The X bit is used to determine the direction of the transfer. Thus, the encoding for the instructions

        AW   R2,LOC1

and

        AW   LOC1,R2

will be identical with the exception of the X bit.

3. Add Word Memory to Register Long Format

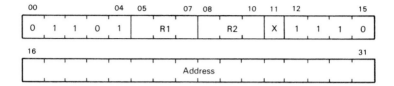

In this format a memory location is added to a register. The effective address is calculated by adding the 16-bit address field to the contents of the register specified by the R1 field, which can be any of the 8 registers. The X bit indicates whether the effective address is the address of the operand or a pointer to the operand.

4. Add Word Memory to Memory

00				04	05		07	08	09	10	11	12	13	14	15
1	0	1	0	0	RB1			RB2		AM1		AM2		0	0

This format allows the optional addition of two 16-bit memory locations. The first operand is specified by a five-bit address and the second by a four-bit address. Therefore, registers R4 through R7 can only be used to address the first operand. Depending on the contents of the addressing mode fields, one or two additional words may be appended to the instruction.

The Add Word instruction can be specified using any of the formats shown earlier. The four different formats demonstrate how the opcode and function fields determine the interpretation of the operand address. Also, the X bit is used in the register/storage format to specify which operand is the destination.

Now that we have examined instruction encoding, it might be interesting to look at the implementation of stacks on the S/1. Like the VAX-11, the S/1 uses stacks for storing local data and for routine linkage.

Instead of using registers to contain stack pointers as is normally done on the VAX-11, the S/1 uses a three-word control block for each stack. In addition to the stack pointer, this control block contains the high and low

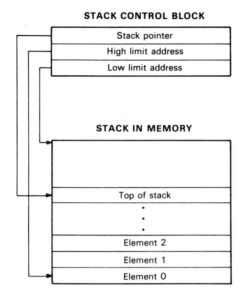

Figure 6-5. Series 1 stack control block.

limit addresses for the stack, as shown in Figure 6-5. When an element is pushed or popped, the hardware can check the limits of the stack to protect against errors.

The S/1 allows for byte, word, and doubleword stacks, and there are push and pop instructions for each. The push and pop instructions contain two operand specifiers. One of the eight registers is always used to contain the element to be pushed or to receive the element to be popped. A four-bit address argument field specifies the address of the stack control block. Thus, the Pop Word instruction:

```
PW      MYSTACK,R3
```

pops the top word of the stack described by the stack control block at memory address MYSTACK. The popped word is stored in R3.

The Series 1 is interesting because of its similarities to the S/370, the PDP-11, and the VAX-11. Efficient encoding was obviously a goal in this machine. The choice of instruction representation is made on an instruction-by-instruction basis. The format of the instruction is specified by the op-code, and the addressing mode field allows for further choices in effective address calculation.

This architecture provides for a large number of addressing modes, but all modes are not allowed for all instructions or operands. Compared to the VAX-11 there is some loss of generality in addressing because of this restriction. This is difficult to evaluate without knowledge of the actual usage of addressing modes with different instructions. Another restriction is in the selection of registers, since four-bit address representation allows only three of the general registers to be used as base registers. However, even with these restrictions, the S/1 is one of the most sophisticated of the 16-bit minicomputers.

SUMMARY

In this chapter, we have introduced the instruction set architectures of three computer systems. The instruction set for each machine was designed based on the goals and constraints for that system, and on the available technology. The designers for each machine made different tradeoffs in addressing capabilities, instruction size, data-types, and generality.

We have focused on the representation of addresses and the coding of instructions. This examination gives us a better basis for comparing computer systems and for evaluating the architecture of the VAX-11. Of course, the VAX-11 is the newest of the systems examined, and benefited from an analysis of previous architectures. However, there are two features of the VAX-11 that are distinctive in comparison. The first is the general structure of the representation of VAX-11 instructions. The VAX-11 architecture allows for up to six operands in an instruction. Instructions are variable length, and any addressing mode can be used to specify the address of any operand. The second important feature of the VAX-11 is the use of indexing as a modifier to other addressing modes. This allows addressing combinations to be used to specify the base address of an array, while the index to the specified entry is computed automatically from the size of the array elements.

REFERENCES

The material in this chapter has been gleaned from the manufacturer's literature. Books like Bell et al (1971), Burr and Smith (1977), Stone (1975), and Tannenbaum (1976) can give the reader a greater appreciation for some of the decisions that go into designing an architecture. The new book by Bell et al (1978) gives an in-depth look at one family architecture, the PDP-11, with the latest machine, the VAX-11, being described in the paper by Strecker (1978). The ultimate authority for all of the material covered here is to be found in the publications by CDC and IBM listed in the bibliography.

EXERCISES FOR CHAPTER 6

1. How are memory addresses represented in IBM 370 instructions? How can the CPU tell which addressing method is being used?

2. What information about the instruction is given by the opcode in a VAX-11 instruction? In an S/370 instruction?

3. What is a System 370 base register? Why are base registers used?

4. What is the difference between index registers on the S/370 and index registers on the VAX-11?

5. Why do we say that the S/370 is a *load and store* machine?

6. The CDC Cyber series has a larger word size than any of the other machines we've examined. Why do you suppose that 60-bit words were chosen, as opposed to 32 or 16?

7. Why do we say that reading or writing memory is a side effect on the CDC Cyber computer?

8. What are some differences between memory addressing on the IBM System 370, the IBM Series 1, and the VAX-11?

9. What is meant by a four-bit and five-bit address on the Series 1?

10. Compare the IBM Series 1 implementation of stacks with the VAX-11 implementation of stacks. How would a stack be implemented on a CDC Cyber computer?

11. What is the major difference between the encoding of addressing modes on the VAX-11 and the encoding of addressing modes on the Series 1? For what reasons would you choose one over the other?

PART TWO

THE SYSTEM ARCHITECTURE

Chapter 7

Physical Input and Output

We have so far been concentrating on the environment visible to the machine language programmer, consisting mainly of the hardware instruction set, memory and its addressing, and the functions provided by the assembler. In this and following chapters, we will begin to examine how the real hardware and the operating system software combine to provide each user with a simple, predictable, logical environment in which to create and execute programs.

Computers and peripheral devices have traditionally been very expensive, although this is changing as the price of memory and processing units rapidly declines. Because of the high price, most users cannot justify owning a dedicated computer. Therefore, the practical solution is to share a computer among many users. A computer that can run several programs concurrently can complete more work, thus becoming a more cost-effective tool.

On a single-user computer, the user has all the physical resources at his or her disposal: the processor, the memory, and the peripherals. On a shared computer, however, resources must be equitably divided among the users so that each user receives a fraction of the total resources available. In addition, it is desirable for each user to be unaware of the other users, that is, for each program to view memory and peripherals as if it were the only program in the system. To permit this, the operating system must transform the physical hardware resources into logical resources that the user manipulates.

The system line printer, for instance, is a logical device that all users share. Each user sees this logical device as being capable of printing program listings and other files on command. (This device automatically prints a header page identifying the user and the listing.) On the other hand, the physical line printer is not so elegant and must be programmed at a basic level. Such line printers must be fed one character or line at a time by a controlling program. Were each user to write directly to the physical line printer at any time, the output would consist of a mess of interspersed lines and characters from different users' files. Consequently, the operating system manages the physical printer, giving each user access to a logical printer, while maintaining the integrity of the material being printed.

Even though direct control of such devices by user programs is not permitted by the operating system, it is still valuable to examine how input/output (I/O) is performed. It is also useful to understand the physical characteristics of some typical devices and the way they are controlled. In this way, we can more easily understand how software transforms physical devices into high level logical devices that programmers can access.

I/O PROCESSING

In requesting an I/O operation, the programmer normally specifies an operation to be performed (e.g., read or write), the main memory address that is to receive data or that contains data to be output, and the amount of data to be moved. The operating system software initiates a data transfer between the device and memory. Early computers required that the processor control the entire I/O operation (as is shown in Figure 2-1, where the CPU must physically move the data). The processor would execute an instruction to transfer the data and would be forced to wait until the operation was completed. During this time, thousands of instructions could have been executed. However, since the program could not continue until the I/O operation was completed, a significant amount of the processor time was lost.

To take advantage of this idle processor time, new computers have *I/O controllers,* as shown in Figure 7-1. A controller contains special hardware to handle device operations. Once an operation has been accepted by the controller, the CPU is free to continue processing. In this sense, a controller is simply a slave computer that performs I/O at the request of the master CPU.

Controllers can control several devices simultaneously because once one device is started, the controller is free to start another device. A computer with several controllers can thus perform computation concurrent with I/O processing on multiple devices.

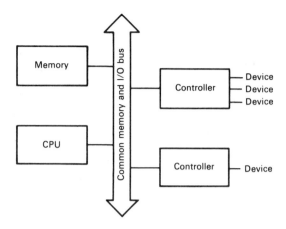

Figure 7-1.   Simple I/O structure.

Instead of waiting in a loop for an operation to complete, some computers periodically *poll* all active devices to check their status. After finding a device that has completed an operation, the processor can initiate another operation and then process the data read or written. Because this still consumes a large amount of CPU processing, interrupts were introduced. An *interrupt* is a signal from a device controller to the processor indicating that the device needs attention. The processor starts the operation, and the controller interrupts when the operation is done. On the VAX-11, an interrupt automatically saves the state of the running program and causes execution of an operating system routine to handle the interrupt. It is thus similar to a subroutine call initiated by the device controller asynchronously to the execution of the currently executing program.

By suspending the program waiting for the completion of the I/O operation, and starting another program to be executed, the processor resource can be shared and more efficiently utilized. Now, however, when an interrupt occurs, the state of the running program must be preserved while an operating system routine is run to handle the interrupt. This saving of state is performed automatically on the VAX-11.

For VAX-11 peripherals, there are two styles of I/O programming. The choice of style depends primarily on the speed of the device. For slow devices such as terminals, *programmed I/O* is used. In programmed I/O, the controller contains a special register, called a buffer register, that the processor loads with a single character to be written out. The device writes the character and then interrupts when it is ready for the next one. Or, on input, the device deposits a single character into a buffer register and interrupts the processor which removes it. Although processing can be overlapped with the operation, the processor must move each byte to or from the controller.

For high speed devices such as disks, the controller normally performs *direct memory access* (DMA) I/O, sometimes called *non-processor request* (NPR) I/O. In this mode, the controller performs a block transfer, in which large blocks of data are moved directly between the device and memory. The entire transfer occurs without processor intervention. To handle such an operation, the controller contains special registers that the CPU loads with information about the transfer. The controller must be told how many bytes to move, where the main memory buffer is located, what device unit and device location to operate on, and what operation to perform. The controller moves the specified amount of data and then interrupts when it is done.

Even though I/O devices can operate independently of the CPU, at times the CPU and the I/O devices contend for the use of main memory. Controllers have internal memories, again called buffers, in which data is placed before being read or written. Because the controller needs to empty its buffer memory before incoming data overwrites its contents, the controller has precedence over the CPU when accessing main memory. The I/O controllers simply cause the CPU to pause while the data is transferred into memory. This process is called *cycle stealing,* because the I/O units steal cycles from the CPU. Cycle stealing works because I/O controllers make memory requests infrequently and tie memory up for only short periods of time.

CONTROL AND STATUS REGISTERS AND I/O SPACE

We have noted that VAX-11 I/O controllers contain special registers for buffering data or holding transfer control information. These are known as *control and status registers* (CSRs) and *data buffer registers* (DBRs). Each I/O device controller contains a set of CSRs that are assigned addresses in the physical address space. The contents of these registers can be manipulated by standard VAX-11 instructions. Therefore, the VAX-11, unlike many other computers, needs no special I/O instructions. For example, the following instruction could be used to store an output character in a device buffer register:

```
MOVB    CHAR,DEVICE_BUFFER_REGISTER
```

0

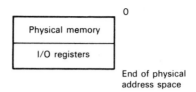

Figure 7-2.   VAX-11 physical address space.

An I/O device driver, which is the software that controls the device, senses the status of the controller and commands the controller by reading and writing the control and status registers. In addition, the device driver reads from and writes to the data buffer registers to obtain input and to initiate output.

I/O device registers have fixed addresses in the upper half of the VAX-11 memory space. The lower half is used for physical memory, as shown in Figure 7-2. Thus, some memory references access physical memory locations, while others access device registers. The VAX hardware is capable of restricting the access to the I/O registers. Normally, user programs are not allowed to read or write CSRs. (For PDP-11 compatibility reasons, most I/O registers must be accessed as 16-bit quantities using word context instructions.)

LOW SPEED DEVICES

Low speed peripheral devices include line printers, terminals, card readers, and some smaller disks. For most of them, device data transfers occur one byte at a time. The device driver writes to the device by moving a character into the output data buffer register of the controller; it reads by moving a character from an input data buffer register. One CSR is normally used to indicate errors and command completion.

The Line Printer

One of the simplest I/O devices is the line printer. For example, the model LP11 line printer controller has two 16-bit I/O registers—one control and status register and one data buffer register—in the physical address space. Figure 7-3 shows the format of these registers. The Error and Done bits of the status register are read-only bits. Software instructions cannot

LINE PRINTER STATUS REGISTER

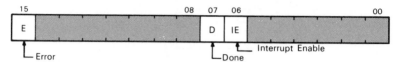

- **Error**—The controller sets this bit when an error condition exists, such as line printer out of paper, printer off-line, or printer on fire.
- **Done**—The controller sets this bit whenever the printer is ready to accept the next character to be printed.
- **Interrupt Enable**—The software sets this bit to tell the controller to interrupt when either D or E is set by the device, i.e., if an error occurs or the printer is ready for another character.

LINE PRINTER DATA BUFFER REGISTER

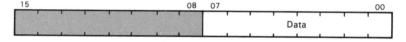

- The software loads bits 0 through 7 with the ASCII character to be output.

Figure 7-3.   Line printer I/O registers.

modify them, and they can only be set or cleared by the controller. To output a character, the software moves an 8-bit ASCII character into the lower byte (bits 0 through 7) of the line printer data buffer register using a MOVB instruction of the form:

```
MOVB    CHAR,LP_BUFFER_REGISTER
```

Although the LP11 controller requires that characters be moved one at a time into the data buffer register, it contains some further internal buffering to reduce the number of interrupts. This buffering allows the controller to hold several characters at a time. Instead of writing one character to the printer and interrupting upon its completion, the controller holds several characters and interrupts only when the entire buffer is written to the printer. If internal buffer space is available when a character is moved to the data buffer register, the controller immediately copies the character into internal buffer storage and sets the Done bit. When the internal buffer is full, the Done bit remains clear until the controller is ready.

What follows is a sample routine to output a string of ASCII bytes to an LP11 line printer. The routine continues inserting characters until the controller fails to set the Done bit. It then waits for an interrupt before continuing.

```
;++
;
; ROUTINE DESCRIPTION:
;
;       This routine outputs a string of ASCII characters to
;       an LP11 line printer.
;
; CALLING SEQUENCE:
;
;       BSB or JSB
;
; INPUT PARAMETERS:
;
;       R0 contains the number of characters to output
;       R1 contains the address of the string
;
; OUTPUT PARAMETERS:
;
;       None
;
; SIDE EFFECTS:
;
;       R0 and R1 are modified
;--

            LP_CSR= ...             ; define CSR address
            LP_DBR= ...             ; define DBR address

WRITELP:
            PUSHR   #^M<R2,R3>       ; save registers
            MOVAW   @#LP_CSR,R2      ; copy CSR address to R2
            MOVAW   @#LP_DBR,R3      ; copy DBR address to R3
10$:        CLRW    (R2)             ; clear Interrupt Enable bit

;
; Begin writing string.
;

            BRB     30$              ; start at end of loop
20$:        BITW    #^X8080,(R2)     ; test Error and Done bits
            BLEQ    40$              ; branch if Error set or Done
                                     ; ...clear (printer not ready)
            MOVB    (R1)+,(R3)       ; output character to printer
30$:        SOBGEQ  R0,20$           ; continue if more to output
            BRW     DONE             ; finish up if done

;
; Either an error exists or printer is not ready.  If not ready,
; then allow interrupts and wait.  R0 must be incremented because
; the SOBGEQ at 30$ decremented it without outputing a character.
;
```

```
40$:    BLSS    ERROR           ; handle error if E set
        INCL    R0              ; update character counter
        BISB    #^X40,(R2)      ; set Interrupt Enable
        .
        <wait for interrupt after line is printed>
        .
        BRB     10$             ; continue
        .
        .
```

Terminal Multiplexing

A typical controller for video and hardcopy terminals is more complicated than a printer controller, because it must handle simultaneous input and output. Users often type while output is still being delivered to the terminal. In addition, because terminals are among the slowest input devices due to human typing speeds, one terminal controller on VAX can handle up to eight lines at a time.

The most common VAX terminal controller is the DZ11, shown in Figure 7-4. It is an 8-line terminal multiplexer that controls eight asynchronous lines for communications with terminals or other computers. Although a DZ11 controller contains nine I/O registers, we will examine only a few registers and fields to see how a multiplexer is controlled. The registers we will discuss are the Control and Status Register (CSR), the Transmitter Buffer Register (TBUF), and the Receive Buffer Register (RBUF). These registers and their important control fields are shown in Figure 7-5.

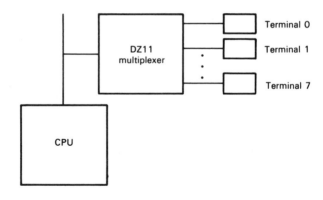

Figure 7-4.   DZ11 terminal multiplexer.

DZ11 CONTROL AND STATUS REGISTER (CSR)

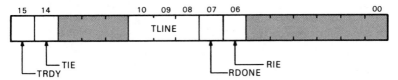

- **Receiver Interrupt Enable (RIE)**—Software sets this bit to cause the controller to interrupt when a character is received.
- **Receiver Done (RDONE)**—The controller sets this bit when a character becomes available in the read buffer. The bit is cleared when the character is read by software.
- **Transmitter Line Number (TLINE)**—The controller loads this 3-bit field with the line number of the line that is ready for transmission of another character.
- **Transmitter Interrupt Enable (TIE)**—Software sets this bit to cause the controller to interrupt when a line is ready for another character to transmit.
- **Transmitter Ready (TRDY)**—The controller sets this bit when a line is ready to transmit a character.

TRANSMIT BUFFER REGISTER (TBUF)

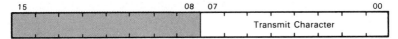

- Software loads bits 0–7 of TBUF with the character to be transmitted to the terminal whose number is in the TLINE field of CSR.

RECEIVE BUFFER REGISTER (RBUF)

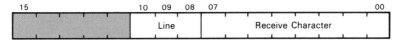

- Bits 0–7 of RBUF contain the character received from the terminal whose number is in the 3-bit LINE field.

Figure 7-5.   DZ11 terminal multiplexer I/O registers.

Output on the DZ11 is similar to the line printer except that the programmer must specify which terminal is to be selected. For each line, a single character buffer holds the character being output. When a buffer for any line becomes empty, indicating that the terminal is ready to receive the next character, the controller loads the line number into the TLINE field of the Control and Status Register and sets the TRDY bit. If transmit interrupts are enabled (i.e., the TIE bit is set), an interrupt is generated. The software handling the interrupt must then move the next character for that terminal into TBUF. Writing the character to TBUF causes the controller to transmit the character to the specified terminal and clear the TRDY bit in the CSR.

Because several terminals may be sending at once, the DZ11 contains a 64-word buffer for input characters called the SILO (for Service In Logical Order). As each character is received, it is placed in the SILO with the line number on which it arrived. RBUF is actually the bottom of the SILO. As characters arrive, they are added to the top of the SILO; characters move toward the bottom as software removes characters from RBUF. Each time RBUF is read, the next character in the SILO is moved to RBUF. Whenever a new character is moved into RBUF, the controller sets RDONE in CSR and interrupts if receive interrupts are enabled.

Terminals can be run in either local-echo or remote-echo mode. In local-echo mode, the terminal itself displays each character as it is typed. In remote-echo mode, the character is merely sent to the computer. The computer must then output it again to make it appear on the screen, a process called *echoing*. Remote-echo allows for more complex terminal functions, particularly for editing, and shows the user that the correct character was received. The echoing can usually be done fast enough that the character appears instantaneously. However, half-duplex is sometimes useful when terminals are connected over slow long-distance lines in which the echo time is long.

HIGH SPEED DEVICES

High speed devices include primarily magnetic disks and tapes. These are known as *mass storage* devices, because, in comparison with primary memories, they have large capacities. A single magnetic disk pack can store up to 600 million bytes of data, which it can transfer at rates of over a million bytes per second. Disks are known as *direct* or *random access* storage devices because any location on the disk is directly addressable. In contrast,

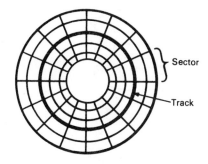

Figure 7-6.   Single-disk platter surface.

tapes are *sequential access* storage devices because they must be scanned to find a given location.

Magnetic Disks

A disk is a rotating flat magnetic *platter* that resembles a phonograph record. Much like the grooves of a record, the surface of a platter is divided into concentric *tracks,* although the grooves do not spiral toward the center. Each track is again subdivided into *sectors* or *blocks* as shown in Figure 7-6. The sector, typically the smallest addressable unit, holds a fixed amount of data. On the VAX-11, most disks have sectors of 512 bytes referred to as *disk blocks.*

To read or write a sector, a magnetic read/write head senses or magnetizes the sequential stream of bits on the track passing beneath it.

Most common disks are *moving-head disks* with one read/write head per surface that must be mechanically positioned over the track to be accessed. The positioning of the head, called a *seek,* usually takes from 10 to 50 milliseconds. In applications in which performance is critical, *fixed-head disks,* which have one read/write head for every track, are used. With fixed-head disks no seeks are required.

Once the read/write head is positioned to the track, it must wait for the correct sector to pass by. Known as *latency time,* this rotational delay can be minimized by increasing the rotational speed of the disk. However, increases in speed are limited by physical tolerances in the balancing of the rotating mass. Most large disks spin at 3600 revolutions per minute, substantially faster than a 33-1/3 rpm record.

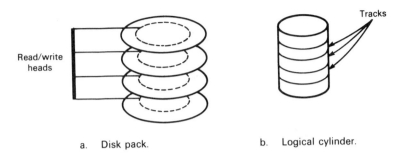

a. Disk pack.   b. Logical cylinder.

Figure 7-7.   Multi-platter disk.

Two techniques are generally used to increase the storage per disk device. The number of bits stored on the surface can be increased, either by storing more bits per inch around a track or by increasing the number of tracks. However, there is always a limit to how much information can be successfully stored and retrieved from a disk. As densities increase, so do error rates.

Another way to increase the storage of each device is to use a number of platters mounted together to form a *disk pack,* as shown in Figure 7-7a. A separate read/write head is used for each surface of each platter. Another benefit of this arrangement is that more data can be read before the heads need to be moved. Indeed, for these multi-platter disks, the concept of a track gives way to that of a *cylinder* formed by the logical grouping of all tracks at the same radius on each platter, as Figure 7-7b illustrates.

Table 7-1 compares performance characteristics of several disks commonly used on VAX-11 systems.

Simplified Disk Control

To gain a better understanding of how software handles a disk, we will examine some of the I/O registers for the RK07 cartridge disk. The RK07 drive is connected to an RK711 disk controller, which is capable of handling up to eight drives. The controller has DMA capability and can move up to 65K 16-bit words of data to or from the disk without processor intervention. The controller is also capable of initiating several simultaneous seek operations, although only one device can transmit at a time.

Table 7-1. Common VAX-11 Disk Characteristics

Characteristic	RX01 Floppy	RK07 Cartridge	RM03 Disk Pack	RP06 Disk Pack
Number of platters	1 (flexible)	2	3	10
Cylinders/ cartridge	77	815	823	815
Tracks/cylinder (R/W heads)	1	3	5	19
Sectors/track	26	22	32	22
Bytes/sector	128	512	512	512
Bits/inch	3200	4040	6060	4040
Bytes/pack	256K	28M	67M	176M
Rotational frequency	360 rpm	2400 rpm	3600 rpm	3600 rpm
Average latency (1/2 revolution)	83 ms	12.5 ms	8.3 ms	8.3 ms
Average seek	380 ms	36.5 ms	30 ms	28 ms
Peak transfer rate (bytes/s)	512K	538K	1200K	806K

The RK711 has 15 I/O registers, several of which are partially described in Figure 7-8. To perform a transfer to or from memory, the device driver performs the following steps:

1. Calculates the disk address of the first disk block of the transfer. The disk address is composed of three parts: cylinder number, track number, and sector number. The cylinder number is moved to the Desired Cylinder Register for head positioning.

2. Loads the Drive Select field in CSR2 with the number of the disk unit.

3. Loads the Function field in CSR1 with the code for a seek function.

4. Enables interrrupts and sets the Go bit in CSR1 to execute the seek for the desired cylinder. The device will interrupt when the seek is complete.

5. When the seek completes, loads the track number and sector numbers into the Disk Address Register and reloads the cylinder number in the Desired Cylinder Registers, in case it has been overwritten by another concurrent disk operation.

DISK CONTROL AND STATUS REGISTER 1 (CSR1)

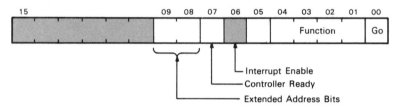

- **Go**—The software sets this bit to cause the controller to execute the specified function on the selected unit.

- **Function**—These bits specify the command to be performed by the controller, e.g., read data, write data, seek.

- **Interrupt Enable**—When this bit is set, the controller will interrupt when (1) a command completes, (2) a drive indicates an attention condition, or (3) any drive or the controller indicates the presence of an error.

- **Controller Ready**—This bit is set by the controller when it is ready to process a new function.

- **Extended Bus Address**—The controller transfers data into a memory buffer specified by an 18-bit address. The low 16 bits are loaded into the Bus Address Register, and the high 2 bits are loaded into this field.

DISK CONTROL AND STATUS REGISTER 2 (CSR2)

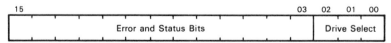

- **Drive Select**—Software loads this field with the unit number of one of eight possible drives on which to perform an operation.

Figure 7-8. RK07 disk I/O registers.

6. Loads the Word Count Register with the number of words to transfer and the Bus Address Register with the bus address of the main memory buffer.

7. Loads the Function field in CSR1 with the code for the operation, whether read or write.

8. Enables interrupts and sets the Go bit to start the operation. The device will interrupt when the transfer completes or an error occurs.

DISK DESIRED CYLINDER REGISTER (DC)

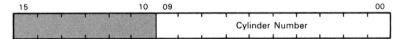

• **Cylinder Number**—Software loads this field with the cylinder number of the first sector for the operation.

DISK ADDRESS REGISTER (DA)

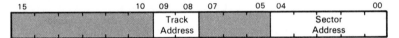

• **Sector Address**—Software loads this field with the number of the desired sector on the selected track and cylinder.

• **Track Address**—Software loads this field with the number of the desired track on the selected cylinder.

DISK WORD COUNT REGISTER (WC)

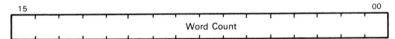

• **Word Count**—Software loads this register with the two's complement of the number of data words to be transferred to or from memory. In other words, the negative word count is stored.

DISK BUS ADDRESS REGISTER (BA)

• **Bus Address**—Software loads this register with the low 16 bits of the 18-bit bus address for the main memory buffer. The low bit is always 0 because it must be the address of a word. The disk transfers only an even number of words.

Figure 7-8.   RK07 disk I/O registers (cont.).

What follows is a simplified code sequence to execute a function on the RK07. The routine is passed a control block containing a buffer address and length, unit number, disk function number, and disk block number. The disk block number must be translated into cylinder, track, and sector address. The routine does no initialization or error checking, but merely loads the registers and starts the operation.

```
;++
;
; ROUTINE DESCRIPTION:
;
;       Routine to execute a specified function on the RK07 disk.
;
; CALLING SEQUENCE:
;
;       BSB or JSB
;
; INPUT PARAMETERS:
;
;       R0 =   address  of  a  control  block  containing  the
;              following fields:
;
;       BUFFER(R0)     = address of the user's buffer (only 18
;                        bits are used)
;       BUFLEN(R0)     = length of user buffer in words
;       BLOCKNUM(R0)   = logical block number of first disk
;                        block of the transfer if the disk were
;                        imagined as a contiguous array of disk
;                        blocks
;       UNIT(R0)       = unit number of disk device
;       FUNCTION(R0)   = code number of disk function to perform
;
;--

;
; Define Disk I/O Register Addresses
;

            RK_CSR1 = ...            ; define first CSR address
            RK_CSR2 = ...            ; define second CSR address
            RK_WC = ...              ; define  Word  Count  Reg.
            RK_BA = ...              ; define Bus Address Reg.
            RK_DA = ...              ; define Disk Address Reg.
            RK_DC = ...              ; define Desired Cylinder

;
; Define Offsets for Input Control Block Arguments
;

            BUFFER = 0               ; offset to buffer address
                                    ; ...argument
            BUFLEN = 4              ; offset to  buffer  length
            BLOCKNUM = 8           ; offset  to  block  number
```

```
              UNIT = 12                  ;  offset  to  unit  number
              FUNCTION = 16              ; offset to Function code

;
; Define Disk Geometry Characteristics for Computing Disk Address
;
              CYLINDERS = 815            ; number of cylinders on pack
              TRACKS = 3                 ; number of tracks per cylinder
              SECTORS = 22               ; number of sectors per track
              BLOCKS_PER_CYLINDER = SECTORS * TRACKS ; just as it says

;
; Calculate the disk address parameters from the disk block
; number and load the appropriate registers.
;
RKDISK:
              PUSHR   #^M<R2,R3,R4,R5>   ; save registers
              MOVL    BLOCKNUM(R0),R1    ; get logical block number
              CLRL    R2                 ; clear next reg. for 64-bit
                                         ; ...divide
              EDIV    #BLOCKS_PER_CYLINDER,R1,R1,R2 ;
                                         ; R1 <- cylinder number
                                         ; R2 <- sectors left on cyl.
              CLRL    R3                 ; clear next reg. for 64-bit
                                         ; ...divide
              EDIV    #SECTORS,R2,R2,R3  ; R2 <- track number on cyl.
                                         ; ...R3 <- sector num. on track
              MOVW    R1,@#RK_DC         ; load Cylinder Register
              MULL    #256,R2            ; shift track number left
              BISW3   R2,R3,@#RK_DA      ; load Disk Address Reg. with
                                         ; ...track and sector numbers
              MOVW    UNIT(R0),@#RK_CSR2 ; load unit number into CSR2
              MNEGW   BUFLEN(R0),@#RK_WC ; load Word Count Register with
                                         ; ...2's complement of
                                         ; ...transfer size
              MOVW    BUFFER(R0),@#DK_BA ; place low 16 bits of address
                                         ; ...in Buffer Address Register

;
; Construct a mask for CSR1 containing the Go bit, the Interrupt
; Enable bit, the Function code field, and the two high order
; address bits from the 18-bit bus address.  Load into CSR1 to
; initiate function.
;
              EXTZV   #16,#2,BUFFER(R0),R4 ; get two high bits of
                                         ; ...bus address
              MULL    #256,R4            ; shift bits to bits <9:8>
              INSV    FUNCTION(R0),#1,#4,R4; insert Function code in
                                         ; ...bits <4:1>
              BISW3   #^X41,R4,@#RK_CSR1 ; enable interrupts, and
                                         ; ...execute the function
              .
              .
              .
```

This routine is a simplified example showing only the loading of some of the important device registers. A real device driver can be extremely complicated. The actual function execution is only a small part of the work to be done. On disk devices, more than half the driver code may be devoted to detecting and recovering from controller or disk unit errors, of which there are many varieties. Another large part of the driver is concerned with interfacing with the operating system and its data structures. However, examples like this do give us some sense of the complexities involved in handling a real device.

Magnetic Tape

Magnetic tape is composed of a 1/2 inch mylar film with an iron oxide coating on one side. A standard 10-1/2 inch reel contains 2400 feet of tape capable of storing up to 40 million characters of data at a density of 1600 bits per inch. Each data byte is written as eight data bits plus one parity bit across the width of the tape, as shown in Figure 7-9. The parity bit is set or cleared to make an even number of one's in the 9-bit character. This is known as *even parity*. When the tape is read, if the character contains an odd number of one's, then a 1-bit error has occurred.

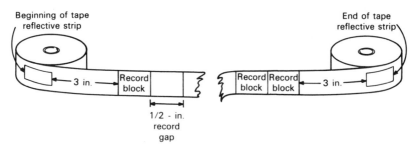

Figure 7-9.   Magtape format.

A tape with the format shown in the figure is known as *nine-track tape* because there are nine data channels. Most drives are also capable of producing seven-track tape that uses six data bits and one parity bit. However, since ASCII characters are eight bits wide, nine-track is more useful on the VAX-11.

Data characters on tape are stored in variable-length blocks called *records*. Industry standards allow records to be from 18 to 2048 characters long. Unlike a disk device, which revolves continuously, a tape must be set in motion before it can be read or written. Because reaching the proper tape speed requires time, a 1/2 inch space, called the *interrecord gap*, is left between records. Hence, the tape is better utilized if longer records are used or if the records are blocked together to reduce the amount of wasted space.

A tape controller normally handles several tape drives. Several drives at a time can be rewinding or spacing although only one may be transferring data at a time. The controller can execute functions to read in the forward or reverse direction, write, space forward or reverse, rewind, unload, or erase. Transfers to or from the tape are DMA. While the tape handles characters one at a time, the controller holds two characters for input or output. As a result, transfers between the controller and memory occur one word at a time.

I/O ADAPTERS

The VAX-11 architecture was constrained to be compatible with PDP-11 I/O devices. A problem arose from the necessity of connecting existing I/O devices that interfaced to existing buses with smaller, slower data paths. To re-engineer these devices would have been costly and time-consuming. The solution was to build *adapters* that would join the existing buses to the new SBI, allowing immediate connection of a host of devices to the VAX.

The function of an adapter is to provide an interface between two data buses, each with its own addressing and data transfer protocol. The adapter is responsible for all communications between the I/O bus and the system bus, including programmed and DMA I/O transfers, interrupts, initialization, and power failure sequences. Moreover, the adapter should handle these communications in a way that takes advantage of the characteristics of the new system bus without hampering its operation.

Figure 7-10 shows the structure of the VAX-11/780 I/O system. Two adapters allow connection between the Synchronous Backplane Interconnect and the two I/O buses: the Massbus and the Unibus.

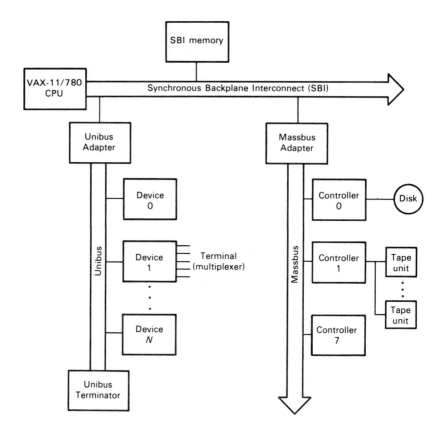

Figure 7-10.   VAX-11/780 I/O structure.

The Massbus Adapter

The Massbus is a high speed data path for connecting high speed mass storage devices to a VAX or large PDP-11 system. The Massbus Adapter (MBA) connects the Massbus to the SBI. A VAX-11/780 can have up to four MBAs, each with up to eight device controllers. Although some device operations, such as disk seeks and tape rewinds, can occur in parallel, only one device can transfer data at a given time on each MBA. Therefore, multiple MBAs allow for simultaneous transfers.

Data transfers on the Massbus occur 16 bits at a time. On the VAX-11/780, the Synchronous Backplane Interconnect (SBI) is designed to move data to and from memory 64 bits at a time. To take advantage of the 64-bit

SBI transfers, the VAX-11/780 MBA contains a 64-bit buffer. On transfers from a device to memory, the Massbus Adapter collects four 16-bit data words before initiating an SBI cycle. On transfers from memory to the device, it prefetches 64 bits, feeding them 16 bits at a time to the device.

The Unibus Adapter

The Unibus connects to all devices except high speed tape and disk units. (One exception is the RK07 disk examined earlier, which connects to the Unibus.) In particular, slower devices such as terminals, line printers, and card readers attach to the Unibus. The Unibus Adapter (UBA) is responsible for buffering data between the Unibus and the system bus.

Unlike the Massbus, which allows only one transfer at a time, the UBA has 16 data paths to the SBI; this allows up to 16 data transfers to be active at once. Each data path buffers data from the 16-bit Unibus data transfers, so that only one system bus cycle is needed for every four Unibus cycles. The software assigns data paths to each device that wishes to transfer data.

THE INITIAL BOOTSTRAP PROBLEM

We have now examined the structure of disks and buses and the logic needed to program them. One problem of any computer system is how it is started. Given the code required to read a disk, how is the machine "smart" enough to load the operating system from disk when it is first plugged in and powered on?

The procedure for bringing up the software from a bare machine is known as *bootstrapping* (booting), because the system is being "brought up by its bootstraps." The booting procedure usually has several stages. On some inexpensive computers, a small program is loaded into memory by hand via switches on the front panel of the processor. This program, known as the *primary bootstrap*, is typically only 10 or 20 instructions long. On most modern computers, the primary bootstrap is stored in a read-only memory (ROM) chip that can be activated by the push of a button.

Every system must have at least one mass storage device, called the *boot device*, which contains more code for starting the system. This code, called the *secondary bootstrap* program, is stored at a known place on the device, such as block zero of a disk. The purpose of the primary bootstrap is simply to load the secondary bootstrap into memory and transfer control. The secondary bootstrap program is large enough to contain logic for locating and loading the rest of the operating system.

Before loading or starting the bootstrap, the computer must be brought to a known state. The processor must be halted, devices must be initialized so that no transfers occur into memory, and memory management must be turned off. The primary and secondary bootstraps operate on a bare processor and physical memory. As more intelligence is loaded, devices are initialized, memory management is turned on, and the operating system takes control. Finally, users are allowed to access the system.

CONSOLE AND FLOPPY

Early computer consoles included rows of lights and switches, much to the delight of the computing center director who could show off the newly acquired machine. With lights flashing and magtapes spinning, the pizzazz of a computer was spectacular! However, trying to keep all the lights working became almost a full-time job for the computer maintenance person.

As a result, it seemed appropriate to replace the lights and switches with a less costly alternative—one that would still allow the operator and system programmer access to the internals of the computer, yet cost less to build and maintain. What developed was called the the ASCII Console. This console terminal, along with some microcode or a microprocessor, allowed the operator to interrogate the status of the machine, and to examine and modify the contents of the registers and memory.

The console subsystem on the VAX-11/780—consisting of an LSI-11, floppy disk, console terminal, and console/CPU interface—includes its own command language, system software, and diagnostics. The console subsystem serves as an operating system terminal, a system console, and a diagnostic console. As an operating system terminal, it is used by authorized system users like any other user terminal. As the system console, it is used for operational control (e.g., bootstrapping, initializing, and software updating). As a diagnostic console, it can access the CPU's major buses and key control points through a special internal diagnostic bus.

The floppy disk drive, which is a part of the every VAX-11/780 system, serves a variety of functions:

1. During system installation, floppy disks hold all of the software components needed to build the system disk.

2. During system booting, the floppy drive acts as a system load device. The bootstrap reads a file from the floppy which, in turn, is used to load the operating system from the system mass storage device.

3. During system start-up, the floppy supplies the system diagnostics, which verify the functioning of the LSI-11, the VAX-11 CPU, the SBI, a memory controller, and a memory module. These diagnostics are run upon command when the power is turned on. Later, they can be again run with the cooperation of the operating system to verify the remaining components of the system.

4. During system updating, the floppy holds the distributed updates or modifications to the operating system software. The updates are provided in machine-readable form so that with a few simple commands from the console, the information on the floppy can be automatically read in and used by the operating system to update itself.

On the VAX-11/780, then, bootstrapping requires an extra step. The LSI-11 console is first booted from a ROM by loading its software from the floppy disk. Once booted, the LSI-11 console allows the operator to specify in a command language how the VAX-11/780 is to be booted. The LSI-11 helps by loading VAX memory with a bootstrap program from the floppy and passing operator-supplied parameters that specify where the operating system is stored.

SUMMARY

In this chapter, we have considered some of the characteristics of VAX-11 input and output devices. We have discussed the functions performed by I/O controllers, which control several devices concurrently and provide for buffering of data between the device and memory. The differences between programmed I/O, where the CPU reads and writes data registers, and DMA I/O, where the device transfers directly to memory, were discussed in light of the speed of the data transfer. Finally, we looked at several typical I/O devices, including their physical characteristics, programming, and logical operation.

The complexity of the devices and the need to share them among many users precludes us from executing code that manipulates these devices directly. Therefore, a controlling operating system is necessary to manage these and other resources. In subsequent chapters, we discuss how the VAX-11 hardware facilitates the management of resources, and examine the characteristics of operating systems in general. We will also take a closer look at one particular operating system, the VAX-11 Virtual Memory System (VAX/VMS).

REFERENCES

The reader can reference the *PDP-11 Peripherals Handbook*, the *Terminals and Communications Handbook*, and the *VAX-11 Technical Summary* for the unique characteristics of the I/O devices for the VAX-11. Descriptions of physical characteristics can also be found in most of the assembly language books already referenced.

EXERCISES FOR CHAPTER 7

1. Explain the concept of contention as it applies to I/O devices using main memory. How can contention be reduced?

2. What is the difference between a device and a device controller?

3. Sketch out the logical flow for the receiving and transmitting of characters for the DZ11 terminal controllers.

4. Explain the differences between a fixed-head disk and a moving-head disk.

5. Why is it best to make a disk a DMA type device?

6. For a disk or tape I/O device, list the functions that should be performed by the device driver.

7. Why are adapters used for peripheral devices on the VAX-11?

8. Flowchart the steps carried out by the bootstrap loader.

Chapter 8

The Support of an Operating System

In Chapter 7 we considered some of the physical characteristics of the VAX-11 I/O system. The complexity of the I/O devices and the need to share them among many users precludes us from executing code that can manipulate I/O devices directly. However, even if we could directly access the physical devices, most applications would find little utility in doing so. Accessing a disk sector is of as little use to the payroll program as it is to the fast Fourier transform program. These programs do not want to handle interrupts or errors from the line printer controller, or worry about sharing the printer. Instead, a controlling program, the operating system, is used to manage these and other physical resources.

The need for an operating system is really a matter of economics. Early computers were batch processing systems. A single program, submitted on a deck of punched cards, would be read into the computer memory and executed. When a program finished printing its results, the next program would be loaded and run.

The main problem with this mode of processing was that a single program could not effectively use all of the expensive resources of the computer system. Some programs were small in size, and most of memory sat empty while they executed. Some programs were I/O intensive, and since the program would wait for each I/O operation to complete, the processor would remain mostly idle. Finally, some programs were totally compute-bound, leaving the I/O devices unused while they ran.

Efficiently utilizing these expensive hardware resources required the sharing of the processor, memory, and I/O devices by several programs at a time. This sharing would allow one program to be computing while another waited for its I/O operations to complete. Several programs would be loaded into memory so that the processor could be quickly switched from one program to another if the current program requested an I/O operation or finished processing.

Sharing of resources as described above was made possible by a multi-programmed operating system. The multiprogramming system allows several programs to compete for computer resources which are divided equitably among the programs. The multiprogramming system creates a logical environment for the programs, which need a simple way to use physical resources. Actually, this simplicity is a consequence of sophisticated software that allows such conveniences as named files instead of disk cylinders or sectors.

To provide these features, the operating system deals with a number of complex issues. First, it must handle complex devices at the physical I/O level, and must be able to recover from unexpected device errors and conditions. Second, it must create an environment for each program, allowing the program to access resources but separating it from other programs. Since several programs share the hardware, they must be protected from each other. Third, the operating system must try to schedule resources in a way that provides fair service to each program while maintaining high utilization of the resources. This is a difficult policy decision-making process, since fair service and high utilization are often mutually exclusive.

One might argue that as hardware prices decline, the economics will no longer justify sharing as they have in the past. In the future, each user may be able to afford a stand-alone computer. However, even the single-user computer of tomorrow will need an operating system to perform the myriad of complex physical housekeeping functions. In fact, tomorrow's operating systems may be more complex because user's demands for new services are increasing as quickly as prices are decreasing.

In this chapter, we examine how an operating system manages the sharing of the processor and memory. Then, we look at how the VAX-11 architecture supports the operating system by providing high level operating system features in hardware.

SHARING THE PROCESSOR

The multiprogramming system must divide the available processor time among its users in a way that is equitable. The *scheduler* is the operating

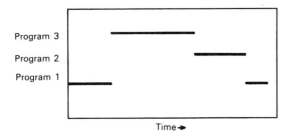

Figure 8-1.   Division of processor time by the scheduler.

system module that selects the programs to be run on the processor and decides how long each should run. The general strategy is to subdivide each second of processor time into a number of units, called *time slices*. Each program in the system is given one time slice to execute, after which it is interrupted so that another program can run. This is shown in Figure 8-1. A new program is also started whenever a running program completes or waits for an I/O operation to finish. Thus, the scheduler attempts to deliver some fraction of the processor time to each program in the system.

In this way, each of the n programs in the system sees a processor with $1/n$ times the power of the actual CPU. From the point of view of the program, it executes continuously on a processor of speed $1/n$. However, a user at a terminal running a highly interactive program (i.e., one that issues a large number of I/O operations) may not be able to tell the difference because the I/O operations are overlapped with the processing of other user's programs.

SHARING THE MEMORY

Just as the operating system manages the sharing of the processor, it also manages the sharing of the memory among several programs. Sharing of memory is more complex because programs address specific memory locations. Therefore, in addition to managing the physical division of memory among the programs, the operating system and hardware must make each program believe that it is the only program in memory. In other words, the system must provide a logical environment for each program that allows the program to operate as if it had been loaded into contiguous physical memory.

This logical environment allows every program to be written for a contiguous, zero-based physical address space. However, since computers must run several programs concurrently to achieve high utilization, the operating system and hardware must provide the logical environment that the program expects.

There are several techniques for hiding the program from its physical location in memory. The simplest scheme for allowing several programs to coexist in memory is relocation through the use of a hardware base register. Using this technique, each program is loaded into contiguous physical memory, as shown in Figure 8-2.

The CPU hardware contains two special registers: a base register and a length register. Before a program is started, these registers are loaded with the base physical address and length of the program. When the program generates an address, the hardware automatically adds in the value of the base register to compute the actual physical address. It also checks the length register to ensure that the program accesses only its own memory. In this way, several programs can reside in memory simultaneously. A program can be located anywhere in physical memory and still address memory as if it were loaded at physical address zero. Of course, there must be sufficient contiguous memory to contain the entire program.

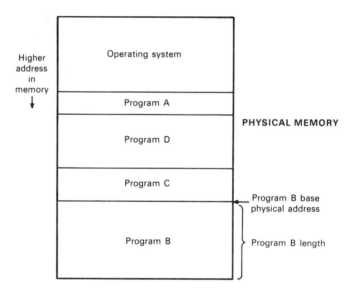

Figure 8-2.   Relocated programs in physical memory.

Program generated addresses are thus called *virtual addresses,* because they refer to the contiguous logical address space, not to the actual physical memory locations. The CPU hardware converts a program generated virtual address into a *physical memory address* through the addition of the contents of a relocation register.

A slight extension of the relocation scheme is *segmentation.* Logically, users write programs and subprograms that can be conveniently thought of as the segments into which a problem has been subdivided. Each program segment in the system is written as if it were loaded into a contiguous memory space starting with memory address zero. To support segmentation, mapping hardware must include a base register and length register for each possible segment, as shown in Figure 8-3. Address translation is more complex because the hardware must locate the appropriate base register for each memory reference.

Segmentation does not require that the program be contiguous in physical memory. Since each segment is mapped separately, it could be loaded anywhere in memory. However, the entire program must still be resident in physical memory.

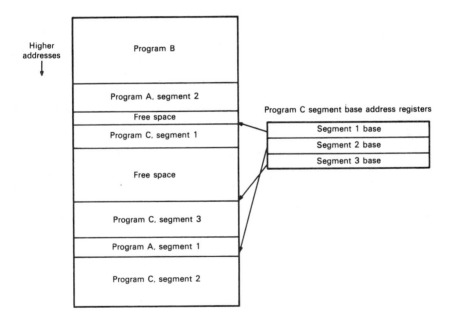

Figure 8-3.   Program segmentation.

The problem with the relocation and segmentation schemes is the complexity of memory management for the operating system. As programs exit or wait for the completion of an event, they are removed from memory, leaving odd-sized holes. Because of this *memory fragmentation,* unoccupied segments may not be large enough to hold new program segments that need to be loaded into memory. The operating system must move segments around to compact all free segments into a large contiguous space. This shuffling of memory is expensive, and, since it involves moving resident segments, the base registers must be changed to reflect the new virtual-to-physical translation.

Managing, compacting, and relocating odd-sized segments is time-consuming. From the operating system viewpoint, a more uniform and more easily handled method of memory management is required. One solution is *paging,* which removes the need for the entire program to be in physical memory; paging also solves the problems of fragmentation and compaction. In the paging scheme, the program is divided into equal-sized blocks called *pages.* Physical memory is also divided into pages. Because both programs and physical memory are divided into pieces of equal size, there is no problem fitting the pieces of a program into memory. Any program page will fit into any memory page. Since a page is usually smaller than a program, many pages are needed to hold the entire program. With paging there is no fragmentation problem. However, the last page of a program may be only partially filled.

For each program, there is a list of mapping registers called a *page table.* The elements in the page table are *page table entries* (PTEs), each containing the base physical address for one page. Each page table entry also contains one bit, the Valid bit, that indicates whether that page is actually in physical memory. The presence of the Valid bit removes the restriction that all of the program must be in memory. If a reference is made to a nonresident or invalid page (i.e., the Valid bit in the corresponding page table entry is 0), the hardware initiates an operating system routine that loads the page from disk. On a paging system with sufficient address space, the programmer need not worry about whether his or her program fits in physical memory. The programmer constructs his or her program for a large contiguous address space, and the operating system does the rest.

Figure 8-4 shows an example of the physical address computation for a paging machine with N-bit addresses and M-bit pages (i.e., 2^M bytes). The virtual address can be viewed as containing two logical components, a virtual page number and a byte offset within that page. The virtual page number, i, is used to select the i'th page table entry, which contains the physical

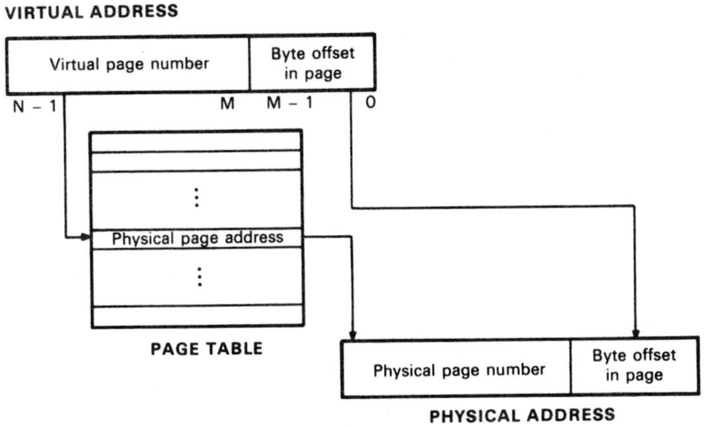

VIRTUAL ADDRESS

Figure 8-4.   Address translation in a typical paging system.

address of the start of that page. The byte offset is appended to the physical page address to form the physical memory address of the referenced byte.

The difference between segmentation and paging is that segmentation is convenient for the user, while paging is convenient for the operating system. In a strict sense, segmentation requires that the range of virtual addresses be no greater than the range of physical addresses because the entire segment must be resident in memory. With several mapping or base registers, the program can be divided into many segments that can be scattered throughout physical memory. If the segments are constrained to be of equal fixed size, multiple segmentation degenerates into paging. And since one advantage of paging is that all pages need not be resident in memory at the time the program is executing, it is possible for a program to reference more pages, and hence more memory, than actually exist.

Of course, the two concepts are not mutually exclusive, and some systems provide both paging and segmentation. In such systems, each segment is divided into a number of pages. The uniformity and consistency of fixed-size pages makes it easier for the operating system to allocate and remove space for different users. For example, in a segmentation scheme with paging, the virtual address can be logically broken into three parts, as shown in Figure 8-5. The segment number is used to select one of the entries in the segment table. The segment table entry contains the address of the page table for that segment. Next, the page number field of the virtual address

VIRTUAL ADDRESS

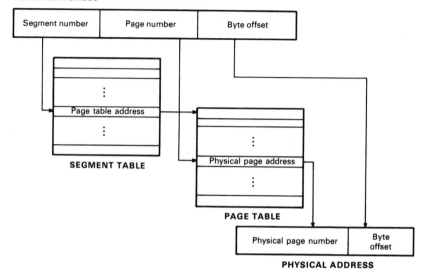

Figure 8-5.   Address translation in a typical segmented paging system.

locates one of the page table entries in the selected page table. The physical address is formed by concatenating the physical page address found in the page table entry with the byte offset from the virtual address.

This extra level of indirection provided by segmented paging simplifies sharing of code segments between programs. With the one-level page table structure of Figure 8-4, each program would need entries in its own page table to map a shared section of code or data. With the segmented structure, however, the two programs could share a page table. Each program's segment table would have an entry that points to the page table for the shared segment. Therefore, a shared physical page would be mapped by only one page table entry. This type of sharing makes it easier for the operating system to account for the page because there is only one descriptor (page table entry) telling whether the page is in memory or on disk.

Virtual memory is the term applied to memory systems that allow programs to address more memory than is physically available. The system disk provides the "virtual" memory by storing pieces of the program that are not currently in use. When one of these pieces is referenced, it is brought into physical memory by the operating system, and some piece of a resident program can, in turn, be moved back to the disk. This loading of pages from disk when a nonresident memory location is accessed is called *demand paging*.

In summary, just as the operating system creates a logical time environment for each program, it also creates a logical memory environment using the memory management schemes described here. Memory can be shared by many programs, with each program operating as if it were loaded into contiguous physical memory. The management of physical memory is done by the operating system to increase memory and processor utilization in a manner that is transparent to the program.

Now that we have examined the basic concepts of processor and memory sharing, in the rest of this chapter we will describe those parts of the VAX-11 architecture that support the VAX-11 operating system and its management of resources. Most of these features are invisible to the executing user program. However, an understanding of this level of the architecture will give us a better appreciation for how computers and operating systems provide the logical environment we see. This chapter deals with the hardware mechanisms that are available for the operating system software to use. In future chapters, we will discuss how this support is used to implement policies and to produce a higher level logical structure for the convenience of the user.

PROCESSES

A user begins a session with a computer by logging into the operating system, that is, by supplying a user identification and a password. After validating this information, the operating system provides the user with an environment in which to edit, run, and debug programs as well as create, update, and maintain a set of permanent files. A *process* is the environment in which these operations are performed. It is the basic logical entity of the hardware and software systems, the environment in which programs execute, and the basic unit scheduled for execution by the operating system.

Each program in the operating system runs in the context of a process. A process is, in effect, a virtual machine that defines the address space and the logical resources for the user. By a virtual or logical machine, we mean a conceptual environment in which the program sees a machine interface that may or may not exist in physical hardware.

A process is represented by its *state,* or context, which tells (1) the location in physical memory of the instructions and data of the process, (2) the next instruction to execute for the process (i.e., its program counter), and (3) the contents of the hardware registers of the process.

Figure 8-6 shows a symbolic representation of the processes in the system. As we shall see, the VAX-11 hardware directly supports the concept of a process. But for the time being, we will use the process concept to understand how the VAX-11 architecture allows the operating system to provide sharing and protection among processes.

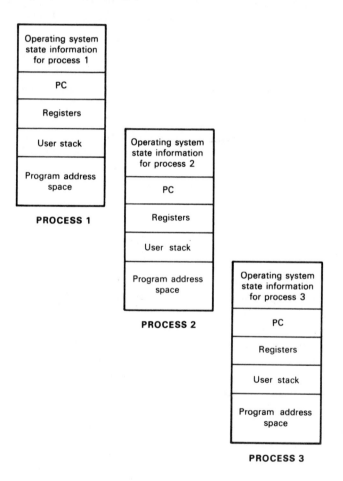

Figure 8-6.   User processes in memory.

PROCESSOR ACCESS MODES

The four *access modes,* known as *Kernel, Executive, Supervisor,* and *User,* provide the basic protection mechanism of the VAX-11 processor. At any point in time, a process executes its instructions in one of these modes. The mode of the process determines its *privilege* for accessing memory and the types of instructions it can execute. For instance, the instruction to halt the processor can only be executed in the most privileged mode, Kernel mode.

Access modes provide *layered protection* for different levels of system software as shown in Figure 8-7. A layered structure is one in which several distinct functional layers are constructed, one upon another. Each lower layer provides primitive functions for the next higher layer to use. As each layer of software is added, a new logical interface is constructed providing higher level features.

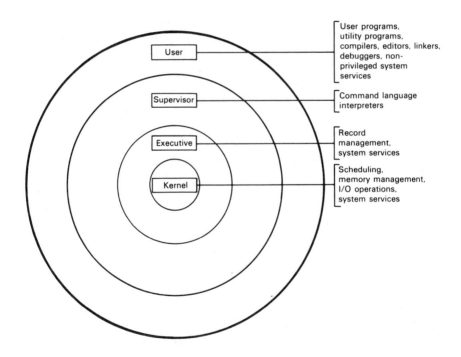

Figure 8-7.   Use of access modes by VMS operating system.

Layering of software simplifies its construction. If careful interfaces are designed between layers to restrict and control the flow of information, layers can be built independently. The VAX-11 access modes allow for the layering of software into four levels. Hardware access modes formalize the structure by providing protection between levels.

In general, routines that execute at a particular mode can protect their code and data from any less privileged mode. Thus, reading or writing certain data structures may require a more privileged, or higher, access mode. Access modes also allow for restricting certain classes of instructions. Running in Kernel mode, the most privileged mode, the program has complete control of the processor and all its instructions, registers, and memory.

Process Access Mode Stacks

When the concept of the stack was introduced in previous chapters, it appeared that a process needed only one stack to handle subroutine and system calls. In fact, each process has four stacks, one for each processor mode. Each stack can be protected against access by less privileged modes. Having separate stacks allows code running at a higher level, that is, in a more privileged mode, to maintain local information on its stack without worrying about interference from another level. For example, a command interpreter that runs in Supervisor mode can use the Supervisor stack for information about its state. Control can be transferred to the user, leaving the Supervisor stack intact until control is returned to the Supervisor level.

The VAX-11 hardware maintains copies of the stack pointer for the four access modes of the current process. The stack pointer register (SP) always contains the stack pointer for the current mode stack. When a mode change occurs (see next section) the hardware automatically stores the contents of SP into its temporary location and loads a new value into SP from the copy of the stack pointer of the new mode.

In addition to the four process stacks, there is a fifth system-wide stack called the *Interrupt stack*. While each user process has four stack pointers for each of the four access modes, there is only one Interrupt stack in the system and only one Interrupt stack pointer. The Interrupt stack is used to service events that occur asynchronously to the execution of a process. When the interrupt occurs, the processor automatically switches to the Interrupt stack. We will examine this further in the discussion of interrupts and exceptions.

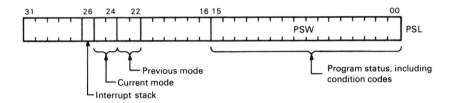

Figure 8-8.   Processor Status Longword.

Changing Modes

Some of the processor state information is maintained in a hardware register called the *Processor Status Longword* (PSL). The upper 16 bits of the PSL are protected and may not be modified by a user program. As shown in Figure 8-8, the PSL describes the current and previous modes of the processor. The modes are encoded in two-bit fields, where

00 = Kernel
01 = Executive
10 = Supervisor
11 = User

The one-bit Interrupt stack field indicates that the processor is executing on the Interrupt stack. When this bit is set, the current mode field must be 00, i.e., the processor must be in Kernel mode.

The processor normally runs at the least privileged mode, User mode. To perform a privileged function (e.g., an I/O operation), the user calls an operating system service routine for assistance. If the system service routine needs to run at a higher mode, the routine executes a Change Mode instruction. For each access mode, there is a Change Mode instruction—CHMK, CHME, CHMS, and CHMU for Change Mode to Kernel, Executive, Supervisor, or User mode, respectively. The instructions have one operand, a code specifying what privileged function or procedure to execute.

When a Change Mode instruction is executed, the processor switches to the stack of the specified mode. It does this by saving the contents of the stack pointer (SP) in an internal register and loading the SP with the saved stack pointer for the new mode. The PSL and the PC of the process are saved on the new stack. The processor then inserts the caller's mode in the PSL previous mode field and loads the new mode in the current mode field.

Now running in the higher mode, the processor transfers to a predefined routine within the operating system. This routine, called the *change mode dispatcher,* examines the code argument and dispatches to the operating system procedure, which performs the requested service. For example,

```
;
; use operating system Kernel mode procedure
; number 10
;

CHMK    #10
```

changes the processor to Kernel mode and invokes the change mode dispatcher to execute a procedure indicated by the argument 10. Normally, the user does not specify a Change Mode instruction explicitly, but instead uses a system call to invoke a system function. The called routine executes the Change Mode instruction if needed.

It is important to note that both the dispatching routine and the final service routine execute within the context of the user's process. They behave as normally called routines similar to local subroutines that a user may call within his or her own program. Therefore, even though the operating system service routine executes in a more privileged mode, it has full access to the user's address space. The Change Mode instructions, then, can be thought of as simple routine calls that cross an access mode boundary. However, because the Change Mode dispatcher intercepts all Change Mode instructions, there is no way for a program to change to a more privileged mode for execution of its own code. Indeed, if a user does execute a Change Mode instruction directly, it will simply call an operating system routine. Theroutine will check to see if correct arguments are supplied and will return an error code if not; otherwise it will execute the function.

When the service routine completes, it must be able to return to the caller. Moving to a less privileged mode is done with the Return from Interrupt (REI) instruction. When an REI instruction is executed, the top of the current stack must contain the PSL and PC for the new mode. The REI instruction causes the CPU to examine the current mode field of the PSL on the stack to ensure that the new mode is the same as or less privileged than the current mode. Therefore, the REI instruction cannot be used to increase privilege. The REI instruction restores the PSL and the PC from the stack and changes the processor and stack pointer to the new mode. Execution continues in the new mode at the instruction specified by the PC.

The Change Mode and Return from Interrupt instructions are used to increase and decrease processor access mode, respectively. Increases in access mode are controlled because they are intercepted by the operating system. Using these mechanisms, the operating system itself can be implemented primarily as a collection of routines that the user calls to perform various functions. These routines execute within the context of the user process either at the user's access mode or at a more privileged mode. The routines have the ability to perform functions that require privilege without allowing the user to have direct access to the privileged resources.

Checking for Accessibility

As we have seen, the Change Mode instructions provide a cross-mode service call facility. When such a call is made, the caller often pushes input arguments on the stack for the service routine. Output arguments are specified as the address of a memory location (or locations) in the user's program to receive an output value from the service routine.

Output arguments may cause a potential problem when the service routine executes in a more privileged mode. The service routine must be able to verify that the caller had access to the memory locations specified. Suppose the service routine executes in Kernel mode and the caller specifies an invalid memory location (e.g., an address in the middle of the operating system). If the Kernel mode routine modifies the memory location, it will not be stopped by the hardware, even though the user mode caller had no authority to reference it.

To protect against such occurrences, two instructions check the accessibility of the previous mode (the caller) to read or write a series of bytes. These instructions are called Probe Read Accessibility (PROBER) and Probe Write Accessibility (PROBEW). A routine executing in a privileged access mode must always check the accessibility of input and output arguments when called by a less privileged mode. In the section on memory management, we will examine in more detail how memory protection is provided on the VAX-11.

PROCESS CONTEXT SWITCHING

The operating system allocates processor time to each process in the system, scheduling each process to run for a given amount of time. When the time expires or if the process waits for an event, the state of the process is saved so that it can be continued at a later time. A new process is then loaded and run. This operation of changing the processor to a new process is called a *context switch*.

Context switching is a common occurrence in a multiprogrammed environment because processes normally wait for the completion of I/O requests. A multiprogramming system may switch processes several hundred times per second. Consequently, the time necessary to perform this operation has a noticeable effect on system performance.

To switch from one process to another, the operating system must save all the state information of the process, including its registers, stack pointers, program counter, etc. This context is stored in a software data structure maintained by the operating system. The context for the new process must then be loaded into the hardware registers from its software storage space before the new process can execute. The VAX-11 architecture has simplified context switching by making the loading and storing of these software data structures a hardware operation.

The Process Control Block (PCB), shown in Figure 8-9, is the data structure that contains all the hardware state information when the process is inactive. The last four longwords in the Process Control Block contain registers that define the address space of the process. These longwords allow the processor to locate the physical memory for each process. (We will learn more about these in the next section.) On a context switch, state information is loaded from or stored into the Process Control Block. Loading and storing of the state information is assisted in the VAX-11 hardware by a privileged register, one that only the operating system can access, called the Process Control Block Base register (PCBB). The PCBB register points to the Process Control Block of the process currently executing.

To perform a context switch, the operating system first executes a Save Process Context (SVPCTX) instruction that causes the hardware to automatically store all the registers of the current process into its Process Control Block, which is pointed to by the Process Control Block Base register. Next, the Process Control Block Base register is loaded with the address of the Process Control Block of the new process to be run. The operating system executes a Load Process Context (LDPCTX) instruction, which loads all the hardware registers from the new Process Control Block. LDPCTX also pushes the PC and PSL of the new process on the Interrupt stack (the operating system must run on the Interrupt stack following an SVPCTX, since there is no process and hence no process stack). Next, the operating system executes a Return From Interrupt (REI) instruction to continue the execution of the new process.

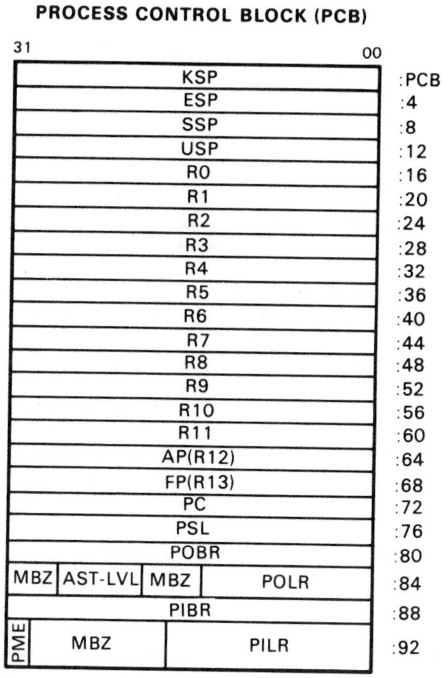

PROCESS CONTROL BLOCK (PCB)

31		00	
	KSP		:PCB
	ESP		:4
	SSP		:8
	USP		:12
	R0		:16
	R1		:20
	R2		:24
	R3		:28
	R4		:32
	R5		:36
	R6		:40
	R7		:44
	R8		:48
	R9		:52
	R10		:56
	R11		:60
	AP(R12)		:64
	FP(R13)		:68
	PC		:72
	PSL		:76
	POBR		:80
MBZ	AST-LVL	MBZ	POLR	:84
	PIBR		:88
PME	MBZ	PILR	:92

Figure 8-9.   Hardware Process Control Block.

The simplified code sequence in Figure 8-10 shows the instructions executed in a context switch. The Move To Processor Register (MTPR) instruction loads the hardware Process Control Block Base register with the physical address of the PCB of the new process.

Since every process in the system has private stacks and stack pointers for all access modes, a process can be context switched even while executing operating system code in Kernel mode. This is unlike many systems, in which the operating system must execute in a special context from which it cannot be interrupted.

SUMMARY OF PROCESS CONCEPTS

We have now covered a number of features that aid the operating system in its management of the processor. First, we found that each program

```
;
; Simplified context switch example.  Assume that this routine
; is entered by an interrupt, as discussed later in this
; chapter.
;

SCHEDULE:
        SVPCTX                          ; save current process state
                                        ; ...in current PCB

        <place current PCB in queue of processes
         waiting for the processor>

        <select next process to be run, load the
         physical address of its PCB into R1>

        MTPR    R1,#PCBB                ; load PCB Base register with
                                        ; ...new process PCB address
        LDPCTX                          ; load hardware registers from
                                        ; ...the new PCB (also pushes
                                        ; ...PC and PSL on the stack)
        REI                             ; continue execution of the
                                        ; ...process
```

Figure 8-10.   Context switch sequence.

runs in the context of a process. The process is the entity scheduled by the operating system scheduler. A process is described by its state information, including its registers, physical memory, program counter, etc.

A process executes instructions in one of four processor access modes. Normal applications programs execute in User mode. However, the user can call operating system service routines that execute at a more privileged mode. The raising of access modes is guarded by the operating system. Although a process can request a service that will be performed in a more privileged mode, it can not execute its own code in that mode.

Finally, the processor maintains the hardware state information for a process in a data structure called a Process Control Block. The operating system scheduler interrupts the execution of one process and begins the execution of another one through the use of special load and store process context instructions.

We have seen how the operating system allows several programs to share the processor. In the next section, we will see how the VAX-11 creates a logical memory environment for each process.

VAX-11 MEMORY MANAGEMENT

Part of the context of each process in the system is its address space. Providing this address space is the job of the operating system *memory management* routines and the underlying hardware.

There are two separable functions required of the memory management subsystem of the operating system. The first gives each user program the impression that it is running in contiguous physical memory, starting at address zero. This is how we have viewed memory since Chapter 2. The second function divides the available physical memory equitably among the users of the system. To obtain efficient memory utilization, the system must allow several processes to exist in memory concurrently. We will now describe how both functions are accomplished by the VAX-11 memory management mechanisms.

VAX-11 Memory Structure

One of the most critical decisions in the design of a computer system is the number of bits to be used for an address, since this determines the amount of memory that can be directly accessed (i.e., the size of the address space). The *address space* is the set of unique memory addresses that a program can generate. On the VAX-11, since addresses are 32-bit unsigned integers, a program can address 2^{32} or 4,294,967,296 bytes.

To the programmer, then, memory is a contiguous array of 2^{32} individually addressable bytes. Of course, programs and data structures are rarely large enough to require even a fraction of this space. Consequently, the VAX-11 address space is divided into several functional regions, simplifying the user-operating system interface with little loss in addressability.

Besides these functional regions, the VAX-11 address space is divided into 512-byte pages. A program is composed of a linear array of pages numbered from 0 to some large upper limit (actually 2^{23} or 8,388,608). For example, the first four pages of the address space of a program are numbered as shown in Figure 8-11.

Because pages are 512 (or 2^9) bytes, the low order 9 bits of the 32-bit virtual address specify the location of the byte within the page being referenced. The high order bits, called the *virtual page number* (VPN), specify the number of the page within the address space as shown:

```
31                                                     09 08                    00
┌──────────────────────────────────────────┬─────────────────────┐
│            Virtual page number             │     Byte offset     │
└──────────────────────────────────────────┴─────────────────────┘
```

For example, in Figure 8-11, virtual address 514 decimal locates the third byte (byte number 2) in the second page (page 1) of the program's virtual memory space. This is shown more readily in the binary representation of address 514 shown below:

```
31                                              09 08                    00
┌───────────────────────────────────────┬─────────────────────────┐
│0              · · ·        0 0 0 0 1   │0  · · ·  0 0 1 0        │
└───────────────────────────────────────┴─────────────────────────┘
```

From this we see that address 514 specifies virtual page 1, byte offset 2.

Figure 8-12 shows a sample allocation of process virtual pages to *physical memory*. Like logical memory, physical memory on the VAX-11 is also divided into 512-byte pages. Physical memory is addressed via a *physical address*. The physical address can also be viewed as having two components: the upper 21 bits specifying the *physical page number,* and the low order 9 bits specifying the byte within the physical page, as shown below:

```
31   29                                       09 08                    00
┌──┬──────────────────────────────────────┬─────────────────────┐
│  │            Page frame number           │     Byte offset     │
└──┴──────────────────────────────────────┴─────────────────────┘
```

Notice that VAX-11 physical addresses are 30 bits, although the maximum amount of physical memory allowed on the processor is implementation specific. Because physical memory can be viewed as a list of physical

Virtual Page Number	Decimal Address	Hex Address
0	0 – 511	0 – 1FF
1	512 – 1023	200 – 3FF
2	1024 – 1535	400 – 5FF
3	1536 – 2047	600 – 7FF

```
┌──────────────┐ 0
│    Page 0    │
├──────────────┤ 512
│    Page 1    │
├──────────────┤ 1024
│    Page 2    │
├──────────────┤ 1536
│    Page 3    │
└──────────────┘
        ·
        ·
        ·
```

Figure 8-11.   Division of address space into pages.

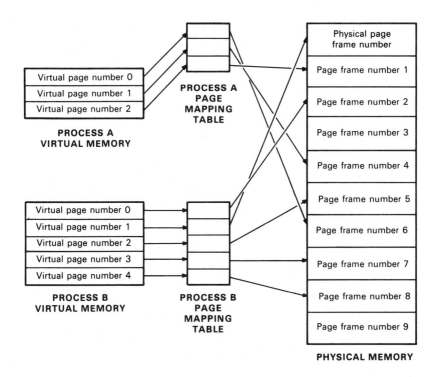

Figure 8-12.   Virtual and physical memory.

frames or page-sized slots that hold program virtual pages, the physical page number is often called the *page frame number* (PFN).

VAX-11 Page Tables

On a paged virtual memory system, a program is allowed to execute with only some of its pages in physical memory. Because each page is addressed independently of the next, the resident pages can be scattered throughout physical memory. However, when a program references an address in virtual memory, the hardware must be able to locate the corresponding physical address. The mechanism for this calculation, called *virtual address translation,* utilizes a data structure called a page table.

A *page table* is an array of longword descriptors, one for each page in the virtual memory of the program. Each descriptor, called a *page table entry* (PTE), indicates

1. What processor access modes can read or write the page.

2. Whether the page is in physical memory.

3. The page frame number of the corresponding physical page if it is in memory.

If the page is not in physical memory, the page table entry can specify where to find a copy of the page on disk. We sometimes refer to a structure like this as a *map* because it gives the directions to (location of) the data in memory.

The VAX-11 page table entry format is shown in Figure 8-13. Bit 31 of the page table entry is the *valid bit*. When set, the valid bit indicates that the virtual page is in memory and that bits <20:0> contain the physical page frame number for the page. If the valid bit is zero, the page table entry does not contain a valid page frame number, and the software can use bits <26:0> to keep information about the page location on the system disk. If a program references a virtual address for which the valid bit is zero, the hardware generates a "translation not valid" fault or *page fault*. This fault causes the hardware to transfer control to an operating system routine to bring the page into physical memory. Faults are described in more detail later in this chapter.

Bit 26, the Modify bit, is set by the hardware on the first write to the page. When the operating system wishes to write a page back to the disk, it first checks the modify bit to see if the page has been modified. If not, the write can be avoided because the disk already contains an up-to-date copy. Bits <30:27> of the page table entry contain a protection mask that indicates which processor access modes, if any, are allowed read or write access to the page. If a process references an address it does not have the privilege to access, the hardware generates an *access violation fault*. Even

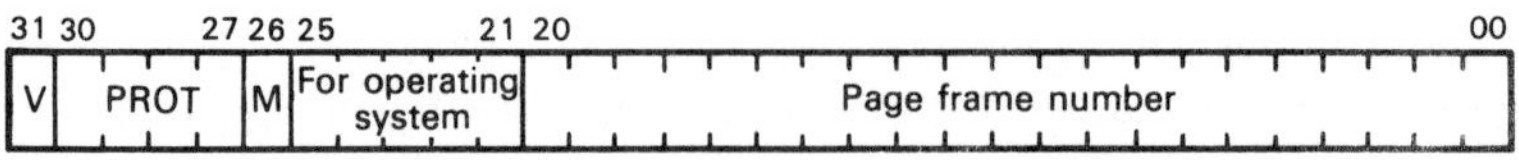

Figure 8-13.   VAX-11 page table entry format.

when the valid bit is zero, the privilege field is checked so that a program cannot cause a page to be faulted for which it has no access rights. Table 8-1 gives the encoding of these bits within the page table entry.

The hardware uses the page table for every program memory access, as shown in Figure 8-14. The virtual page number of the virtual address is used to locate the appropriate page table entry within the page table. If the valid bit is set and the protection check succeeds, then the page frame number in the low 21 bits of the page table entry is appended to the low 9 bits of the virtual address, forming the 30-bit physical address.

Table 8-1. PTE Protection Encoding

Code Decimal	Binary	K	E	S	U	Comment
0	0000	—	—	—	—	No access
1	0001	Unpredictable	—	—	—	Reserved
2	0010	RW	—	—	—	
3	0011	R	—	—	—	
4	0100	RW	RW	RW	RW	All access
5	0101	RW	RW	—	—	
6	0110	RW	R	—	—	
7	0111	R	R	—	—	
8	1000	RW	RW	RW	—	
9	1001	RW	RW	R	—	
10	1010	RW	R	R	—	
11	1011	R	R	R	—	
12	1100	RW	RW	RW	R	
13	1101	RW	RW	R	R	
14	1110	RW	R	R	R	
15	1111	R	R	R	R	

— = No access	K = Kernel	
R = Read only	E = Executive	
RW = Read write	S = Supervisor	
	U = User	

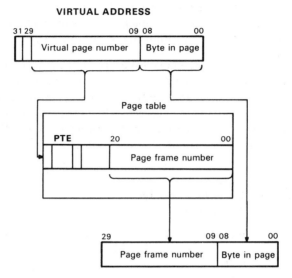

Figure 8-14. Virtual address translation.

VAX-11 Address Space Regions

On the VAX-11, the virtual address space is actually broken into several functional regions or segments. Figure 8-15 shows the division of the virtual address space into two halves called system space and process space. Process space is again broken into the program (P0) and control (P1) regions. The high-address half of system space is reserved for future use. The arrows in Figure 8-15 show the direction of dynamic growth in each region.

Each region has its own page table. Each page table is described to the hardware by two registers: a base register containing the page table starting address and a length register containing the number of page table entries in the table (i.e., the number of pages mapped within the region).

The two high order bits of a virtual address, as shown in Figure 8-16, specify the region containing the address. When a memory reference is made, the hardware examines bits 31 and 30 of the virtual address to determine which page table to use. The selected base and length registers are then used, along with the virtual page number, to locate the page table entry.

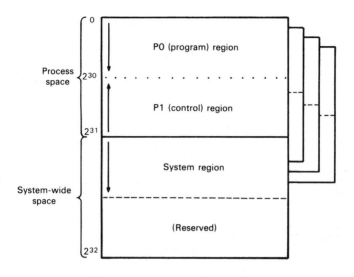

Figure 8-15. VAX-11 process virtual address space.

System Space

The high-address half of the address space is called *system space*, because it is shared by all processes in the system and because the operating system runs in this region. In other words, there is only one page table for system space, called the System Page Table (SPT), that translates all system space references. All processes referencing a virtual address in system space will access the same physical location. The operating system is located in system space, and is shared by all processes. Thus, the operating system is in the same section of the address space of each process. In fact, as stated earlier, the operating system is simply a collection of routines located in the system address space that user programs can call on to perform services.

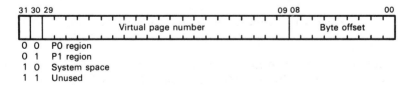

Figure 8-16. VAX-11 virtual address.

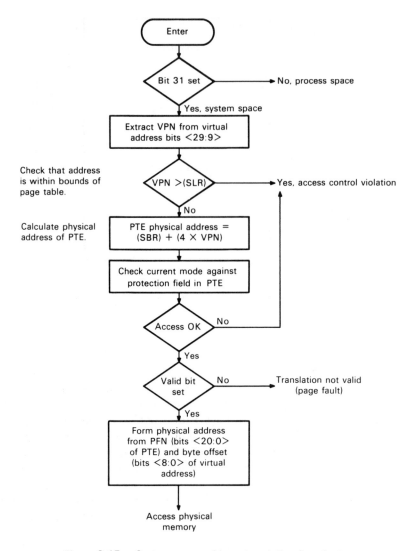

Figure 8-17. System space address translation flowchart.

The System Page Table is described by its two hardware registers, the System Base Register (SBR) and System Length Register (SLR). These registers are loaded by the software when the operating system is booted. The System Base Register contains the starting physical address of the System Page Table, which must be contiguous in physical memory. Note that the

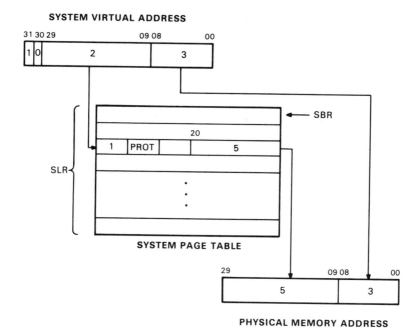

Figure 8-18.   System space virtual address translation.

hardware must reference the System Page Table directly by physical address, since there can be no virtual-to-physical conversion without the page table itself.

The hardware uses the translation process shown in Figure 8-17 to calculate a physical memory address from a system virtual address. The physical address of the page table entry is computed using the contents of the System Base Register and the virtual page number in the specified system virtual address. Figure 8-18 shows an example of the formation of a physical address from a system space virtual address.

Process Space

The low-address half of the VAX-11 address space, in Figure 8-19, is called the *process space*. Process space itself is divided in half by bit 30 of the virtual address. The lower half of process space (bit 30 = 0) is known as the *program* region, the upper half (bit 30 = 1) as the *control* region.

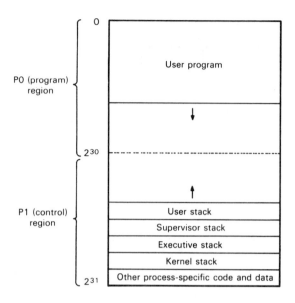

Figure 8-19. Process space.

Unlike system space, which is shared by all processes, process space is unique to each process in the system. In other words, each process has its own page tables for its private program and control regions. Different processes referencing the same process space virtual address will access different physical memory locations.

The reason for having two process regions is to allow for two directions of growth. The program region, P0, is used to hold user programs. This segment provides the zero-based virtual address space into which most programs expect to be loaded. The program can expand dynamically toward higher addresses. The control region on the other hand, conveniently accommodates the User mode stack of the process since stacks grow toward lower addresses. Operating systems can also use the control region, P1, to contain protected process-specific data and code, as well as the stacks for the higher access modes.

The P0 and P1 page tables are described by the hardware base and length registers, P0BR and P0LR, and P1BR and P1LR, respectively. These registers are always loaded with the address and length of the page tables for the process in execution. Unlike the System Page Table, which is stored in contiguous physical memory and can not be paged, the process page tables are stored in contiguous virtual memory in system space and can be paged. The base registers thus contain system space virtual addresses.

Because the process page tables exist in virtual memory, a process space translation demands extra work. The hardware must first use the System Page Table to compute the physical address of the process page table. Once the physical address of the process page table (P0 or P1) is located, the translation process proceeds as it does for system space. Figure 8-20 shows the extra steps in process address translation.

As we saw in Figure 8-9, the P0 and P1 base and length registers are part of the Process Control Block. Thus, the process address space is automatically switched by the execution of the VAX-11 context switch instructions.

Privileged Registers

In this chapter we have seen a number of special registers used to support the operating system data structures, for example the Process Control Block Base register (PCBB), P0 Page Table Base register (P0BR), and P0 Page Table Length Register (P0LR). These registers are known as privileged registers on the VAX-11. A *privileged register* is one intended for use only by the operating system. Privileged registers can not be accessed or modified by user programs.

Each privileged register on the VAX-11 has a privileged register number, as shown in Table 8-2. The column labelled Scope tells whether the register contains information about the state of the CPU or the current process.

The Move From Privileged Register (MFPR) and Move To Privileged Register (MTPR) instructions can be used to read or write privileged registers. The source (for MFPR) or destination (for MTPR) is specified by the register number. For example, to store the current value of the P0 Length Register in R1 and load a new value from R2, the following instructions would be used:

```
MFPR    #9,R1          ; load P0LR into R1
MTPR    R2,#9          ; load new P0LR from R2
```

The move to and from privileged register instructions is protected, and execution from any mode other than Kernel causes a fault.

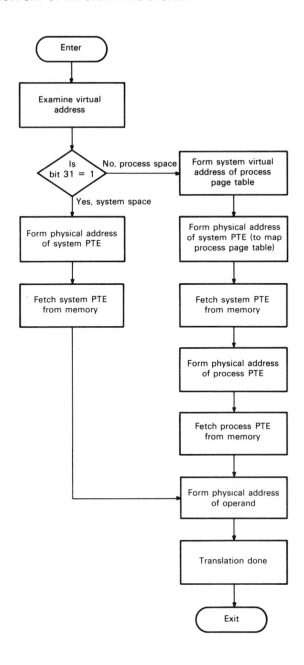

Figure 8-20. Process space vs. system space address translation.

Table 8-2. VAX-11 Privileged Registers

Register Name	Mnemonic	Number	Scope
Kernel Stack Pointer	KSP	0	Process
Executive Stack Pointer	ESP	1	Process
Supervisor Stack Pointer	SSP	2	Process
User Stack Pointer	USP	3	Process
Interrupt Stack Pointer	ISP	4	CPU
P0 Base Register	P0BR	8	Process
P0 Length Register	P0LR	9	Process
P1 Base Register	P1BR	10	Process
P1 Length Register	P1LR	11	Process
System Base Register	SBR	12	CPU
System Length Register	SLR	13	CPU
Process Control Block Base	PCBB	16	Process
System Control Block Base	SCBB	17	CPU
Interrupt Priority Level	IPL	18	CPU
Asynchronous System Trap Level	ASTLVL	19	Process
Software Interrupt Request	SIRR	20	CPU
Software Interrupt Summary	SISR	21	CPU
Interval Clock Control	ICCS	24	CPU
Next Interval Count	NICR	25	CPU
Interval Count	ICR	26	CPU
Time of Year	TODR	27	CPU
Console Receive CSR	RXCS	32	CPU
Console Receive DBR	RXDB	33	CPU
Console Transmit CSR	TXCS	34	CPU
Console Transmit DBR	TXDB	35	CPU
Memory Management Enable	MAPEN	56	CPU
Transmit Buffer Invalidate All	TBIA	57	CPU
Transmit Buffer Invalidate Single	TBIS	58	CPU
Performance Monitor Enable	PMR	61	Process
System Identification	SID	62	CPU

Summary of Memory Management Concepts

In this section we have seen how the VAX-11 hardware provides for the logical program address space and the sharing of memory by several programs. VAX-11 programs reference a linear virtual address space. The virtual address space, as well as the physical memory address space, is divided into 512-byte pages. As part of its private state information, each process has data structures, called page tables, that describe the physical memory location of each virtual page. While a process is running, the CPU uses the process' page tables to translate program-generated addresses into physical memory addresses.

The VAX-11 process address space is divided into several regions. The low-address half is unique to each process. The high-address half is a system-wide address space, used for the operating system, that is shared by all processes. Because system space is part of the address space of every process, a program can directly call operating system routines for service. In addition, since the operating system routine runs in the context of the calling process, it has access to that process' virtual memory (and only that process' memory). The fact that the operating system exists in the process address space and runs in the context of every process greatly simplifies operating system construction.

Here we see the need for the processor access modes described earlier. The operating system code and data must be protected because they can be directly addressed by users. The access modes permit the operating system to protect its code and data from user observation and tampering, while still allowing users to call operating system routines for service. The Change Mode instructions provide a protected crossing between user programs and operating system services that operate on protected data structures.

I/O CONDITION HANDLING

So far we have described the VAX-11 architecture features that support the management of the processor and memory. The management of I/O devices is handled at a different level than the management of the processor and memory. For nonshared devices, the program allocates the device while it is in use. The operating system ensures that no other program can use the device while it is allocated. For shared devices such as disks, the operating system maintains a logical file structure. A request for a file I/O operation is checked against the user's privileges. However, in either case, the operating system does not usually worry about guaranteeing fair service. I/O requests are usually processed in order, or sequenced according to the priority of the program.

The problems associated with input and output functions are related to the real-time nature of devices. In this chapter, we will look at how interrupts are used to service devices with real-time requirements.

Interrupts and Exceptions

Chapter 7 explained that an interrupt is a signal from an I/O device to the CPU. The interrupt causes the CPU to suspend the current process and execute a special operating system service routine to handle the external condition. Interrupts save the processor from having to examine (poll) each device periodically, to see whether there has been a change in its state. Other conditions that occur within the running program, called exceptions, also require special handling by the operating system. We have already seen one exception condition, the page fault.

Interrupts

An *interrupt* is an external event asynchronous to the current process execution that causes the processor to change the flow of control. In a sense, it is like an externally triggered subroutine call. Because the interrupt is not related to the running process, the routine initiated by the interrupt executes on the system-wide Interrupt stack. The PC and PSL of the running process are saved on the Interrupt stack so that the process can be resumed later with a Return from Interrupt (REI) instruction.

Because interrupts occur asynchronously and because there are many devices that may require service, the processor must be able to arbitrate interrupt requests. Associated with each interrupt request is an *interrupt priority level* (IPL). Since some events have more time-critical requirements than others, the processor grants an interrupt to the request with the highest priority. When that request is serviced, requests with lower priority are granted.

The VAX-11 architecture recognizes 32 interrupt priority levels. The lowest priority, IPL 0, is used for all user mode and most operating system code. The next fifteen levels are reserved exclusively for the operating system. The highest sixteen levels are used for hardware interrupts. Peripheral devices interrupt at levels 16 through 23, the system clock interrupts at level 24, and levels 25 through 31 are used for urgent processor error conditions, such as power failure.

The interrupt priority level of the processor is contained in bits 16 through 20 of the PSL. Thus, when the processor is interrupted by a higher priority interrupt request, the current interrupt priority level is saved within the PSL on the stack. When the higher level routine executes an REI instruction, the PSL of the lower priority routine is restored, and the processor returns to the lower priority level.

Exceptions

An *exception* is an unusual condition resulting from the execution of an instruction that causes the processor to change the flow of control. Because exception conditions are caused by the running process, they are usually serviced within the context of that process on one of the process stacks. The VAX-11 recognizes three types of exceptions: traps, faults, and aborts.

A *trap* is an exception condition that occurs at the end of an instruction. Some instructions explicitly request an exception. For example,

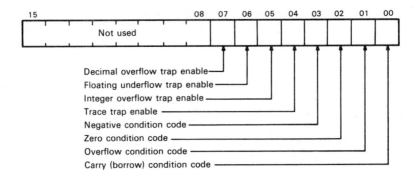

Figure 8-21.   Program Status Word.

Change Mode instructions always trap to an operating system routine for handling, as explained previously. However, there are really two kinds of traps that concern the user process. First is the *trace trap,* used to debug programs. The trace trap allows the debugger to gain control following the execution of every instruction. Second is the *arithmetic trap,* which can occur after the completion of an arithmetic operation, including

1.   Integer, floating-point, or decimal string overflow, in which the result was too large to be stored in the given format.

2.   Integer, floating-point, or decimal string divide by zero, in which the divisor supplied was zero.

3.   Floating-point underflow, in which the result was too small to be expressed by the floating-point format.

Because some routines may not want to trap for all of these arithmetic conditions, the programmer may disable some of the traps by clearing bits in the PSW, shown in Figure 8-21.

Note that there is no way to disable division by zero and floating-point overflow. Also, because each routine has its own expectations about arithmetic conditions, the VAX-11 calling mechanism allows the called routine to specify the condition of the integer overflow and decimal overflow bits. We learned in Chapter 4 that the word call mask at the call entry site contains bits specifying which registers should be saved on entry. However, the full format of the call mask is shown in Figure 8-22. Only registers 0 through 11 may be specified (the others are automatically saved in the call frame). The high two bits of the entry mask specify the condition of the integer and

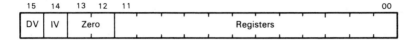

15	14	13	12	11							00
DV	IV	Zero					Registers				

Figure 8-22.   VAX-11 call entry mask.

decimal overflow bits. Since the PSW is saved in the call frame, a Return instruction automatically restores the previous state of the overflow bits.

An exception condition that arises in the middle of an instruction is a *fault.* A page fault, for example, may occur during instruction operand fetching. The registers and memory must be preserved so that the instruction can be restarted and still produce the correct results. Therefore, the PC is left pointing at the instruction that caused the fault. If the operating system routine is able to clear the condition, the instruction is restarted from the beginning.

Finally, an exception condition arising in the middle of an instruction that cannot be restarted because of the condition of the registers or memory is called an *abort.* Aborts are terminating conditions. For example, if, while pushing information onto the Kernel stack, the processor determines that the Kernel stack pointer contains an illegal address, an abort condition is signaled. This usually indicates an operating system error. Because the Kernel stack pointer is invalid, the abort condition is handled on the Interrupt stack, and the instruction cannot be restarted.

Traps, faults, and aborts are the three types of exceptions recognized by the VAX-11 hardware. Both the exception and interrupt mechanisms handle special conditions and have the same effect, namely, switching the processor to a special routine to handle the condition. The differences between interrupts and exceptions are summarized in the following list.

Interrupts	Exceptions
Asynchronous to the execution of a process.	Caused by process instruction execution.
Serviced on the system-wide interrupt stack in system-wide context.	Serviced on the process local stack in process context.
Changes the interrupt priority level to that of the interrupting device.	Does not alter interrupt priority level.
Cannot be disabled, although lower priority interrupts are queued behind higher priority interrupts.	Some arithmetic traps can be disabled.

Vectors

When an interrupt or exception occurs, the hardware transfers to a predefined routine to service the condition. A *vector* is a longword that dictates the action to be taken when a specific condition occurs. The vector specifies both the address of the service routine and how the condition is to be handled.

The System Control Block (SCB) is a data structure that contains vectors for each of the various traps and exceptions and for each software and hardware interrupt level. The System Control Block Base register (SCBB) is a privileged register containing the physical address of the System Control Block. Figure 8-23 shows the layout of the vectors in the SCB.

The vectors are divided into two fields. Bits <1:0> contain a code specifying how the interrupt should be serviced. The binary encoding is as follows:

- 00—If the processor is already running on the Interrupt stack, it continues on the Interrupt stack; otherwise, it services this event on the Kernel stack. Bits <31:2> of the vector contain the virtual address of the service routine. For this and the next encoding, note that the service routines must begin on a longword boundary, because the virtual address is formed by appending two 0 bits to the address contained in bits <31:2> of the vector.

- 01—This event is serviced on the Interrupt stack, and the IPL is raised to 1F hex if this is an exception. Bits <31:2> of the vector contain the virtual address of the service routine.

- 10—This code is for events handled by writeable control store (WCS) microcode. Bits <15:2> are passed to the microcode. If WCS does not exist, this operation causes a halt on the VAX-11/780.

- 11—This code is reserved. It causes a halt on the VAX-11/780.

Software Interrupts

As stated earlier, the VAX-11 processor provides 15 interrupt priority levels (IPLs) for use by the operating system software. Since the hardware contains a separate vector for each interrupt priority level, the operating system can use software interrupts as routine calls, where the service routine for each level performs a specific function. A Kernel mode routine can invoke the service by requesting an interrupt at the appropriate level. The

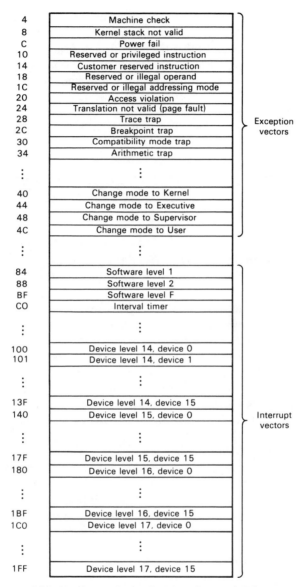

Offset from System Control Block Base Register (HEX)

Figure 8-23.   System Control Block.

interrupt priority levels also allow the operating system to synchronize different levels of execution. If a particular operation is only performed at one level, software can guarantee that the operation does not occur by executing at a higher level. For example, if context switching is always done at interrupt priority level 3, an operating system routine can ensure that a context switch does not occur while it executes at level 4.

The management of software interrupts uses three of the privileged registers. The first register is the Software Interrupt Summary Register (SISR) shown below:

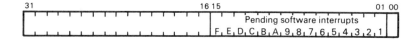

The Software Interrupt Summary Register contains a bit for each of the 15 software interrupt levels (1–15). When the processor priority level drops below the highest level for which a bit is set in the Interrupt Summary Register, an interrupt occurs at that level.

The Software Interrupt Request Register (SIRR) is used to request an interrupt at a given level. The software requests an interrupt by writing the desired level into the SIRR using the Move To Privileged Register Instruction. If the requested level is less than the current processor priority level, the appropriate bit is set in the Software Interrupt Summary Register described above. If the requested level is higher than the current processor level, an interrupt is immediately generated at the requested level.

Finally, the Interrupt Priority Level Register (IPL) is used to read or set the processor priority field of the Processor Status Longword (PSL). Kernel mode software can raise or lower its processor level by writing this register. If the instruction specifies a higher level than the current IPL, the processor is raised to the specified level. If a lower level is specified, the processor priority level is lowered. However, lowering the processor level may cause an interrupt for any pending levels set in the Software Interrupt Summary Register.

Summary of I/O Condition Handling Concepts

In this section we have examined the VAX-11 mechanisms for dealing with special conditions: interrupts and exceptions. The interrupt is an external device-generated signal that tells the operating system to service a device. The exception is the result of an unusual condition in the execution of a program instruction. The existence of both exceptions and interrupts reduces the work required of the processor. The software does not have to constantly check for special conditions, completion of device operations, or erroneous arithmetic results. Instead, the hardware automatically reports the occurrence and prioritizes its servicing. Through the use of vectors, the operating system tells the hardware what action to take when a special condition occurs.

SUMMARY

In this chapter, we have seen how the VAX-11 architecture helps the operating system in the physical management of its three major resources—the processor, the memory, and the I/O devices. The VAX-11 hardware provides process support through the context switching instructions and layered protection through the processor access modes. It supports a virtual memory environment that protects process local data while allowing efficient sharing of the operating system. And, it contains an efficient mechanism for servicing external events and conditions. All of these features greatly simplify the job of the operating system. In a later chapter, we will examine how the operating system uses these mechanisms to build a logical user environment.

REFERENCES

The *VAX-11/780 Hardware Handbook* and *VAX-11 Architecture Handbook* describe some of the features covered in this chapter. Additional material on VAX/VMS can be found in the *VAX-11 Technical Summary* and the *VAX-11 Software Handbook*. The book by Organick (1972) and the paper by Daley and Dennis (1968) discuss operating system support in the MULTICS system.

EXERCISES FOR CHAPTER 8

1. List some of the functions provided by an operating system.

2. What is a process? Why are processes useful? Explain the context of a process.

3. What are the VAX-11 processor access modes and what are they used for?

4. What is process context switching? List the steps involved in a VAX-11 context switch.

5. Explain the difference between virtual and physical memory. Can you have physical page faults? Why must the VAX-11 System Page Table always be resident in contiguous physical memory?

6. Why is the VAX-11 address space divided into several regions? How many memory references are needed to access a location in system space on the VAX-11? How many for a location in process space?

7. If 90% of all references are to process space addresses, what is the average number of memory references required to access a location?

8. Given the process (P0) page table below

E0000028	Virtual page 0 page table entry
70000105	Virtual page 1 page table entry
D0000064	Virtual page 2 page table entry
38000012	Virtual page 3 page table entry

what will happen when a user mode process attempts to write a long-word to each of the following virtual addresses? For those writes that succeed, what physical address will be accessed? What effect, if any, does the access have on the page table entry?

a. 0000006E
b. 000001FE
c. 00000214
d. 00000720
e. 00000436

9. What is the difference between a fault, a trap, an abort, and an interrupt?

10. Why can't *all* arithmetic traps be disabled?

11. What is the System Control Block? Does the System Control Block reside in physical or virtual memory? Why?

12. The privileged register MAPEN is used to enable VAX-11 virtual memory. When the VAX-11 is first powered on, an initial bootstrapping routine is read into memory. Memory management is turned off, and the routine executes in physical memory. That is, all generated addresses specify physical memory locations directly. What must this routine do before it enables the use of virtual memory?

13. What happens if a Kernel mode routine running at interrupt priority level 0 executes the following code sequence?

```
PR$_IPL  = 18              ; define IPL privileged reg.
PR$_SIRR = 20              ; define interrupt request reg.
 .
 .
 .
MTPR    #8,#PR$_IPL
MTPR    #5,#PR$_SIRR
MTPR    #3,#PR$_SIRR
 .
 .
 .
MTPR    #0,#PR$_IPL
```

Chapter 9

The Structure of a
VAX-11 Operating System

In the previous chapter, we began to consider an operating system and its management of physical resources. We then took an in-depth view of the VAX-11 architectural features that support an operating system and its creation of a logical programming environment.

This chapter describes the use of those architectural features by the VAX/VMS (Virtual Memory System) operating system. In particular, this chapter discusses the strategies used by the VMS operating system kernel in its resource management activities. The material provides a close view of the implementation of the VMS operating system. VMS presents an interesting example because it was designed in parallel with the VAX-11 architecture and takes advantage of the features described in the previous chapter.

PROCESS SCHEDULING

We have already seen the details of process management in the VAX-11 hardware and briefly described the operating system scheduler, which allocates processor time to executable processes. In a multiprogrammed system, when the scheduler gives the CPU to a process, the process is usually allowed to compute for an interval of time called a *quantum*. If the quantum expires or if the process suspends itself by waiting for an event such as an I/O completion, the scheduler saves the state of the current process and selects another process to execute.

The job of scheduling is one of selecting a process to be run in a way that gives users equitable service. There are many strategies that can be employed to select a process to be run, including priority, memory residency, size, and readiness to run. The schedulers for different systems may favor different user processes depending on the environment. For example, some systems favor interactive users, others favor computational batch users, while others favor the service of time-critical events.

In the simplest scheme, a single queue of executable processes is maintained and processes are scheduled *round-robin*. That is, when the processor becomes available, the scheduler chooses the process at the head of the execute queue. When that process' quantum expires, the scheduler places that process on the tail of the queue and chooses the next process from the head. Thus, the scheduler cycles through all executable processes, giving each process an equal chance to execute.

If the operating system wishes to favor different types of processes, it usually adopts a priority ordering scheme. Processes with higher priorities are favored over lower priority processes. Each user might have an initial fixed priority based on a system manager assigned job class (e.g., depending on the amount of money the user pays), and the priority may be modified as a result of the activity of the process. Or, processes could be given priorities depending on the expected remaining service time. Thus, the scheduler may choose to run jobs that are expected to complete quickly. This gives users response time commensurate with the resource requirements of the job. Regardless of the policy implemented, when the quantum expires, the scheduler must again select the next process to be run.

VMS Process Scheduling

In the VMS operating system, the scheduler maintains a data structure called the Software Process Control Block (PCB). Just as the Hardware Process Control Block contains all of the hardware context information, the Software PCB contains the software context information for each process. The Software Process Control Block is part of the context of every process and describes the condition of a process at any point in time. For example, the Software PCB contains the user's privileges, accumulated resource usage information, username, etc. The scheduler keeps track of the condition of each process by maintaining queues of Software PCBs organized by process state and priority. Each process' Software Process Control Block is linked onto one of the scheduler's queues.

Picking a new process to run in VMS is very simple. Each process in the system has an associated priority between 0 and 31. (Process priorities are defined by the operating system and are not related to the processor interrupt priority levels discussed in the last chapter.) When a memory-resident process is ready to compute, it is placed on one of the 32 corresponding runnable priority queues maintained by the scheduler for executable processes, as shown in Figure 9-1. When selecting a new process to run, the scheduler always chooses the process from the head of the highest priority queue that is non-empty. The Software Process Control Block of each process contains a pointer to its Hardware PCB, which is used in performing the context switch to restart the program.

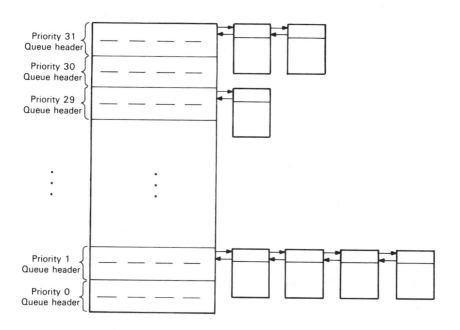

Figure 9-1.   VMS executable process queue headers.

This means of selecting a process to run implies that the highest priority processes could execute forever without allowing lower priority processes access to the CPU. The problem does not normally occur, however, because the VMS scheduler changes process priorities dynamically. When a process is created during login, it is given the base priority assigned to the user by the system manager. As the process runs, its priority can be raised or lowered depending on its activity. For example, if a process computes until its quantum expires, its priority is reduced, and it is placed on the tail of a lower priority queue. (A process is never lowered below its initial priority, however.) Alternatively, if an I/O request completes for a waiting process, its priority is raised to a higher level so that it has a greater chance of computing.

The events that cause priority re-evaluation are:

1.   Quantum expiration (priority is decreased).

2.   Terminal input completion (priority is increased).

3.   Terminal output completion (priority is increased).

4.   Other input, output, or page fault completion (priority is increased).

5.   Resource availability, wake, resume, or deletion (priority is increased).

As a process runs, then, its priority is modified as events occur. Figure 9-2 shows a possible graph of process priority fluctuation over time. The VMS system favors interactive users by raising a process' priority following an interaction (terminal I/O completion) and reducing its priority as the process becomes computational (quantum expiration). The largest priority boost occurs following the completion of a terminal input operation.

The scheduler only manipulates the priorities of processes whose base priorities are between 0 and 15. The priorities of these processes (known as timesharing processes) are never reduced below their base priority or raised above 15. Processes whose base priorities are between 16 and 31 are *real-time* processes. Real-time processes deal with time-critical events and can only be run by suitably privileged users. They execute until they reach completion, suspend themselves to wait for an I/O operation, or until a higher priority real-time process becomes runnable, and they are not interrupted by quantum expiration.

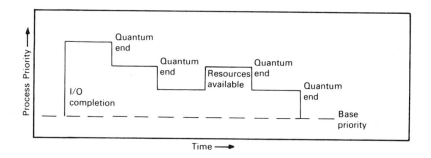

Figure 9-2.   Changes in process priority with time.

Besides selecting the next process to execute, the VMS scheduler is responsible for managing all process state transitions. In VMS, the *state* of a process is part of its context that describes its condition. The first process state we discussed was the executable and in memory state, for which the scheduler maintains 32 priority queues. There are also 32 queues for processes that are in the executable state but are currently out of memory. An operating system process called the swapper, to be discussed later, is responsible for moving processes between memory and the disk under command of the scheduler.

The remaining states include non-executable processes that are waiting for event occurrences, such as the completion of an I/O operation or page fault completion, or the availability of a hardware or software resource. These processes are linked onto one of the 11 scheduler wait queues described in Table 9-1. As events occur for a process, the Software Process Control Block is moved between queues to reflect the state of the process. The differentiation of processes into queues reduces the work needed to locate a waiting process when an event occurs that affects it. For example, when a page fault completes, the scheduler knows that the waiting process can be found on the Page Fault Wait queue. Its Software Process Control Block would then be linked onto the appropriate executable queue, based on its priority and whether or not it is in memory. Figure 9-3 shows the possible states and transitions for a process in the VMS system. The arrows in Figure 9-3 show the events causing a process to move from one state to another.

Table 9-1. VMS Process Wait Queues

Process State	Process Condition
Collided Page Wait	Processes faulting a page in transition (usually a page in the process of being read or written).
Common Event Wait	Processes waiting for shared event flags (event flags are single-bit interprocess signalling mechanisms).
Free Page Wait	Processes waiting for a free page of physical memory.
Hibernate Wait	Processes that have requested hibernation and are resident in memory.
Hibernate Wait, swapped out of memory	Processes that have requested hibernation and are swapped out of memory.
Local Event Wait	Processes waiting for local event flags (most likely for I/O completion) that are resident in memory.
Local Event Wait, swapped out of memory	Processes waiting for local event flags that are swapped out of memory.
Suspended Wait	Processes that are suspended and resident in memory.
Suspended, swapped out of memory	Processes that are suspended and nonresident.
Resource Wait	Processes waiting for miscellaneous system resources.
Page Fault Wait	Processes waiting for a faulted page to be read in.

VMS, then, attempts to provide equitable service by preempting long running jobs and by modifying process priorities to allow other processes to execute. It does this in a way that favors highly interactive users. When a program is preempted, its state information is saved in system data structures (the Hardware and Software Process Control Blocks) so that the process can be resumed later. All this is done in a way that is invisible to the process and the user.

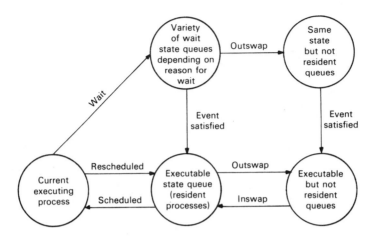

Figure 9-3.   VMS process state transitions.

VMS Scheduler Context Switch Example

It is interesting to look briefly at how the VMS context switch routine (called the rescheduler) is implemented. Chapter 8 mentioned the use of software interrupts in the operating system as function calls. In VMS, the rescheduler is actually a service routine that executes in response to an interrupt at software interrupt priority level 3.

Routines that detect a process state change or a quantum expiration execute at software IPLs above 3. If the quantum expires or if a detected event causes a process of higher priority than the current process to become executable, then a context switch will be initiated. To cause the context switch, the event reporting routine simply requests an IPL 3 interrupt using the Software Interrupt Request Register, described in Chapter 8. When the event reporting routine returns to a priority level below 3, an interrupt will occur, causing the rescheduling routine to perform a context switch.

We have included a listing of the VMS rescheduling code in Figure 9-4. This routine is really quite simple, although it may look complex at first glance because of the long symbol names. The frequently used notation $W^\wedge symbol$ tells the assembler to generate word-relative addressing. (By default, the assembler uses longword-relative addressing for variables not

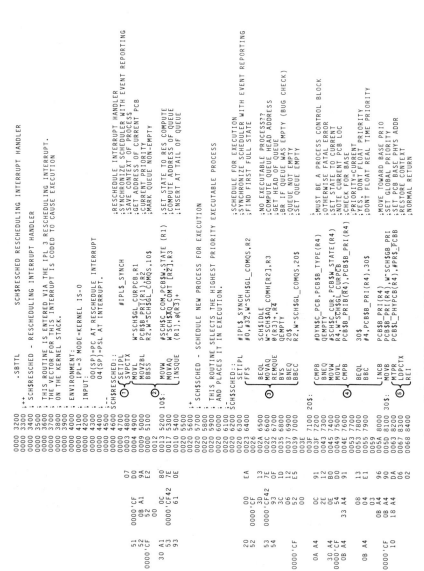

Figure 9-4. VMS rescheduling interrupt handler.

defined in the same module. Forcing word-relative addressing saves space if the variable is within reach.) To understand what the routine does, we must first define the following symbols that it uses:

1. SCH$GL _ COMQS   The address of the 32-bit Compute Queue Status (COMQS) longword. Each bit in COMQS represents one of the 32 executable process queues shown in Figure 9-2. In the actual implementation, both the queues and the bits are ordered from highest to lowest priority. Thus, bit 0 and queue header 0 represent the highest priority queue, priority 31. Using the Find First Set (FFS) instruction to scan the longword and locate the highest priority non-empty queue is quite effective. (In fact, the FFS instruction, which scans a field of 32 bits, was included for just this purpose.)

2. SCH$AQ_ COMH   The address of the first header in the array of 32 computable queue headers is shown in Figure 9-2. The bit number from a bit found in SCH$GL _ COMQS can be used as an index into the quadword array to address the queue header of a priority queue.

3. SCH$AQ_ COMT   The address of the tail pointer in the first (highest priority) of the 32 queue headers.

4. SCH$GL _ CURPCB   The address of a pointer to the Software Process Control Block of the process currently executing.

The following notes refer to the numbers in the listing. It is not important to understand every instruction. Rather, this routine is a good demonstration of the use of the VAX-11 architecture by the operating system.

1. The routine is entered as a result of an IPL 3 interrupt. It immediately raises its interrupt priority level to the VMS synchronizing level (IPL 7, shown symbolically as IPL$_ SYNC) to synchronize with event reporting routines. This ensures that no process state changes or data base changes will occur while rescheduling is underway.

2. The routine stores the address of the Software PCB of the current process into R1, and stores the priority of the process in R2. The Process Control Block will be placed on the end of the executable

queue for its priority. The corresponding bit in the Compute Queue Status longword is set to note that a process will be placed in the queue. The address of the queue header for this priority is computed, and the PCB is added to the tail.

3. The Find First Set (FFS) instruction locates the first bit set in the Compute Queue Status longword. This indicates the highest priority non-empty queue. The address of the header for that queue is computed and the first Software PCB is removed. This is the new process to be run. If this PCB was the last entry in the queue, the corresponding bit in the Compute Queue Status longword is cleared.

4. The priority of the process is reduced so that it will automatically be placed on a lower priority queue if its quantum expires. (This is done with an increment because the queues and bits and internal priority representations are backwards, i.e., 0 is highest priority.)

5. The address of the Hardware Process Control Block of the process is loaded in the Process Control Block Base register. A Load Process Context instruction then causes the hardware registers to be loaded for the new process. Finally, the Return from Interrupt instruction returns from the original interrupt priority level 3 interrupt. If there are no lower priority interrupts pending, the processor will return to IPL 0 and continue executing instructions for the new process.

The Load Process Context (LDPCTX) instruction at the end of the reschedule routine is the only use of this instruction in the VAX/VMS operating system. The Save Process Context instruction does not enjoy quite such a restricted usage. The event reporting routines will execute a Save Process Context if the current process must be placed in a wait queue. They will then enter the rescheduling code in Figure 9-4 at SCH$SCHED to start the next process.

PROCESS PAGING

In Chapter 8, we examined the VAX-11 hardware support for memory management. The VAX-11 architecture provides for a number of features, including:

1. A linear logical program address space
2. Protection of memory

3.   Sharing of operating system code and data
4.   Trapping of references to nonresident pages

Although these architectural features provide the basis for the memory management system, there is a large number of issues and problem areas in the control of memory. For example, the architecture does not help in deciding how program pages should be loaded or removed from memory. This support must be handled by software, and there are many different strategies that can be chosen for handling memory management, depending on the requirements for the system.

In general, virtual memory is not a performance feature, i.e., there is a performance cost in providing the virtual memory service. First, there is the cost of the extra memory references introduced by page tables, although this can be significantly reduced by additional hardware as we shall see in Chapter 11. Second, and more important, is the cost of a reference to a nonresident page. A page fault can require both a disk read and a disk write operation. This is time-consuming to the program and requires some amount of processing by the operating system. Thus, the difficult job of the virtual memory management system is to optimize performance by trading off the amount of physical memory for each process, which reduces its paging activity, with the number of processes allowed to share memory, which reduces the swapping activity.

The number of page faults generated by a program depends on the memory reference pattern of the program and on the physical memory allocation and page replacement policies of the operating system. Normally, the operating system places some limits on the physical memory available to a program. Figure 9-5 shows a graphic representation of program page fault rate plotted against the ratio of virtual-to-physical memory. Of course when the virtual-to-physical ratio is 1, there are no page faults once the program is resident in memory (the total number of faults is equal to the program size). As the ratio increases, the fault rate increases. Figure 9-6 shows a similar graph of total program page faults versus the program physical memory limit. We see here that there is a point beyond which additional physical memory allocation does not provide any significant decrease in the number of page faults. This point often occurs much before the program becomes fully resident. Therefore, the operating system needs to avoid overcommitting memory to a program. Overcommitting memory will reduce the memory available to others, while not benefitting the receiving process.

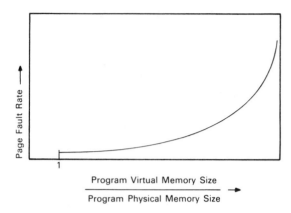

Figure 9-5. Program page fault rate versus virtual/physical memory size ratio.

As a program executes, pages are faulted into physical memory until the program reaches the physical memory limit imposed on it by the operating system. At this point, when the program references the next nonresident page, the operating system must choose a page to remove from memory in order to bring in the newly referenced page. The strategies for selecting a page to remove are known as *page replacement algorithms*.

The optimal replacement strategy, described by Belady, requires full knowledge of the program's future behavior. This method removes the page that will not be referenced for the longest time in the future. Of course, this knowledge is generally not available. Most methods, then, use past program behavior as a predictor of future behavior. For example, in the *Least Recently Used* (LRU) scheme, the page removed is the one that has not been accessed for the longest time. It is hoped that this page will not be needed in the near future. To implement LRU requires that the hardware maintain some amount of usage information on each page. Usually, each page table entry will contain a bit called the *reference bit* that is set whenever a reference is made to the page. If the software periodically turns off the reference bit, it can keep track of the number of periods since a page has been accessed.

Denning's working set model for program behavior provides better intuition concerning the pages required by a program to execute efficiently. Denning defines the *working set* of a program, $W(T,t)$, to be the set of pages referenced in the interval $(T - t, T)$. For different sizes of the interval, $t,$ the

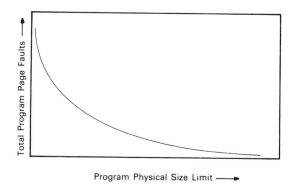

Figure 9-6.   Program page faults versus physical size limit.

working set is the set of pages referenced in the last t seconds, and the working set size, $w(T,t)$, is the number of pages referenced. Both the membership of the working set and the size of the working set can be expected to change during the execution of the program, that is, as T increases. If the window size t has been appropriately selected (by considering CPU speed and paging device capacity), then the objective of the memory management mechanism should be to keep the pages belonging to the program's working set resident in memory at all times.

Therefore, this model describes a basis for selection of program pages to remain in memory. For a given interval size t, pages that have not been accessed in the last t references are removed from memory in an attempt to keep exactly the working set in memory at all times. Notice that with this definition, a page can be removed without the occurrence of a page fault.

There is a tradeoff between the cost of page faults and the complexity of the algorithm required to reduce them. If the replacement algorithm is successful in reducing faults, but requires excessive processor time, then it may not be worth the effort. Some simpler but less successful schemes for replacement are Random replacement, in which the page to be removed is chosen at random, and First In First Out (FIFO) replacement, in which the page removed is the page that has been in memory for the longest time. In FIFO, the system just keeps a queue of pages. A new page is added to the bottom of the queue and the oldest page is removed from the top of the queue.

No matter how intelligent the replacement strategy, there is no substitute for physical memory. Regardless of the strategy, the page fault rate is likely to be high if a process has too little physical memory, as we see in Figure 9-5. Therefore, the main advantage of virtual memory is that it allows processes to operate on a larger address space than would be otherwise possible, but at the cost of performance. The cost, of course, rises with the size of the "virtual" memory needed by the process.

VMS Memory Management

Memory management in VMS actually consists of two parts. The first part of the memory management subsystem is the *pager*, which handles the reading in of faulted pages and the writing out of resident pages from the memory of a process. The pager, which executes within the context of the process, is basically a subroutine shared by all processes in the system and is called implicitly when a nonresident page is addressed. The second part of the VMS memory management subsystem is the *swapper*, a process whose function is the removal or loading of entire processes from or into memory. The swapper is closely related to the scheduler since both must cooperate to determine which processes will be moved, or "swapped," between memory and disk.

Paging under VMS

In VMS, each process in the system has a quota or limit for the number of pages of physical memory that it may occupy. This number is called the *resident set limit*. The VMS *resident set* is the set of pages a process has in memory. (The resident set is called the working set in VAX/VMS documentation.) The memory management system maintains a list for each process called the *resident set list* that points to these pages.

When a new process is initially run, the process load file is examined, and page tables are built from information contained there. At first, all page table entry Valid bits are zero since none of the process pages have been loaded. The resident set of the process is empty, and the resident set list has no entries. When the operating system transfers control to the starting address of the process, a page fault occurs. The page fault causes a transfer of control to the pager so that the first page of the process can be loaded into memory.

When the pager gains control following a page fault, the hardware has pushed the program counter that points to the faulting instruction, and the virtual address that caused the fault, onto the stack. From the virtual address, the pager is able to locate the process page table entry for the faulted page. This page table entry contains information leading to the disk address of the page. The pager obtains an empty page of physical memory and initiates a read of the page from disk. The corresponding page table entry is changed so that the Valid bit is set and the page frame number field points to the physical page into which the read will occur. If this is the first faulted page, then it will be the first page in the resident set of the process and the first entry in the resident set list. When the read completes, the pager returns to user level to restart the instruction that faulted.

As the program continues to execute, more and more pages are faulted into its resident set. Each time a fault occurs, the pager reads the page from disk and creates a valid page table entry to map it. If the program has a large virtual size, the resident set size will eventually reach the resident set limit for the process. At this point, the process may not use any more physical memory, and reading a new page forces it to return a page from its resident set to the system.

VMS does not use a least recently used page replacement strategy because VAX page tables do not have a reference bit (although this could be simulated in software). Instead of selecting pages to be removed from the system as a whole, VMS pages the process against itself. That is, the page that is removed must come from the process that caused the page fault if it has reached its resident set limit. The page removed from the resident set is selected in round-robin style (first in, first out) from the resident set list. A pointer circles through the resident set list to determine the next page to be removed. Although this method is not optimal, the cost of making an error (i.e., throwing out a page about to be referenced) is low, as we shall see.

The VMS memory management system maintains two lists of physical pages called the *free page list* and the *modified page list*. The free page list is the source of physical pages for the system. When a process needs a physical page to receive a faulted page, it takes the entry from the head of the free list. The system tries to keep at least some minimal number of pages free at all times.

The free list also acts as a cache (a fast backup store) of recently used pages. When a page is removed from a resident set, it is placed on the tail of the free page list or the modifed page list, depending on the condition of the Modify bit in the page's page table entry. If the Modify bit is 0, then there is already an exact copy of the page on disk and the page need not be written back. Such a page is placed on the tail of the free page list. If the Modify bit is set, then the page must be written back to disk and is placed on the tail of the modified page list. The pages of the modified list are not written back to disk until the list reaches a predefined threshold.

A page removed from a resident set remains on the appropriate list for some period of time before it is reused. If a process faults a page that is on one of the lists, the page is simply returned to the resident set at little cost. Depending on the list sizes and activity of the system, these caches have a significant effect on system and process performance by reducing fault time and paging I/O. However, they also have an inherent unfairness because a heavily faulting process can cause a rapid turnover of the lists.

Besides being a cache for pages, the *modified page list* serves another important purpose. By delaying the writing of modified pages, the system can write pages to the paging file in clusters or groups instead of individually, significantly reducing the number of I/O operations and thereby minimizing the time the disk is busy. Moreover, by waiting some period of time, many pages never have to be written at all because they are referenced again or because the program is terminated.

In addition, since many pages are written at one time, the system can attempt to write virtually contiguous process pages on contiguous disk blocks. This way, the system can also cluster reads from the paging file. When the process accesses a page, the system may choose to bring in several pages (a cluster) if they are located together on the disk.

The biggest gain from clustering of pages on reads occurs when a new program is started. Typically, programs fault heavily when they start until a reasonable working set has been established. When the program faults the first page, VMS actually reads many pages into memory, reducing the high program startup faulting.

A common technique for both reducing paging and optimizing the sharing of programs is to dynamically adjust the resident set size of a program. Some schemes attempt to equalize the fault rate across all processes. Following each quantum expiration, VMS checks the process' fault rate for the past interval. Based on this rate, the process' resident set limit may be increased or reduced. Processes that are faulting heavily will receive an increment in their physical memory limit, while processes not faulting will have their resident set limit reduced. This takes memory away from processes that don't need it, and gives physical memory to processes that make heavy use of virtual memory.

Swapping under VMS

In addition to paging, VMS also swaps entire processes between memory and disk. Swapping is performed by the swapper, a separate process that runs at a high priority and, of course, is never swapped itself.

When the resident set of a process is in memory, it is a member of the *balance set*. While the resident set is the collection of pages for a particular process, the balance set is the set of all resident processes. VMS swaps entire resident sets between the balance set and disk to make room for swapping in resident sets of other processes. Some virtual memory systems force a non-resident process to page itself back into memory. However, before it allows a process to execute, VMS loads the entire resident set as it existed when the process was interrupted. This reduces the number of page faults and the number of disk I/O operations, since all of the resident set pages can be written in or out with a minimal number of disk transfers.

When a process is brought into memory, it is guaranteed at least one quantum before it becomes eligible to be swapped out. The algorithm for determining which process to swap in is quite simple. The swapper checks the nonresident executable queues to find the highest priority process to be brought in. Having selected a process, the swapper must then find enough free pages to hold the resident set of the selected process. Free pages may be located by:

1. Taking them from the free page list

2. Writing the modified page list back to disk, thereby freeing those pages

3. Swapping out a process of lower or equal priority.

Sometimes several processes have to be swapped out to make room for one large incoming process.

INPUT AND OUTPUT PROCESSING

The input and output processing routines are often the most complex in the operating system. This is due in part to the asynchronous nature of I/O devices and the synchronization problems caused by the parallelism inherent in their operation. In addition, many I/O devices have real-time service requirements, and the I/O system must be carefully tuned to meet these constraints.

The control of I/O devices differs significantly in its purpose from the processor and memory handling described previously. Processor and memory management operations are generally provided invisibly to the user. They exist to increase resource utilization. On the other hand, I/O operations are initiated at the request of the user program.

A user requests an I/O operation by calling an operating system routine. For high-level languages, the user codes an OUTPUT or WRITE statement (for output), and the language run-time system generates the low-level operating system call (or calls). The call generally specifies the type of operation to be performed (e.g., read or write) and the address and length of a user memory buffer for containing the data to be read or written. The I/O service routine then passes the arguments to a separate process, called a *device driver*, that is responsible for invoking the physical I/O operation. In most systems, the calling process is then suspended and placed in a process wait queue until the I/O request completes. In other systems, the process is allowed to continue processing while the I/O operation is in progress.

It is possible for several driver processes to be in various stages of I/O processing at any time. Before a device driver can initiate device activity, it may need to allocate hardware or software resources. For example, if there are several devices on a single-transfer bus, the driver processes need a mechanism to determine which driver can cause a transfer. Thus, there must be a mechanism that allows a driver to coordinate with other driver processes. There must also be a mechanism for informing drivers when a resource becomes available.

In this section, we will examine the basic structure of the VMS I/O system. The VMS I/O system is quite complicated and we will not cover all of its functions or components. Our goal is to show how VMS uses the hardware architecture. To this end, we will concentrate on the flow of an I/O request between the user process and the system and the use of VAX-11 interrupt priority levels to schedule and synchronize I/O processing.

The VMS I/O System

The VMS input/output system is composed of several layers. Each layer provides a higher-level interface to the level above it, as shown in Figure 9-7. At the highest (most general) level are the record management and data base systems that manage named objects such as files, records, fields, and so on. At the lower levels are the kernel routines that interface directly to physical devices. This is the level discussed in this section.

In general, VMS I/O is asynchronous. In other words, a program can issue an I/O request and continue processing while the request is in progress. Sometime later, the program can check to see if the I/O operation has completed, or can be notified when the completion occurs. If the program

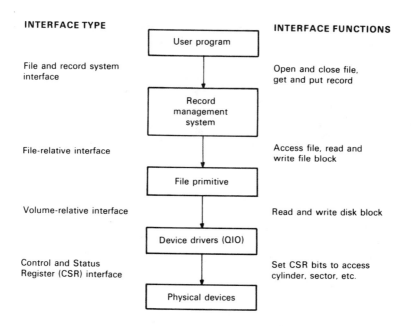

INTERFACE TYPE

File and record system
interface

File-relative interface

Volume-relative interface

Control and Status
Register (CSR) interface

INTERFACE FUNCTIONS

Open and close file,
get and put record

Access file, read and
write file block

Read and write disk block

Set CSR bits to access
cylinder, sector, etc.

Figure 9-7. VMS file system layers.

wishes to wait until the I/O completes, it calls another operating system routine to request suspension until the I/O operation is done. However, the suspension is not part of the I/O requesting procedure.

VMS I/O Data Base

Before we begin the discussion of the functioning of the I/O system components, we will introduce a simplified model of the I/O data base. The I/O data structures tell as much about the system as the code does.

We have already seen the Process Control Block, which describes the state of each VMS process. In the I/O system, there are control blocks that describe every bus adapter (e.g., Unibus), every controller (e.g., terminal multiplexer), every device unit (e.g., terminal), and every outstanding I/O request (e.g., a terminal read operation). These control blocks are linked into a structure that represents the topology of the hardware I/O system.

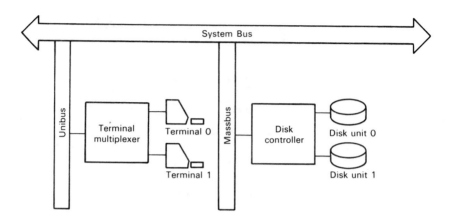

(a)   Sample system hardware structure.

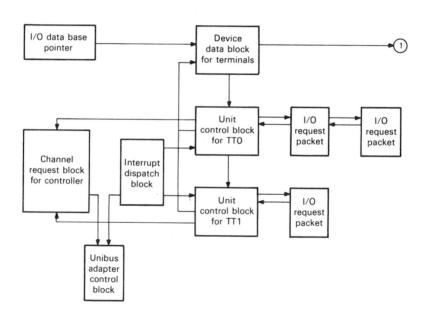

(b)   Sample VMS I/O data base.

Figure 9-8.   VMS I/O organization and data base.

For example, Figure 9-8b shows a simplified VMS I/O data base for the hardware configuration shown in Figure 9-8a. The arrows indicate pointers from one control block to another. The six control blocks shown are briefly described below.

1. The Device Data Block (DDB) contains information common to all devices of a given type connected to a single controller, such as the device name string (e.g., TTA for terminals attached to terminal controller A).

2. The Unit Control Block (UCB) describes the characteristics and state for a single device. It also contains the context for the device driver process that controls the device.

3. The I/O Request Packet (IRP) describes a single user I/O request. For example, the packet contains an identifier for the requesting process, the type of operation requested, and the address and length of the user's memory buffer.

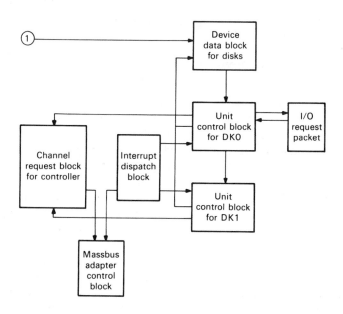

(b) Sample VMS I/O data base (cont.).

Figure 9-8. VMS I/O organization and data base (cont.).

4. The Channel Request Block (CRB) defines the state of a controller. The Channel Request Block is used to arbitrate requests for a shared controller. The CRB indicates which device unit is currently transferring and which units are waiting to transfer when the current transfer is complete.

5. The Interrupt Data Block (IDB) describes the current activity on a controller and is used to locate the responsible device when an interrupt occurs. It is a logical extension to the Channel Request Block.

6. The Adapter Control Block (ADB) defines the characteristics and state of a Massbus or Unibus adapter.

The arrows in Figure 9-8b show the static relationship of the data base. However, some control blocks may contain other pointers or be members of other queues, depending on the state of the devices. For example, when a unit is waiting for a free controller on which to transfer, its Unit Control Block is queued to the Channel Request Block for the controller. Thus, the contents of these control blocks precisely define the state of the I/O system at any point in time.

VMS I/O System Components

The VMS I/O system can be logically separated into three components. First is the Queue I/O (QIO) system service, which is called to request all I/O operations on VMS. QIO is a procedure called by the user program. Although it executes in Kernel mode, QIO runs within the context of the user's process and has access to the process address space of the caller. The basic function of QIO is to validate the user-supplied arguments and build a data structure in system dynamic memory called an I/O Request Packet (IRP). The I/O Request Packet contains all of the information needed by the device driver to perform the physical I/O function. QIO also checks that the calling process is allowed to perform the requested function on the specified device.

Within the Unit Control Block of each device is a header for a queue of outstanding I/O requests, as shown in Figure 9-8b. Once QIO has validated the request and built the I/O Request Packet, it inserts the packet onto the queue for the proper unit and returns control to the caller. (Queue I/O earns its name because it queues the I/O request to the driver.) The calling process may then continue processing or request suspension until the I/O completes. A success indication from QIO means only that the parameters were supplied properly and that the I/O request has been queued to the driver. To see if the I/O has completed successfully, the user program must specify a memory location in which the final status will be placed when the operation completes.

The second component of the I/O system is the device driver. A device driver is a set of routines and data structures that control the operation of a single type of device. VMS uses the routines and data structures in the execution of an I/O request.

When an I/O request is issued for an idle device, VMS creates a driver process to handle the request. A driver process is a limited context process. By limited context, we mean that the driver is restricted to system space addressing; it does not execute within the context of a user process. Its state is completely described by its program counter, several registers, and the device data base.

The device driver executes at a high processor priority level. Since it cannot be interrupted by the scheduler, a driver executes until it either terminates, performs an explicit wait request, or is interrupted by a driver at a higher IPL. User processes do not run until all driver work is completed. The context for each driver, its registers and program counter, are kept within the Unit Control Block for the device.

Thus, the Unit Control Block is to the device driver as the Process Control Block is to the process. For each active device, the unit's Unit Control Block contains the state information of the executing driver process, as well as the status of the unit.

The third component of the VMS I/O system is the I/O postprocessing routine that completes the I/O operation within the caller's address space. Postprocessing, like Queue I/O, is a common routine used for final processing of all device requests. Postprocessing routines are used to return the final status and data to user process memory.

I/O Control Flow

The I/O request begins as a call to QIO. The QIO routine creates an I/O Request Packet, queues it onto the device Unit Control Block, and returns to the user. The I/O Request Packet is the embodiment of the request, and is passed between various components of the I/O system. It contains all of the information needed to perform the operation independently of the requesting process and to later complete the operation within the context of the requesting process.

The operations performed by the VMS I/O system to process a request can be shown in the flow diagram in Figure 9-9. The user calls the QIO

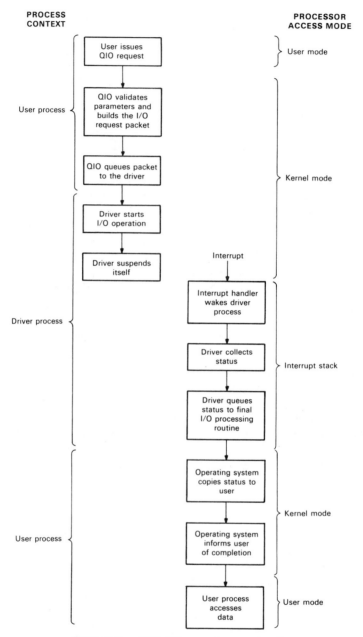

Figure 9-9.   VMS I/O request processing flow.

service routine, which executes in Kernel mode within the context of the user's process. QIO locates the Unit Control Block and associated data base for the device. It checks device-independent parameters and calls driver sub-routines to validate device-specific parameters. Then, QIO builds an I/O Request Packet and queues it for the driver by placing it on the Unit Control Block request queue.

The driver process dequeues the request and starts the device. The driver suspends itself by placing its UCB in a wait queue so that other processing can continue while the I/O operation proceeds. When the device interrupt occurs, the operating system resumes the driver process. The driver collects any status information from the device and controller registers, and copies them into the I/O Request Packet for the request. The I/O Request Packet is then placed on a queue for the I/O postprocessing routines.

I/O postprocessing examines the I/O Request Packet to determine how the I/O should be completed. Because the postprocessing routine returns status information into user memory buffers, it must execute with the address space (the context) of the requesting process. Finally, the postprocessing routine notifies the process that the I/O operation has completed.

The Use of Interrupt Priority Levels

The scenario in the previous section showed the sequence of events with respect to a single I/O request. Of course, at any time there are many processes executing, and many I/O requests in various states of completion. The I/O system has a number of tasks to perform to manage all of the simultaneous operations. It also tries to optimize throughput while also retaining real-time device responsiveness. It does this by keeping as many devices busy as possible. For example, as soon as an I/O transfer completes on a device, a new transfer will be started if one is queued for the device.

VMS uses the software interrupt priority levels to keep the devices busy while also maintaining responsiveness. This is done by performing different I/O processing functions at different priority levels. Therefore, the I/O system will not process an I/O request sequentially, but will perform all the critical work for each outstanding request at a given level. Then the lower priority work can be done for each request, and so on. This requires a mechanism for suspending a driver process at one level and continuing its work sometime later at another level.

Figure 9-10 shows the work done at each of four levels of processing. The VMS I/O system is structured so that all work is completed at the highest level before the next level executes.

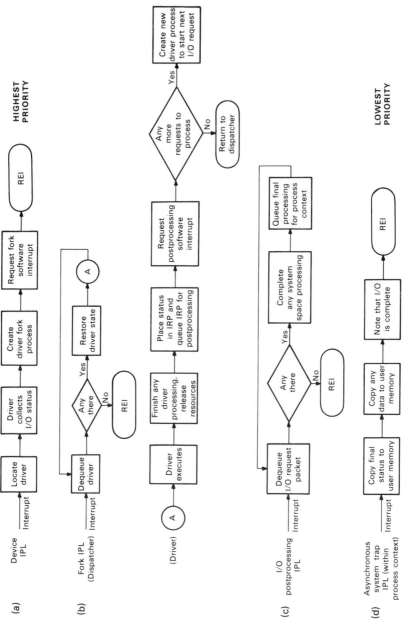

Figure 9-10.   I/O system use of IPLs.

The highest priority activity in VMS is the response to a device interrupt. Figure 9-10a shows the flow when an interrupt occurs. The interrupt dispatcher locates the responsible driver and initiates a routine within the driver to service the interrupt. It is a goal of VMS driver interrupt service routines to spend as little time as possible at the device IPL because other hardware interrupts may be locked out. Therefore, VMS device drivers only execute at device IPL long enough to copy any CSR status information into the Unit Control Block. Staying at this IPL ensures that the registers do not change while being copied. As soon as the registers are copied, the driver asks the operating system to continue its execution at a lower level.

The lowering of a driver IPL is known as a *fork* in VMS. It is a continuation of the execution of a process at a different level and time. To initiate a fork, the operating system saves all of the driver context (its PC and registers) in the Unit Control Block for the device. The Unit Control Block is placed on a queue for the lower IPL, called the device fork level queue. The operating system requests a software interrupt at the fork IPL and returns from the hardware device interrupt, allowing other devices to interrupt.

When the processor priority level drops below the IPL requested for the driver, an interrupt occurs. Figure 9-10b shows the actions at this level. An interrupt dispatcher dequeues the first Unit Control Block from its queue and restores the state of the driver process. The driver process continues execution and releases any resources, such as controller data paths, which it has acquired, so as to increase the level of concurrency possible.

The fork IPL is also used to synchronize driver data bases. Any driver wishing to access some of the shared data base components for a device or controller must operate at the fork IPL of the device. By forcing all drivers to queue at a given level, VMS ensures that only one driver process can access the data base at a time. Following an interrupt, drivers are queued to the lower IPL by the operating system. Thus, the forking mechanism is a forced serialization (e.g., queuing) of activity. A driver does not have to worry about synchronizing with other driver processes. It knows implicitly that it is the only process active at that level.

Although there may still be processing needed to complete the I/O request, VMS again defers much of it to a lower level. The driver process places any final status in the I/O Request Packet. This time, the I/O Request Packet is used to propagate the execution of the I/O request. The packet is placed on a queue for the I/O postprocessing routine that executes at the lowest IPL for I/O postprocessing.

After queueing the I/O packet and requesting a software interrupt at the postprocessing IPL, the driver checks its Unit Control Block request queue to see if any more requests are waiting. If so, the driver begins processing the next request. This way, a new request can be started on the device as soon as possible. After the driver initiates the next I/O operation, if there is one, it returns to the fork interrupt dispatcher. The dispatcher checks to determine if any other driver fork processes are waiting to execute at that level.

Once VMS has seen that all possible I/O requests have been initiated, postprocessing can occur. Postprocessing is initiated by a software interrupt. The postprocessing routine dequeues an I/O request packet to finish any processing that can be done in the operating system context, as shown in Figure 9-10c. Then, it must switch to process context to perform any final copying of data and status into user memory.

The switch to process context (address space) is done with an *Asynchronous System Trap*. An Asynchronous System Trap (AST) is a call of a routine within the context of a process, asynchronous to the execution of that process. For example, when a process issues an I/O request, it can specify a routine to be called when the I/O is completed. This routine is called an Asynchronous System Trap routine, because it is called when an asynchronous event occurs. If the process is executing when the event occurs, it will be interrupted and the AST routine will be called. When the AST routine returns, program execution continues from the interrupt point.

The operating system maintains a queue of AST control blocks in the Software Process Control Block of each process. Each entry in the queue describes one requested AST and contains the address of a routine to be called when a specified event occurs. The I/O postprocessing routine queues the address of one of its subroutines, to be executed in Kernel mode when the appropriate process next executes. It also notes in the Hardware Process Control Block that a Kernel mode AST is pending for the process. When the process next executes, the VAX-11 hardware automatically causes an interrupt at the AST level IPL so that the operating system can execute the Asynchronous System Trap routine.

This final AST routine executes in user mode to copy any information into the user's address space. It may also inform the process that the I/O operation has completed. For example, if the process asked to have its own AST routine executed following the I/O completion, the Kernel mode routine will queue an Asynchronous System Trap for the user.

We have seen that there are two ways to consider I/O processing. First is the sequential flow of a single I/O request through the system, as shown in Figure 9-9. Second is the actual servicing sequence used by VMS to increase response time, as shown in Figure 9-10. In Figure 9-10 we can see how a number of work queues allow for the propagation of a request through several prioritized levels. VMS uses the software interrupt priority levels and the software interrupts to schedule work at each level. However, it is the hardware that automatically generates an interrupt at the highest level with work to do. Also, because access to the driver fork level is serialized through a queue, drivers do not have to explicitly synchronize for the access to a shared driver data structure.

SYSTEM SERVICE IMPLEMENTATION

We discussed the use of an operating system service routine while examining Change Mode instructions in the previous chapter, and in this chapter we have considered the most frequently called system service in VMS, the Queue I/O service. In this final section, it will be instructive to discuss how control is actually transferred to a VMS service.

We have already stated that VMS system services are called via the Call instruction. In VMS, macros are available at the assembly language level to access system services. For example, the $QIO macro generates a call to the QIO routine. The name of the QIO entry point in the operating system is SYS$QIO. A high-level language program can call this routine as it would call any other procedure, e.g., CALL SYS$QIO(parameters).

Once a program containing a system service call is translated and linked, it contains the system space virtual address of the service routine entry point. One might ask whether this means that each service routine always remains at the same virtual address or whether the user has to reassemble or relink the program each time a new version of the operating system arrives. The answer to each question is no. VMS was designed so that user programs would run without relinking or reassembling across VMS versions, even though the service routines might be relocated in the system address space. The first few pages of system address space in VMS are reserved for system service *vectors,* which are the pointers into the system service routines. These vectors are similar to the interrupt vectors in that they give directions to where a routine or system service actually resides in system space.

For each system service, there are several instructions in the vector region to transfer control to the actual service routine. The instructions in the vector region for each service are at fixed virtual addresses for the life of VMS. Consequently, if a new version of VMS is issued in which the service procedures have moved, user programs can still run unchanged because the vectors remain at the same address although they transfer control to different locations.

For example, SYS$QIO is the address of the vector for the Queue I/O system service. The vector contains instructions to transfer control to the system service routine in system space. If the service routine runs with the access mode of the caller, the vector contains only the 16-bit register save mask (remember that the vector was called as if it were a procedure) and a Jump instruction. The following is an example of a system service routine called NAME executing in the same mode:

```
SYS$NAME:
        .WORD   ^M<R2,R3,R4,R5>    ; register save mask
        JMP     EXE$NAME+2         ; transfer to service
```

The Jump instruction transfers control to the first instruction of the service routine in system space, which is at address EXE$NAME+2. This calling method forces the first instruction of the service to be two bytes past its entry point, since the actual service routine has a copy of the register save mask at its beginning. When the service routine executes a Return instruction, it will return directly to the user.

If the system service routine executes in a different mode than the user program, then the vector contains the Call mask followed by a Change Mode instruction and a Return instruction:

```
SYS$NAME:
        .WORD   ^M<R2,R3,R4,R5>    ; save registers
        CHMK    #code              ; dispatch to service
        RET                        ; return to caller
```

The Change Mode instruction causes an exception, changing the mode of the processor and transferring control to a special dispatching routine within VMS. This routine examines the code number, which tells which system service should be called. It also copies arguments from the caller's stack to the stack of the new, higher access mode before calling the system service routine. When the system service routine executes a Return instruction, it returns to this dispatcher. The dispatcher executes a Return from Interrupt (REI) instruction, lowering the access mode and returning to the instruction following the Change Mode. Now running in the caller's access mode, the Return instruction in the service vector executes, returning control to the user.

SUMMARY

In this chapter we have looked closely at the implementation of the VMS operating system. In particular, we have examined the operating system's use of the architectural support for managing the processor, memory, and I/O.

VMS uses the hardware process as the basis for program execution. Processes are scheduled to run by VMS using a preemptive priority scheme, where the highest priority process is always run. However, process priorities are modified by VMS as the process executes. The VMS scheduler maintains a number of data structures to manage the scheduling procedure, including the Process Control Block introduced in the previous chapter.

The memory management support is used to implement separate process address spaces and to allow sharing of the operating system. VMS uses both paging, to allow processes to access large address spaces, and swapping, to allow sharing of memory by many processes. A number of optimizations are used in an attempt to decrease the number of I/O operations, including the use of memory lists of recently used pages, reading and writing of pages in clusters of several pages at a time, and swapping.

Finally, VMS uses the software interrupt capability to schedule events in the I/O system. The use of software IPLs simplifies the synchronization requirements of the I/O system, and helps to reduce the response time to hardware interrupts.

REFERENCES

Two works have already been referenced in this chapter: the articles by Belady (1966) and by Denning (1968). In fact, the May 1968 issue of CACM that contains the Denning paper has a number of other interesting papers on operating systems. A later paper by Denning (1971) describes "Third Generation Operating Systems." Books by Brinch Hansen (1973), Donovan (1972), Haberman (1976), Holt (1978), Katzan (1973), Organick (1972), Shaw (1974), and Watson (1970) make interesting reading for those who wish to learn about operating systems in more detail. Spirn's book (1977), while somewhat advanced, gives a thorough treatment of program behavior.

EXERCISES FOR CHAPTER 9

1. How does an operating system scheduler ensure that a single process does not consume the entire CPU, once it has begun executing?

2. What is meant by a real-time process in VMS? How are real-time processes treated differently from timesharing processes?

3. Contrast the scheduling policies you might use when trying to optimize response time with those you would use to optimize throughput.

4. What are the primary states that a process can be in as it makes progress from initiation to completion?

5. Name three page replacement algorithms and describe the differences.

6. What is the resident set? What algorithms are used to change or replace pages in the resident set? What is the balance set?

7. What is the difference between working set and the VMS resident set?

8. What is the difference between paging and swapping? Why does VMS use both paging and swapping? Are both paging and swapping needed to implement a VAX-11 virtual memory system?

9. What is the difference between a *modified bit* and a *referenced bit* in a page table entry? What is the use of each?

10. What are the functions performed by the VMS I/O device driver?

11. Why does the VMS I/O system use the interrupt priority levels for processing I/O requests?

12. What is an asynchronous system trap?

13. Why do users call VMS system service routines through vector instructions, instead of calling the routines directly?

Chapter 10

The Operating System Interface

Nearly every modern computer system, including the small microprocessor, comes with an operating system and associated utilities. Our impressions of each computer—its ease of use, its friendliness, and its efficiency—are due to the machine we see through the eyes of the operating system. Each operating system has its own personality. But all operating systems share a common purpose: to hide the user from the complexities of the physical hardware.

Figure 10-1 shows several of the hardware, firmware (microcode), and software layers of a computer system. Just as the computer hardware architecture presents a well-defined interface for programming, the operating system presents a high level architecture to the user and the user program. The operating system architecture is defined by a number of interfaces: one for the terminal user, one for the program wishing to perform I/O operations on files, one for the utility making a system call, and so on. This chapter will examine some of those interfaces and some of the utilities provided by an operating system. Again, we use the VMS operating system as an example.

USER-LEVEL INTERFACE: THE COMMAND LANGUAGE

In the days of the early batch processing system, users entered instructions to the computer on punched cards. The card deck contained programs, data, and control cards. Control cards were usually recognized by special

319

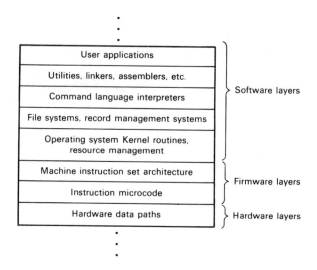

Figure 10-1. System hardware and software layers.

characters in the leading columns, such as slashes (//) in the first two columns, and contained system access and job control information. The system was not very tolerant of errors, and any error was likely to terminate the job because there was no way to query the user for appropriate action.

With today's interactive computers, the terminal has replaced the card reader, and the *command language* is the modern equivalent of control cards. The user communicates with a timeshared operating system through a terminal. Command languages have evolved to become more English-like and more forgiving for the novice, while allowing extensions and abbreviations for the sophisticated user. Some command languages allow a programming language syntax for problem solving and command processing.

At the terminal, the user can request services of the system, and the command language can help the user by requesting information needed to perform the service. The *command language interpreter* is the program that reads commands and executes requests. Although most operating systems have only one command language, some allow for several command languages to deal with different user application requirements.

Commands can generally be categorized into several varieties, including commands that:

1. Manipulate files such as: Copy, Rename, Directory, and Delete.

2. Provide information, such as the time, date, accounting usage, and system status.

3. Allow users to execute own programs or system utility programs.

In the following sections, we will examine some of these commands for the VMS operating system in more detail.

Communicating with the System

Communications with an operating system usually begin with a validation procedure called *login*. The user identifies himself or herself to the system by supplying a username and a password. The password is used to verify that the user has the right to use a given username account, as in

```
USERNAME:  sally
PASSWORD:  xyzzy      (The password is not
                       echoed by the terminal.)

WELCOME TO VAX/VMS VERSION  X
$
```

Following the login procedure, the VMS command interpreter prompts with a dollar sign ($), showing that it is ready to receive commands.

In VMS, commands are of the general form

```
command_name   parameter_1  parameter_2  ...  parameter_n
```

where the command__name is a verb describing the action to be performed and the parameters are usually objects of the command. For example, the command

```
$ print myfile1.lis
```

directs the system to print the file named myfile1.lis on the system line printer. Commands sometimes contain qualifiers that modify the behavior of the command. Qualifiers are appended to the command verb or to one of the parameters by a slash character (/). For example, the command

```
$ print/delete myfile1.lis
```

causes the system to print the file myfile1.lis on the line printer and then delete it from the storage device. Finally, VMS prompts interactive users for required parameters that are not supplied on the command line. For instance, in the example

```
$ pri
FILE:   myfile1.lis
```

the user types only the verb pri, and the command interpreter requests the file name specification with the prompt FILE:. This example also illustrates that VMS allows command names to be abbreviated.

File Conventions

For most operating systems the file is the basic logical container of information. A user creates a file using an editor or a program, gives it a name, and writes information into it. Alternatively, a user may read information from a file previously created and named. The information in a file is usually organized as a series of records whose size and meaning is defined by the user. A file may contain text, such as a source program or a chapter of a book, or it may contain binary data.

File names on VMS have the format

```
name.type;version
```

where:

1. *Name* is a one- to nine-character descriptive name for the file.

2. *Type* is a three-character string describing the type of information contained there, such as LIS for a listing file.

3. *Version* is an integer that identifies the history of the file.

Commonly used file types include:

BAS	Basic source programs
COM	Command procedure files
DAT	Data input or output files

DIR   Directory files
EXE   Executable program image files
FOR   FORTRAN source programs
LIS   Files suitable for printing on the printer
MAR   VAX-11 Macro source programs
OBJ   Assembled or compiled binary object programs
PAS   Pascal source programs

Normally, the user does not type a version number when specifying the name of a file; the system automatically uses the latest version. When a file is created, it is assigned version number 1. Each time the user changes the file with a text editor or creates a file with the same name, the new file is given a version number one greater than the previous version's. Several examples of valid file names are:

PROBLEM1.DAT

TEST.MAR

TEST.OBJ;1

TROUBLE.LIS;6

So that users can name and keep track of their files independently, each user is given a *directory*, which is a catalog of files. A directory is itself a file that contains file names and pointers to the locations of the files on a mass storage device. A user finds the names of all the files in his or her directory by issuing the Directory command:

$ directory

Directory [JONES]

ADVENT.EXE;1   DUNGEON.EXE;1   FILE1.DAT;3   PRIMES.EXE;4
PROGRAM.EXE;2   PROGRAM.FOR;8   PROGRAM.OBJ;2   RAINDROP.PAS;2
TICTACTOE.FOR;5

Directories in VMS have names that are shown syntactically in brackets ([]). To specify a file in a particular user directory, the file name is appended to the directory name. For example, the file specification

[JONES]TICTACTOE.FOR

specifies the FORTRAN source program TICTACTOE in directory [JONES]. Each user has a default directory that the system uses if no directory name is supplied in a file command. Therefore, the directory name need not be specified if all work is done within the default directory.

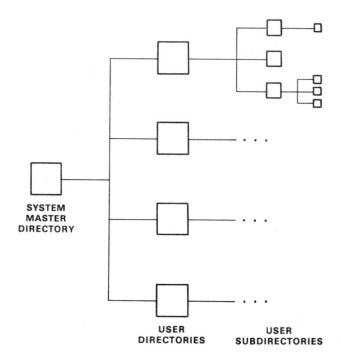

Figure 10-2. VMS subdirectory structure.

A user can also specify the device volume on which the file resides. A device name is specified by the device type, controller number, and unit number. Device types are indicated by a two-character name such as TT (terminal), LP (line printer), DB (large mass storage disk, such as RP06), or DK (smaller cartridge disk, such as RK07).

Controllers are named alphabetically, and since some systems have only one disk controller, disks commonly have names like DBA0. The format of a full file specification, including device, is

```
Device:[directory]file.type;version
```

where a colon (:) follows the device name. Just as with the directory name, each user has a default device. When specifying files on the default device, the user may omit the device name.

Each VMS user can define any number of *subdirectories* to help organize his or her files. Subdirectories can be created in tree-like structures up to nine levels. Each subdirectory, as shown in Figure 10-2, is actually just a directory file that appears as an element in a higher level directory.

Examples of full directory names include:

```
[JONES]
[JONES.GAMES]
[JONES.GAMES.SOURCE]
[JONES.GAMES.LISTING]
```

Each user, to simplify the specification of directories, can set a default directory string. To access a subdirectory, the user merely specifies the directories below the default, preceded by a dot (.). For example,

```
$ set default [jones.games]
$ directory [.source]

Directory DBA1:[JONES.GAMES.SOURCE]

ADVENT.FOR     TICTACTOE.FOR
```

File Manipulation Commands

Much of the work done on operating systems is in the creation and manipulation of files. VMS supports a set of commands to manipulate and examine files. Each command takes one or more file names as parameters. If a directory specification is not given, the default directory is assumed. Table 10-1 describes the basic VMS file manipulation commands.

A brief terminal session using some of the commands of Table 10-1 is shown below:

```
$ show default            ! ask for default directory
DBA0:[FRED]
$ dir                     ! look at current files
Directory DBA0:[FRED]

PRIME.EXE;1     PRIME.FOR;1     PRIME.LIS;1     PRIME.OBJ;1

$ create/dir [fred.sources]   ! create source subdirectory
$ copy prime.for  [.sources]  ! copy file to subdirectory
$ delete prime.for;1          ! delete from main directory
$ set default [.sources]      ! set default to subdirectory
$ dir

Directory DBA0:[FRED.SOURCES]

PRIME.FOR;1
$
```

Table 10-1. VMS File Manipulation Commands

Name	Parameters	Function
APPEND	inputfile1,inputfile2, . . .	Append some number of files to the end of the first file named.
COPY	inputfile outputfile	Copy inputfile into a file named outputfile.
CREATE/DIR	directory _ name	Create a directory or sub-directory.
DELETE	file1,file2, . . .	Remove the named files from the mass storage device.
DIRECTORY	directory _ name	List the names of the files contained in the supplied directory or the default directory if none is given.
PRINT	file	List the given files on the system line printer.
PURGE	file	Delete older versions of the file.
RENAME	oldname newname	Change the name of the file from oldname to newname.
TYPE	file	List the given files on the user's terminal.

The example also shows that comments can be included in VMS command lines using the exclamation (!) character.

Informational Commands

A number of commands are available just to provide status information on the user's process or on the system as a whole. The most general VMS informational command is Help, which gives the user information about how to use the commands that the system understands. Typing

Table 10-2.   VMS Show Commands

Option Name	Function
DAYTIME	Display current date and time.
DEFAULT	Display default device and directory string.
DEVICES	Show status of devices in the system.
PROCESS	Display status of the user's process.
STATUS	Show status of the user's program (image).
SYSTEM	Show status of all processes in the system.
TERMINAL	Display characteristics about a terminal.

"Help" at the keyboard solicits a list of the keywords about which the user may obtain additional information. Typing "Help keyword" gives more information about that particular keyword:

```
$ help type

TYPE

        Displays the contents of a file or group
        of files on the current output device.

        Format:

                TYPE file-spec

        Additional Information Available:

        Parameters Qualifiers

        /output=file-spec
```

The other general command that returns information is Show. Show displays process, status, and device information at the user's terminal. Some of the available Show options are listed in Table 10-2.

Extending the Command Language

After using the command language and taking advantage of the defaults provided by the system, the user may wish to provide his or her own defaults, to simplify the commands, or to define a private set of commands. This can be done in several ways, including:

1. Establishing synonyms for use in place of command names or command strings.

2. Setting default qualifiers.

3. Creating command procedures to perform predefined sets of commands.

The following examples demonstrate how the command language can be extended using the VMS command interpreter.

An *assignment statement* allows the programmer to equate numeric values and character strings with symbols. Thus, instead of typing:

```
$ show time
```

the programmer, using the special character pair :==, can equate the symbol "time" to this string:

```
$ time:==show time
```

Thereafter, the user simply types the newly equated symbol

```
$ time
```

to cause the system to print the current time and date.

A command with qualifiers can also be shortened in the same manner, for instance:

```
$ pd:==print/del
$ pd file.lis,file2.dat
```

Each user has sequences of commands that he or she issues frequently. To simplify the repeated issuing of a sequence of commands, command procedures are used. *Command procedures* are files that contain lines and possibly data to be used as sequences of commands. For example, to assemble, link, and run a VAX-11 Macro program, the programmer can create a command file (with file type COM) that looks like the following:

```
$ macro/list squaroot
$ link squaroot
$ run squaroot
```

If the programmer names this file exe.com, the command file can be executed by using the execute operator of the command interpreter (the @ sign):

```
$ @exe
```

This causes the system to locate the file exe.com and execute the commands it contains. The process is similar to the macro expansion process we discussed earlier in the book. The command interpreter simply executes each line as if it were typed in at the terminal.

While the example command procedure simplifies the user's typing, it lacks flexibility since it works only with the VAX-11 Macro program named squaroot. Fortunately, the command procedures can be generalized by allowing parameters to be supplied when the procedure is invoked. When the command procedure is executed, the real arguments are substituted for the symbolic parameters. This procedure is similar to the substitution of arguments in macro expansions.

VMS command files are parameterized by including "dummy" arguments P1 through P8 within the command file. The actual arguments are automatically equated with the symbols P1, P2, . . . , P8 within the command file when it is processed. Thus, exe.com can be changed to

```
$ macro/list 'P1'
$ link 'P1'
$ run 'P1'
```

and executed as

```
$ @exe squaroot
```

The quote (') characters tell the command interpreter that the following symbol should be replaced by an actual argument. Using the command level symbol mechanism along with this command file, we could define

```
$ exe:==@exe
```

and then simply type

```
$ exe tictactoe
```

to remove the need for the @ character. Thus, we have simply created our own command.

Usually, one of the first acts of the frequent VMS user is to create a *login command procedure.* When a user logs into the system, the system automatically searches for and executes a file named LOGIN.COM if it is found in the user's default or login directory. This file can be used to set up the user's defaults and symbols. For example, LOGIN.COM might contain

```
$ time:==show time
$ exe:==@[sally]exe
$ mail:==run [system]mail
$ type [system]dailynews.dat
$ set def [sally.pascal.sources]
```

where the file EXE.COM has been created in directory [sally]. Following login, the user would be able to use any of the symbols defined in the command file, and would have the default directory [sally.pascal.sources].

PROGRAM DEVELOPMENT SOFTWARE

Now that we have seen how the command language is used to manipulate files, provide information, and execute programs, we will briefly look at the components or utilities of the program development process. The steps involved in this process are shown in Figure 10-3. The utilities shown include the editor, the compiler or assembler, the linker, and the debugger.

The Editor

The editor on a development system is used to create and make changes to source programs and text files. As the most heavily utilized software program, good human engineering and ease of use are a critical part of the editor's design. Of course, almost every user will debate the fact that his or her favorite editor is the best or easiest to use.

Although editors differ greatly, almost all editors have some capabilities in common, including the abilities to:

1. List or display some contiguous string of characters within the file on a hardcopy terminal or video screen.

2. Locate a specified character string within the file.

3. Insert a string of characters at any position within the file.

4. Delete a string of characters from the file.

5. Replace a string of characters with another.

6. Change the current position or field of view within the file.

7. Exit the editing session, creating a new file with the changes or additions made.

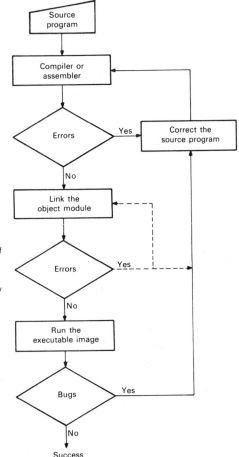

Use the *editor* to create a disk file containing the source program statements. Specify the name of this file to invoke the compiler or assembler.

The compilers and assemblers check syntax, create object modules, and if requested, generate program listings.

If a processor signals any errors, the editor is used to correct the source program.

The *linker* searches the system libraries to resolve references in the object modules and create an executable image.

The linker issues diagnostic messages if an object module refers to subroutines or symbols that are not available or undefined. If the linker can not locate a subroutine, the LINK command must be reissued to specify the modules or libraries to include. If a symbol is undefined, the source program may need to be corrected.

The *RUN* command executes a program image. While the program is running, the system may detect errors and issue messages. To determine if the program is error-free, its output is checked.

If there is a bug in the program, the cause is determined and the error is corrected in the source program.

Figure 10-3. Steps in program development.

The most basic editors are for use with hardcopy terminals, although they can also be used with video terminals. Often these editors are line-oriented. That is, the user specifies a line of text or a series of lines to be examined or modified. Changes are made on a line-by-line basis. The editor keeps track of the current line under examination. Some editors, however, are character-oriented and view the file as a continuous stream of characters. The user still specifies which characters are to be displayed or modified.

Many modern editors make use of the fact that most users access computers through high-speed video terminals. *Screen editors,* also called *window* or *keypad editors,* take advantage of the high-speed display by maintaining a current "window" of the file on the screen at all times. Usually, the sequence of lines in view (the window) is the size of the screen (about 24 lines by 80 characters for most terminals). Commands to the editor are normally single keystrokes that allow the user to position a cursor anywhere in the file. The cursor shows the position where modifications will take place. Commands may allow cursor movement based on any logical or physical structure. For example, the user may be able to move the cursor right or left or up or down by a number of characters, words, lines, sentences, paragraphs, etc. If the user inserts text, it is inserted into the window as it is typed, and all following text on the screen is moved down or off the screen.

Because of the number of single keystrokes involved in this type of editor, screen editing is being supported by hardware (intelligent terminals) in newer terminal devices. This relieves the host computer of the job of servicing individual cursor movement commands and simple editing commands.

The Production of the Object File

Once the user creates a source file with the editor, a compiler or assembler is invoked to read the user's source program and create an object program. We discussed the creation of an object program by the two-pass assembler in Chapter 2. However, the object program contains more than just the binary machine code for the user's program. For example, it contains information for the *linker,* the program that combines object modules and prepares them for execution.

One of the goals of modular programming is to be able to separately produce and maintain parts of a single program. Instead of writing one monolithic program, the program is divided into small independent units. Each separate module consists of one or more routines that may refer to other routines (or possibly variables) outside of its own module. The assembler or compiler can not generate the complete binary machine code because it does not know the addresses or symbol values for symbols not locally defined. The assembler or compiler also does not know where in the program's virtual memory the module will be placed. Therefore, the compiler may have to leave address fields blank in some instructions to be filled in later by the linker.

In addition to binary instructions, then, the object program typically contains some of the following information:

1. The name and attributes of the object module, for example, the creation data and time, the name of the compiler that produced the object module, etc.

2. The name and attributes of each program section within the module, for example, whether the program section is read/write, read only, etc.

3. A global symbol table describing all global symbols defined within the module. These are the symbols and routine entry points that can be referenced by other modules. Each symbol name, value, data-type, etc., must be specified.

4. Records describing all references that could not be resolved by the compiler or assembler. For each unresolved reference there is information on the symbol name, type, and the location of the instruction that could not be completed.

5. Some amount of information for the debugger so that the user can specify symbolic names for variables and routines. For some languages, this information may also describe how the program was compiled, for example, it may give addresses corresponding to FORTRAN line numbers.

All of this information is needed by the linker to produce a runnable program from the object file.

The Linker

The linker is the software that combines separately compiled or assembled modules into a single executable program. The ability to separately maintain modules that are later linked together greatly facilitates modular programming.

In the VMS operating system, the linker performs all the duties of resolving symbolic references between modules and allocating virtual memory for the program. When a module is compiled, the compiler does not know where the module will reside in the address space. Thus, modules may need to be relocated within virtual memory. The use of position-independent coding and relative addressing on VAX makes this task much simpler. The linker examines the requirements of each object module to be linked and forms the virtual memory image of the program. Each module may contain several program sections with different attributes. The linker groups program sections with similar attributes, such as read-only, read/write, etc., together in the address space. Once the address space is laid out, the linker can resolve symbolic references between modules.

In addition to resolving references between user-specified object modules, the linker also searches operating system libraries for referenced symbols and modules. A *library* is a file containing a collection of object modules and symbol definitions. The library has a symbol table at the start for easy searching and access. When references can not be resolved from the supplied object modules, the VMS linker checks the VMS system library. This library contains system symbol definitions, such as the addresses of entry points for VMS system services. It also contains object modules that may be needed by compiler-generated code at run time. For example, modules that perform I/O for Pascal or FORTRAN programs may be taken from the library and linked with the user program. The user does not have to specify or know the names of these modules, since the compiler generates the reference or routine call, and the linker automatically locates the object module containing the routine.

The final job of the VMS linker is to build the executable file to be stored on the disk from which the program can be run. This file (called the *image* file in VMS) contains the now complete program, along with some information for the VMS memory management system. This information describes the sections of the program, their attributes, sizes, addresses in virtual memory, and locations in the file. When the program is run, the virtual memory system uses this information to build page tables for the program.

All systems do not have linkers like VMS. On some systems, the compiler performs more of the work needed to resolve addresses and a *loader* program completes the task while loading the program in memory. (The

Run command is the loader in VMS.) Having a separate linker simplifies the job of the compiler, and the address resolution logic need not be duplicated in each compiler. On other systems, *dynamic linking* is performed. With dynamic linking, global references are resolved as the program runs. In this case, the compiler leaves trap instructions in place of instructions that contained address references that could not be resolved due to undefined symbols. When one of these instructions is executed, a trap occurs and special software is invoked to resolve the address. This software computes the correct instruction from available symbol tables, and replaces the trap with the correct instruction.

The tradeoff of separate linkers versus dynamic linking depends on the requirements of the system. For program development, dynamic linking is better, since recompilations are frequent. For applications that are run over and over again, it is better to link once and not require the overhead of dynamic linking each time the program is run.

Debugging

As every programmer finds out, newly created programs rarely run the first time, no matter how careful one is. Debugging is one of the most difficult stages in program development and a good debugger is invaluable. There are several types of debuggers: some that are linked with the program and run in its address space, and some that run in a separate process from the program being examined. However, some of the common features available in most debuggers are:

1. The ability to examine or set the contents of locations in the user's program. The user can examine or change both variables and instructions.

2. The ability to set breakpoints. A *breakpoint* is an instruction address at which the program will stop execution to allow user examination. By setting breakpoints, the user can examine the state of the program at critical points.

3. The ability to perform arithmetic, expression evaluation, and radix conversion.

4. The ability to single-step the program through each instruction.

5. The ability to set watchpoints. A *watchpoint* is a specific location that is under examination by the debugger. The debugger causes the program to stop execution whenever the location is modified. This allows the user to find out if a variable is being incorrectly modified.

With these features, the user can control and examine the program's execution and ensure that the operations taking place are as expected.

THE SYSTEM SERVICE LEVEL INTERFACE

We have already seen one operating system interface, that provided by the command interpreter. In this section we examine the system service calling procedure and the interface provided by the operating system to user programs. The VMS system service routine interface allows a user program written in any language to request services of the operating system.

VMS System Service Interface

VMS system services are operating system routines residing in the system half of the virtual address space. These routines may be called by a user program to perform desired functions. All system services are called by a standard call instruction. The user program communicates with the service routine by passing arguments, either on the stack (CALLS) or in a predefined argument list (CALLG). From high level languages, the routines are called just like any user-written routine or subprogram.

We will describe only the Macro level CALLS form because it is the more common linkage between an assembly language program and a service routine.

All arguments to system services are longwords. The arguments are either values, pointers to user input arguments, or pointers to user memory in which the service routine will store output arguments.

When strings must be passed to or returned from a system service, the user supplies the address of quadword string descriptors as arguments. As Figure 10-4 shows, a *string descriptor* is a two-longword array in which the low order word of the first longword contains the length of the string and the second longword contains the virtual address of the string. To pass a string to a system service, the user simply specifies the address of the string descriptor as an argument. If the service must return a string, the user specifies two arguments. The first is the address of a word (remember that strings may be as long as 65K bytes on the VAX-11) in which the service will return

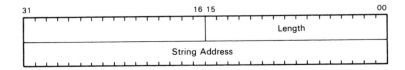

Figure 10-4. VMS string descriptor.

the length of the output string that it writes. The second argument is the address of a string descriptor for the buffer in which the service will write the output string. If the user's buffer is not large enough to hold the output string, the service truncates the string to fit the buffer.

System Service Macros

To simplify coding system services using the VAX-11 Macro assembler, VMS has macros defined for each system service. We will discuss only the macro forms that push the system service arguments onto the stack and then generate a CALLS instruction, since these are the most commonly used form.

All system service macros are of the form

```
$NAME_S         KEYWORD1=argument1,-
                KEYWORD2=argument2,-
                .
                .
                KEYWORDn=argumentn
```

where

1. NAME is the descriptive name of the macro.
2. KEYWORD1 is a descriptive name of the argument.
3. ARGUMENT1 is a value or address to be passed to the service.

An example of a system service macro is

```
$GETTIM_S       TIMEADR=mybuffer
```

which invokes the Get Time system service. This service returns the 64-bit internal representation of the time into the user's buffer. The keyword TIMEADR specifies that the time value should be returned to the user's buffer at address mybuffer. Of course, keywords are much more important in calls to services with many arguments because they eliminate the need for supplying arguments by position. The $GETTIM macro in the previous example will actually generate the instructions

```
PUSHAQ   mybuffer
CALLS    #1,SYS$GETTIM
```

Interestingly, the macro generates a Push Address instruction with quadword context, since this argument is the address of a quadword to receive the time. The user could as well specify the address with several different addressing modes, such as

```
$GETTIM_S     TIMADR=mybuffer      ;
$GETTIM_S     TIMADR=(R8)          ;
$GETTIM_S     TIMADR=timearray[R5] ;
```

In the third example, R5 must contain an index into the quadword array timearray.

Status Return Codes

When the system service routine returns, the calling program must be able to determine if the function was completed successfully. By convention, all routines in VMS return status in R0. For high level languages, the return code is the value of the function or procedure. The status code returned indicates whether the service completed successfully, and, if not, what error condition occurred. Bit 0 of the status code contains the success or failure indication. If bit 0 is set, the return value is a success code; otherwise, it is an error code. This makes it simple to test for successful completion with a single instruction or statement such as:

```
BLBC    R0,error_routine
```

or

```
IF NOT SERVICE(parameters) THEN error_path;
```

for a language that only tests the low bit for true or false. Actually, the low order three bits <2:0> together represent the severity of the condition by the following encoding:

0	Warning
1	Success
2	Error
3	Reserved
4	Severe error
5–7	Reserved

Note that all error codes are even (bit 0 = 0) and all success codes are odd (bit 0 = 1). Each 32-bit error code is actually an identifier for a system error message string that describes the error. This string can be obtained by the Get Error Message system service ($GETMSG).

VMS provides a macro, $SSDEF, to define symbolic names for all status codes. All the names are of the form SS$_name, where name describes the condition. For instance, SS$_NORMAL is the symbolic name for the normal success code; SS$_INSFARG is the name for the error code indicating that too few arguments were supplied to the service. A user can check for a specific status condition using these names, for example,

```
        $SSDEF                      ; define names
        .
        .
        .
        <system service call>
        CMPL    #SS$_INSFARG,R0     ; too few arguments?
        BEQL    special_routine     ; branch if so
        .
        .
        .
```

VMS SYSTEM SERVICES

In Chapter 9 we described the VMS Queue I/O system service and the implementation of system service vectors in VMS. Besides I/O operations, operating systems can perform many commonly required functions for the user, all of which are initiated by system service calls. We will now take a closer look at some other functions provided by VMS system services.

Information Services

The first category of system services we will consider includes those by which a process can determine system or process information. We have already explained the SYS$GETTIM system service that allows the programmer to get the time and date. Since VMS uses a particular format for this, which might not be convenient for a user, there are also system services that manipulate this format. Thus, a process that must print the date or time on a report can get the time in binary (as supplied by VMS) and then request that another system service translate the time into a more suitable format, such as ASCII. Beyond merely telling time, a user can also request notification at a particular time or after some interval of time has passed (such as 30 seconds from now). Another alternative is to request that a process be notified at some absolute time, such as noon Friday.

The following list includes some of the informational system services provided by VMS:

1. Get the time.

2. Convert binary time to numeric format.

3. Convert binary time to ASCII format.

4. Get Job Process Parameters (returns system or accounting information about a process).

The final service, Get Job Process Parameters, allows a process to determine almost any process-specific information kept by the operating system, such as its defaults, quotas, resource usage, etc. A suitably privileged process can also determine this information about other processes in the system.

Memory Management Services

In addition to finding information about itself, a process has a great deal of flexibility in managing its environment. In the memory management area, a process can control its usage of address space, its memory residency, and the residency of its pages. VMS provides services for a process to:

1. Create or delete pages of its physical address space.
2. Lock and unlock certain pages in its resident set.
3. Lock and unlock certain pages in physical memory.
4. Lock and unlock the process in physical memory.
5. Adjust its physical memory quota.

The Create and Delete Virtual Address Space system services are among several system services that allow a process to dynamically define its physical size. For example, an assembler that requires a large symbol table does not have to pre-allocate the table in its address space. Instead, the assembler expands its physical size as it runs. This is a more efficient usage of program space since the program only uses what it needs.

Another feature of the memory management system services is that they allow several processes to communicate through shared memory pages, called *global sections* in VMS. Using global sections, two processes can map the same physical page into their individual virtual address spaces, thereby sharing the same page of code or data. We consider global sections as an interprocess communications (IPC) facility later in this chapter.

A process also has some degree of control over its utilization of memory. A suitably privileged process can lock itself into memory to preclude being swapped out. This facility is useful for time-critical processes that may be dormant most of the time, but must respond immediately upon being activated. Such a process should never be swapped out, regardless of whether or not it happens to be momentarily waiting. Alternatively, a time-critical process may need only a few pages of the service routine and its buffer kept in memory. For such cases, VMS allows a process to lock certain pages into memory.

Process Control Services

While a process can control itself (using memory management services), a suitably privileged process can also control other processes in the system. For example, a process can

1.   Create and delete a (sub)process or detached process.
2.   Set the priority of a (sub)process.
3.   Force a (sub)process into a wait state (suspension).
4.   Resume a suspended process.
5.   Hibernate.

A process can also create a new process (a subprocess) that executes concurrently with the creating process. In addition, the owner process can define, within limits, the base priority at which the subprocess executes. An owner process might therefore create a lower priority subprocess to handle lower priority tasks to be completed when that subprocess is activated. Or an owner process might create a higher priority subprocess to perform a parallel task whose completion is urgent to the owner process.

There are other controls over a process or subprocess that involve wait states called *hibernation* and *suspension*. Hibernation is less drastic than suspension in that a wider variety of events can awaken a hibernating process. Only a Resume Process Request issued by another process can bring a process out of suspension. A process can also suspend itself or, more commonly, be suspended, whereas hibernation is strictly voluntary.

Interprocess Communication

Both general-purpose and real-time systems require the exchange of data and timing signals between cooperating processes. VMS provides several mechanisms, some high speed and specific, some slower but more general, to synchronize processes and pass information.

Event Flags

The simplest VMS interprocess communication mechanism is the event flag. An *event flag* is a bit that can be set or cleared to indicate the occurrence of an event. The flag can be used to synchronize an event within the process or among multiple processes. Each event flag is contained within a 32-bit *event flag cluster* and each process has access to four clusters (numbered zero through four). Two of the clusters are reserved for synchronization within the process. Cluster 0 is reserved for use by VMS on behalf of the process, and its flags are set or cleared only by the system. Cluster 1 is for local use by the process itself.

Event flag clusters 2 and 3 are called *common event flag clusters*. They are created dynamically by system service request and can be shared with other cooperating processes in the system. When a user creates a common event flag cluster, the cluster is given a cluster name. Other processes may *associate* with the cluster, given that they know its name and have proper privilege. Common event flag clusters are protected in a manner similar to files on VMS.

System services are provided by VMS to

1. Create or associate with a common event flag cluster.
2. Clear an event flag.
3. Set an event flag.
4. Wait for an event flag.
5. Read an event flag cluster.
6. Wait for the logical OR of event flags within a cluster.
7. Wait for the logical AND of event flags within a cluster.
8. Disassociate from a common event flag cluster.
9. Delete a common event flag cluster.

Figure 10-5 shows two cooperating processes that synchronize by using event flags. The first process to execute the Associate with Common Event Flag Cluster ($ASCEFC) service actually creates the cluster, while the second one associates with it. Each process sets a flag telling the other that it is ready, then waits for its own flag to be set. In the Associate Common Event Flag Cluster service call, the event flag number (EFN) parameter is the number of any flag in the cluster to be associated.

Mailboxes

For more general interprocess communication, VMS provides a mailbox facility. A *mailbox* is a record-oriented logical device. That is, it is read or written just like a file or physical device, but the records are actually buffered in system dynamic memory. Users may open a mailbox using file system primitives and read or write using Get or Put.

Process 1

```
$ASCEFC_S EFN=#64,NAME=cluster_name   ; create or associate
                                      ; ...cluster 2
$SETEF_S EFN=#65                      ; notify process 2
$WAITFR_S EFN=#66                     ; wait for proc. 2 signal

    .

    .

    .
```

Process 2

```
$ASCEFC_S EFN=#64,NAME=cluster_name   ; create or associate
                                      ; ...cluster 2
$SETEF_S EFN=#66                      ; notify process 1
$WAITFR_S EFN=#65                     ; wait for proc. 1 signal

    .

    .

    .
```

Figure 10-5. Synchronization with event flags.

Figure 10-6.   VMS mailbox message queue.

Illustrated in Figure 10-6, the mechanism is called a mailbox because it is used to store and pass messages just like a real mailbox in which letters are placed in at one end and removed from the other. When someone wishes to send a message, he writes a message which is placed in the back end of the mailbox. As more messages arrive, they are stacked behind each other in order of arrival. Someone who wishes to see if any messages have arrived reads the mailbox, getting either the oldest message in line or a notification that the mailbox is empty. The reader can also request to be notified whenever a message is placed in the mailbox.

Mailboxes are of limited size. When a mailbox is created via the Create Mailbox system service, the creator specifies the maximum message size and the maximum number of messages that the mailbox can hold. The creator can also control who may write to the mailbox. Mailboxes are protected in the same method as VMS files.

Shared Memory

The third and most general interprocess communication mechanism is *shared memory,* shown in Figure 10-7. VMS allows processes to share memory in the process half of the address space through global sections. A *global section* is a named area of memory that can be mapped into the address space of several processes. It is created or mapped by the Create and Map Global Section system service ($CRMPSC). Processes using shared memory must invent their own synchronization although they may choose to use event flags along with shared data structures. Processes realize the best performance with shared memory because data need not be buffered by the operating system.

Combining Interprocess Communications Mechanisms

The various interprocess communication mechanisms can be combined so that events, data, and messages may all be used to control multiple processes cooperating on a complex task. For example, imagine the three-process scenario:

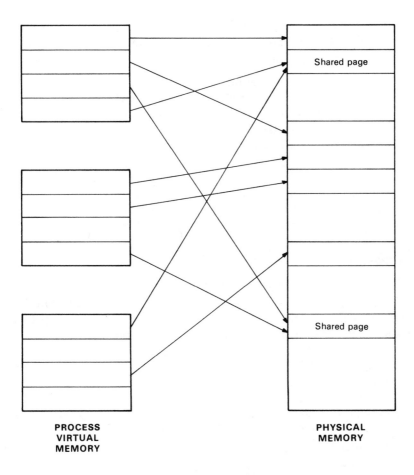

Figure 10-7.   Shared memory mapping.

1. Process A periodically samples a laboratory experiment under control of the timer, which signals the process by means of event flag 1.

2. Process A writes its sample data into a global section and notifies process B that it has done so by means of event flag 2. Process B then analyzes the data and writes it out to a disk file.

3. Process B determines that the current sample indicates the need for additional control of the experiment and sends a data message to process C's mailbox.

4. Process C, obtaining the message from process B, adjusts the parameters of the experiment to bring it back within the range of acceptable conditions. Process C also prints a message on the terminal to notify the experimenter that corrective action was needed and has been taken.

This is just one example of the possible use of multiple interprocess communication mechanisms. In each case, the mechanism is selected depending on the requirements of the communication, such as the size of the data to be transmitted and the desired speed of transmission.

I/O Services

As mentioned in Chapter 9, VMS provides a variety of I/O services through the Queue I/O system service. In addition, the VMS Record Management System (RMS) provides file and record maintenance capabilities necessary in many applications. A variety of file organizations and access methods are supported by RMS, which appears as an integral part of the operating system. RMS also offers a high degree of data security through validating I/O requests and checking access rights to data files. Finally, RMS allows the programmer to write device-independent programs. That is, I/O is performed on logically named files that can be associated with particular devices when the image is run. The user can decide at run time whether the program output should go to a file, a line printer, or the terminal. This is possible because RMS performs the necessary translation of logical names and performs I/O on the specific device according to the characteristics of that device in a way that is transparent to the user.

The QIO system service allows a programmer to perform I/O operations at a level that requires the selection of specific device functions and direct interaction with the I/O system. The QIO system service is used only when a programmer needs to perform I/O at the device level.

Before a VMS program can initiate an I/O operation, it must establish a logical pathway to a physical device. The logical pathway is called a *channel*. When the program wishes to perform I/O, it first assigns a channel to the device by calling the Assign Channel system service ($ASSIGN). The user supplies $ASSIGN with a string descriptor for the device name, such as

TTA1 or SYS$DISK, and the service returns a 16-bit *channel number.* Actually an index into a process data structure pointing to the physical device data base, the channel number is supplied as an argument when future I/O requests are issued to the device.

In general, the Record Management System should be chosen over the Queue I/O system service because of its generality and device independence. Only in situations requiring high performance asynchronous I/O or physical device manipulation is the user forced to employ the QIO service.

HANDLING ASYNCHRONOUS EVENTS

In time-critical systems, a process must be able to respond to events that occur asynchronously to its execution. These events may result from actions by other processes in the system, by peripheral devices, or by the operating system itself. When the program requests a service that may complete asynchronously, such as a terminal I/O request or a time notification, it can specify the address of an Asynchronous System Trap (AST) routine. The Asynchronous System Trap routine is a procedure within the user's program that is called when the event or request completion occurs. If the user's program is active at the time, it is interrupted, and control transfers to the AST routine. The Asynchronous System Trap routine is thus really a process interrupt routine. When the AST routine returns, the program resumes where it left off. Or if the program was in a wait state, it will return to the wait state. However, the AST routine can execute services to cause the state of the program to change.

ASTs are queued to the process. That is, several ASTs may be outstanding for a process at any one time. In addition, each process logically has four AST queues, one for each access mode (Kernel, Executive, Supervisor, and User). The VMS operating system often queues Kernel mode ASTs in order to execute code on behalf of a process within the address space of that process. ASTs are processed on a first-come, first-served basis from the most to the least privileged mode. In other words, a User mode AST may be interrupted to allow a Kernel mode AST to execute. Whenever an AST is active, all other ASTs of the same mode must wait until the AST completes before they are allowed to run.

All system services that allow the specification of an AST routine also take an associated argument called the AST parameter. This 32-bit parameter is available on the call stack to the AST routine. If a user wants to use one AST routine to process events from several sources, the AST parameter may be used to distinguish the responsible source. For instance, a program handling several terminals can issue read requests on all of them, requesting an AST when a read completes. The AST parameter would indicate on which terminal the read completed.

When the AST routine is entered, it is called by the Call instruction with the *argument pointer* (AP) pointing to the following list:

31		00
		5	◄── AP
AST parameter		
Saved R0		
Saved R1		
PC of interrupted program		
PSL of interrupted program		

The AST parameter is the one specified to the service when this AST was requested. The AST routine can change control at program level by modifying the PC contained in the argument list.

In previous chapters we saw how Asynchronous System Traps are handled by the architecture and used by the operating system. However, the AST is also the basic mechanism used by programs that service asynchronous events. This is a particularly useful mechanism for time-critical or real-time processing.

SUMMARY

In this chapter we have discussed some of the operating system interfaces and operating system services. We also described the components of the program development process. The interfaces described form a user architecture, just as the instruction set forms a programming architecture.

At the start of this chapter, Figure 10-1 showed the layers of the software and hardware architectures. The VAX-11 architecture is currently defined by its instruction set. As we have seen, parts of the instruction set operate on operating system data structures. As technology changes and components and memories become cheaper, it is easy to speculate about how architectures will evolve. The hardware architecture could someday support any of the levels we now see above the instruction set. It will become increasingly difficult to draw that line in Figure 10-1 between hardware and software.

REFERENCES

The best introductory information about VAX/VMS is contained in the *VAX-11 Primer, VAX-11 Technical Summary*, and *VAX-11 Software Handbook*. Most of the operating systems books referenced at the end of the previous chapter also contain sections on operating system features and interfaces.

EXERCISES FOR CHAPTER 10

1. What are the major parts of the user architecture provided by the operating system? Why are these interfaces also architecture?

2. What are file directories and subdirectories used for?

3. What is a command file? Why are command files useful?

4. What is the difference between a screen editor and a line editor? Why would you prefer one over the other?

5. What information is contained in the object file in addition to binary instructions?

6. What is the purpose of the linker? What is dynamic linking and how is it different from the linking method used on VMS?

7. What is the purpose of operating system service routines? Why are these routines part of the operating system? Do you think that they should be part of the operating system?

8. Contrast the three interprocess communication primitives available to VMS processes.

Chapter 11

The Efficient Implementation of an Architecture

For any computer architecture, there are many implementations spanning a wide range of price and performance. For example, versions of the PDP-11 are now available for less than one thousand dollars per unit for the LSI-11, up to hundreds of thousands of dollars for a PDP-11/70 system with a large number of peripherals. The implementation of each version requires the designer to choose a computer structure that meets cost constraints while providing the best possible performance and reliability. This structure must be built with readily available component technologies and, typically, must be modifiable to accept newer technologies as they become proven.

In this chapter, we consider some of the choices the hardware implementor has in the design of a member of a computer family. We will focus on the features of the VAX-11/780, shown in Figure 11-1, other than the instruction set architecture. Although invisible to the executing program, these features have a significant effect on system performance and cost.

CHOICE OF MEMORY TECHNOLOGY AND STRUCTURE

Throughout the rapid evolution of the computer, the cost of memory has been a major factor in overall system price. Although memories have become relatively inexpensive, there are and always will be memories with

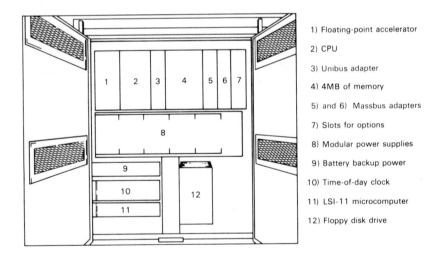

1) Floating-point accelerator

2) CPU

3) Unibus adapter

4) 4MB of memory

5) and 6) Massbus adapters

7) Slots for options

8) Modular power supplies

9) Battery backup power

10) Time-of-day clock

11) LSI-11 microcomputer

12) Floppy disk drive

Figure 11-1.   VAX-11/780 internal view.

varying storage capacities and performance characteristics available at different costs. Since memory speed has a substantial influence on the execution speed of the CPU, selecting a particular memory technology and memory structure is a critical aspect in designing a given computer family member.

If cost were no object, the entire memory system would be constructed from the fastest available memory, as was done for the CRAY-1 computer. For low cost computers, this is obviously impossible. However, one option for less expensive systems is organizing the memory system into a layered hierarchy composed of different memory technologies. If this is done with a knowledge of the statistical characteristics and patterns of typical programs in execution, a significant increase in memory performance can be obtained at little added cost.

The Fastest Technology Approach

One way to structure the total memory system is to implement one segment of the memory with the fastest technology available. Exemplifying this strategy, the PDP-11/55 provides for up to 64 Kbytes of bipolar memory, which the user can fill with data or executable code. For many real-time applications, this is a perfect solution. The user locks his or her most time-critical code and data in high speed memory at program load time, allowing him or her to predict his or her performance exactly. This method, however, is unlikely to benefit a time-sharing system, in which physical memory is allocated and reallocated among users and time slices. Another disadvantage of this approach is that it requires the programmer to be familiar with the physical memory structure.

Cache Memory Approach

A more common structure for the memory system is the *cache memory* (pronounced "cash," from the French *cacher,* to hide). In this scheme, a small, high speed buffer memory, called the *cache,* holds the most recently used instructions and data items. When a program makes a memory request, the CPU first checks to see if the data is in the cache. If so, the data can be brought quickly without using main memory.

Programs, of course, do not execute randomly, but exhibit some locality in their generation of addresses and use of memory. Memory generally is accessed in a logical order, often sequentially, as in processing an array or sequencing through the instructions of a program. Alternatively, a program may repeatedly flow through a loop of instructions, then move to another

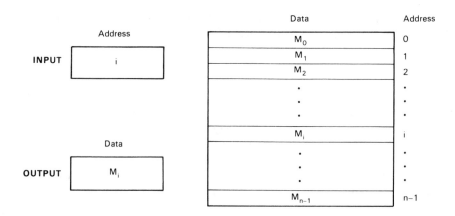

Figure 11-2.   Random access memory.

localized area. In either case, if the cache can hold enough data to avoid a large number of references to slower memory, not only does execution speed substantially increase, but contention for the memory or system bus is also reduced.

Associative Memories

A typical computer memory system is composed of a number of consecutive storage elements, usually bytes, each with a unique physical address. To read the data from a given storage location, the CPU places this unique address in an internal register on the memory bus (often referred to as the memory address register or input register) and receives the return data in another register (the memory buffer register or output register), as shown in Figure 11-2. Note that each address uniquely specifies one memory location to be selected, and no searching is required.

Human memories function not by using addresses but by associating or chaining related information together. We often recall an item committed to memory by remembering something else we associated with the item. Thus, to recall an acquaintance's name, we conjure up the image of a cat so that the name Felix pops into our heads. Such an *associative memory* is represented by the phone book in Figure 11-3. Here we have a list of names and associated information. Although the information could be listed randomly, it is usually presented in alphabetical order. For each name, or *tag*, there is some associated information. Each entry is "addressed," not by its number or position within the list, but by its name or tag field.

Name or Tag	Data Item(s)
Arnold Apple	856–2031
Bob Blackberry	356–8123
Cal Cauliflower	281–5610
Dora Dandelion	413–1213

Figure 11-3.   Associative list.

Notice that if the tags do not uniquely identify the object, then duplications may occur. For instance, the Chicago phone book contains many entries for the name Peter Smith, because the name does not uniquely identify the person. Thus, an associative search can yield several alternatives from which one must be selected based on additional information (e.g., street name).

A computer memory structure could be similarly constructed as shown in Figure 11-4. Each entry consists of two parts, a tag and an associated data item. The computer presents a tag to memory by writing it into the TAG register. If a match (called a *hit*) is found anywhere in the A half, the associated data item from the B half is returned to the output DATA register. If

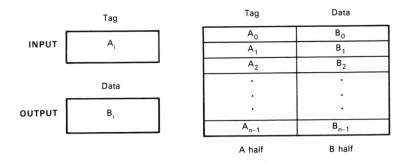

Figure 11-4.   Associative memory cache.

no match is found, memory reports a *miss*. This type of memory is termed *fully associative* because the data being searched for could be stored in any of the *n* locations. A complete memory search would be slow if the comparisons were made sequentially from the beginning to the end of the list. Consequently, it is more common for the system to be constructed to perform parallel comparisons, that is, parallel searches, at a substantial increase in complexity of the system.

It is also possible to use some bits from the tag as an index into the memory, forming a *direct mapped cache* as illustrated by the example shown in Figure 11-5. The figure shows a 32-element associative memory. The 5 low-order bits of the tag are used to locate one of the 32 cache entries. For example, if the value of the 5-bit field is the integer *i*, then the *i*th cache entry will be selected. Once this cache entry is selected, the 27 high-order bits of the tag are compared with the contents of the A half of entry *i* (A_i). If a match occurs, data B_i is returned. Depending on the uniformity of the distribution of the 5 low-order bits, some loss of generality can occur. For instance, if all 5-bit values are even, then only half of the cache will be used. However, the direct mapped cache is significantly less expensive than the fully associative cache.

CACHE MEMORY ON THE VAX-11/780

If data were fetched from memory and stored in the cache byte by byte, time would be saved only on a hit to a previously referenced byte. A better method is to fetch several bytes on each miss. On the VAX-11/780, memory is accessed in 64-bit quadwords. When the CPU reads the first byte in a quadword from memory, the entire quadword is fetched from memory and stored in the cache. If the processor then accesses any of the next seven

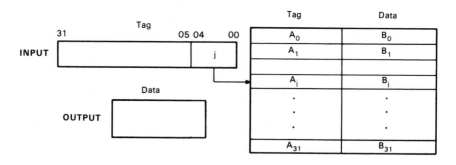

Figure 11-5.   Direct mapped cache.

bytes, they are read from the high speed cache rather than from the main memory, thereby avoiding the slower access time of main memory. The inherent savings of fetching several bytes rather than one byte must be weighed against the additional cost, and a good tradeoff must be chosen. For the VAX-11/780, the quadword fetch was found to be that point.

On the VAX-11/780, an 8-Kbyte high-speed cache memory is arranged in a two-way *set associative* organization. This structure is similar to the direct mapped cache shown in Figure 11-5, but in this organization two possible locations exist for each tag. Figure 11-6 is a block diagram of the cache for the VAX-11/780. The cache is divided into two parallel sets, termed Group 0 and Group 1. Each group consists of an address part (the

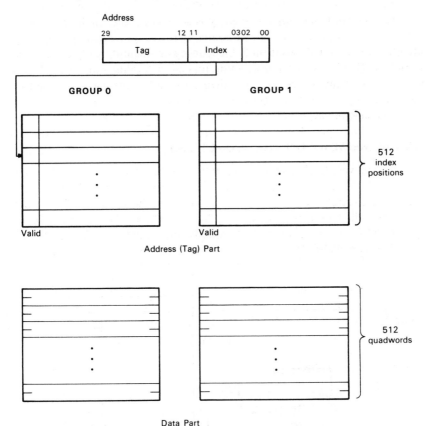

Figure 11-6.   VAX-11/780 set associative cache.

top half) containing 512 address tags, and a data part (the bottom half) containing the associated quadword for each tag. When a physical address is presented to the cache, the lower 9-bit field of the address, bits <11:3>, selects parallel tags in the two groups. The upper bits of the physical address, bits <29:12>, are then compared with the tag stored in the selected locations. If there is a match, a cache hit occurs, and the data is read out of the associated data part of the group in which the hit occurred.

In the case of a cache miss in both groups, the data must be read from main memory. A memory read fetches a quadword to be stored in the cache in either the Group 0 or Group 1 set. When a new read replaces data in the cache on the VAX-11/780, one of the groups is selected at random for replacement.

The VAX-11/780 cache uses a *write-through* strategy on write requests. When a write request is made, the new data is written in both the cache and main memory. In this way, both the cache and memory always have valid copies of all data. Although some performance loss may occur because of the time to perform the write, the processor can continue operation while the write into memory proceeds.

Another method used to handle writes in some cached systems is the *write-back* strategy. With write-back, the new data is written only to the cache and not to main memory. A separate bit that is part of the cache tag is set, thereby "remembering" the cache modification. This method, faster than write-through, reduces the number of writes to main memory. The hardware, however, is more complex because it is required to know when a write to main memory must occur. If a user process with cached data were to be paged out, modified cache information would first have to be written back to main memory.

Other problems are also associated with the write-back strategy. Device controllers require more intelligence because memory can not be read until the device examines the cache. In addition, during power failure the write-back cache holds the only correct copies of the modified data. This presents a problem because high speed caches are implemented using bipolar semiconductor technology which, by its very nature, is volatile.

THE TRANSLATION BUFFER

On a virtual memory system such as the VAX-11, a reference to a single virtual address can cause several memory references to occur before the desired information is finally accessed. For example, a reference to a system space address requires one reference to the system page table, which then yields the final physical address. This extra reference is part of the overhead associated with a virtual memory system. Similarly, a process space access requires references to the system and process page tables to compute the actual physical address.

To reduce the apparent overhead of these levels of indirection, the VAX-11/780 contains a high speed associative memory called the *translation buffer,* which caches the most recently used virtual-to-physical address translations. The 128-entry translation buffer contains copies of the page table entries (PTEs) for the current translations, including the valid and modify bits, the protection field, and the physical page frame number. The overhead of translating a virtual address can thus be considerably reduced to simply finding a hit in the translation buffer.

Figure 11-7 shows the translation buffer block structure. Like the memory cache, the translation buffer is two-way set associative; as a result, there are two possible slots in which a particular page table entry can reside. Moreover, the translation buffer is separated into two parts. In Figure 11-7, the upper 32 entries are used for system space translations (system PTEs), the lower 32 for process space translations (process PTEs). This structure was chosen because while system space is shared among all processes, process space translations are local and must be invalidated when a context switch occurs. If these entries are not invalidated, the next process could access the wrong physical memory location by generating a process virtual address when a previous process translation was in the buffer. Dividing the translation buffer provides a simple structure for invalidating all process translations while leaving system translations unaffected.

The translation of a virtual address is shown in Figure 11-8. Bit 31 of the virtual address selects the top or bottom half of the translation buffer for system or process space. Since there are 32 entries in each half of the buffer, bits $<13:9>$ are used to select one of these entries in both the Group 0 and Group 1 buffers. A validity check is made, and address bits $<30:14>$ are checked against the tag field stored in the buffer. If a match is found, the physical page frame number bits stored in the associated data field for the matching entry are appended to the byte-within-page bits $<8:0>$ of the original virtual address, forming the physical address. At the same time, the protection field is compared with the current mode to see if the process has the appropriate privilege to access that page. If not, an access violation fault is generated.

If the operation to be performed is a write, a check must be made to see whether the Modify bit was set. If it was not, this is the first write to the page, and the Modify bit must be set on both the translation buffer and main memory versions of the page table entry.

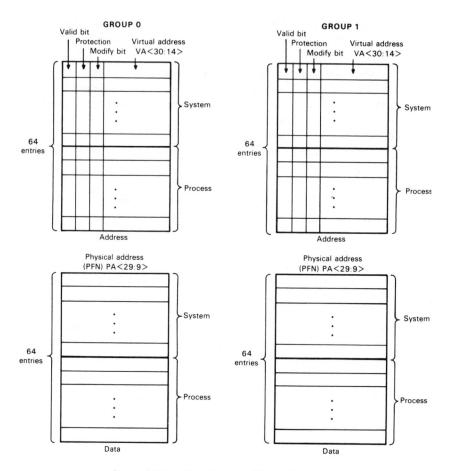

Figure 11-7.   Translation buffer block structure.

THE INSTRUCTION BUFFER

One area in which the processor particularly benefits from buffering and overlapping operations is in fetching and decoding the instruction stream. Despite occasional traps or subroutine calls, instructions are almost always executed in a linear or sequential order. If the processor can fetch the next instruction from memory while the current instruction is executing, it almost never has to wait for the memory system between execution of sequential instructions.

VIRTUAL ADDRESS

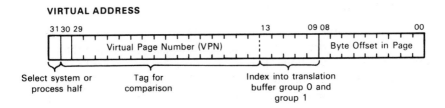

Figure 11-8.   Translation of a virtual address.

An eight-byte *instruction buffer* on the VAX-11/780 handles the fetching and decoding of instructions. It is capable of requesting and rearranging data from memory as well as decoding instruction and operand specifiers. Although instructions may begin on any byte boundary, the instruction buffer reads only longwords from the cache. For example, when the instruction buffer wishes to fetch an instruction that begins at hex address 401, the longword at hex 400 is actually fetched; the bytes within the buffer are rotated so that the first byte of the instruction at hex address 401 is first in the buffer. Associated with each byte in the buffer is a Valid bit, which notes whether that byte contains useful data.

Byte zero of the buffer always contains the opcode of the instruction being executed. Operands are shifted to the lower bytes and evaluated. As each operand is evaluated and dispatched, new operands are shifted in. Then, as the higher bytes of the buffer empty, a fetch is started to bring in the next instruction(s) held in main memory. If a branch is executed, the buffer has to be purged so that it can begin fetching new instructions from the new branch destination.

Another optimization in the VAX-11/780 is the Instruction Physical Address (IPA) register, which contains the physical address of the next instruction to be executed. This register makes address translation and many instruction fetches unnecessary. Because most instructions are executed sequentially, IPA allows the hardware to translate only the first instruction executed within a page. Whenever a branch is taken or when IPA is incremented across a page boundary, a translation must be done to calculate the physical address and verify protection. Following the translation and loading of IPA, subsequent sequential instructions fetched within the same page do not require virtual address translation.

INSTRUCTION ACCELERATORS

Another implementation optimization is the instruction *accelerator*. Certain machines provide for optional hardware to increase the speed of some classes of instructions. The accelerator contains special hardware that intercepts the normal instruction flow and provides a high-speed path for execution of the selected instructions.

For example, the VAX-11/780 has an optional floating-point accelerator that greatly increases the speed of the VAX-11 floating-point instructions, including the polynomial evaluation. It also speeds up the integer multiply, which is frequently used in routines utilizing floating-point instructions extensively. Users who write programs with large amounts of floating-point computation can benefit from this accessory.

I/O IMPLEMENTATION

In Chapter 6 we examined the control of I/O devices on the VAX-11. At that point we presented the device Control and Status registers as if they were normal memory locations. Later, we learned that the physical memory space is partitioned, providing a space for physical memory addresses and a space for device control registers.

The exact structure of the physical memory space is implementation specific. Different implementations of the VAX-11 may allow for different amounts of physical memory and I/O space. The VAX-11/780 has 30-bit physical addresses as shown in Figure 11-9, although the maximum amount of physical memory is determined by the number of boards that can be attached and the semiconductor technology (e.g., 16K- or 64K-bit memory chips). The VAX-11/780 SBI (Synchronous Backplane Interconnect, the common memory and I/O bus) uses 30-bit addresses to access physical memory and I/O registers. However, the SBI is not part of the architecture, and other implementations can have other bus structures and other physical addressing requirements.

Since the memory bus is implementation specific, device interfaces must be engineered for each implementation. This is not as much of a problem as it seems, since most devices do not attach directly to the memory bus but to an I/O bus such as the Unibus or Massbus. Still, a new Unibus adapter and Massbus adapter must be designed for each specific implementation.

The VAX-11/780 Unibus and Massbus adapters must allow devices to address SBI physical memory. However, most Unibus and Massbus devices were designed for the PDP-11 and use 16- or 18-bit addresses to refer to

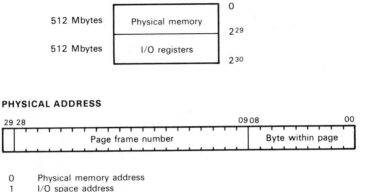

Figure 11-9.   VAX-11/780 physical address space.

physical memory locations. The adapters must be able to translate these addresses into 30-bit SBI memory addresses. To do this, both adapters contain a set of internal mapping registers.

The Unibus adapter contains 496 mapping registers to translate 18-bit Unibus addresses into 30-bit SBI addresses. Each mapping register maps one 512-byte page. A device reads or writes memory using an 18-bit address, while the adapter uses the mapping registers to perform the translation. As shown in Figure 11-10, the upper 9 bits of the Unibus address are used to select one mapping register. The register contains the page frame number of the VAX-11 physical page. The page frame number in the mapping register and the low order bits of the Unibus address together specify the byte in physical memory.

Similarly, the Massbus adapter contains 256 mapping registers. Each register contains the page frame number for one page, and can be used to map transfers to and from physical memory.

Before a transfer can begin using either the Massbus or Unibus, the operating system must allocate a set of contiguous adapter registers to map the transfer. A transfer of n pages requires n or $n + 1$ mapping registers, depending on whether or not the user's memory is page aligned. The registers are loaded with the physical page frame numbers for consecutive virtual pages from which data will be be read or written. The device data address register is loaded with the Unibus or Massbus address that specifies the first of the mapping registers allocated for the transfer.

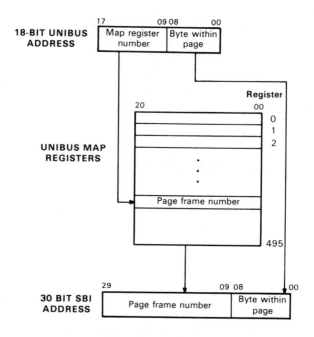

Figure 11-10. VAX-11/780 Unibus to SBI address translation.

New devices that connect directly to the VAX-11 buses have another option besides mapping registers. These devices can use 32-bit addresses to refer to VAX-11 virtual memory. If the device can find the physical address of the System Page Table (which the software could load into an internal device register), it can use the VAX-11 page tables directly to locate physical memory for data transfers.

THE EVOLUTION OF THE VAX-11 ARCHITECTURE

The architecture of a computer is determined by the technological, economic, and human aspects of the environment in which the computer is designed and built. Most of these factors are not entirely under the control of computer designers. In addition, the factors may change with time. Consequently, a design must not only take these factors into account; it must also be flexible enough to allow for evolution and refinement of the design.

Some factors that influenced the design of the earlier PDP-11—including limited addressing capability, lack of a sufficient number of registers, inadequate character handling, complex I/O, and interrupt handling—influenced the design of the newer VAX-11 architecture. The first implementation of that architecture, the VAX-11/780, represents the tradeoffs that could be made with current technology in order to maintain a proper balance among price, speed, packing density, heat dissipation, reliability, and so forth.

With time, the technology will change, thereby offering the VAX-11 designers three alternatives:

1. To use the new technology to build cheaper systems with the same performance.

2. To hold the price constant and use the technological improvement to obtain an increase in performance.

3. To push the design to its limits, increasing both price and performance.

The market life of a computer is determined, in part, by how well the design can gracefully evolve to accommodate new technologies and innovations. New implementations of the architecture will appear, and older designs will be retired in favor of newer versions utilizing improvements in memory and semiconductor technology.

THE FAMILY CONCEPT

Taking advantage of these three alternatives leads to the production of a "family" of CPUs with varying price and performance. Each family member, while exhibiting the same basic architecture, in general, represents a different implementation. However, because of common architecture, software compatibility at the machine language level is made possible. Thus, as the user's needs grow, software that evolves can be moved from a smaller machine to a larger one, and, conversely, newer software can be expected to run on earlier members of the family.

With time, two changes typically occur in family architectures. First, shortcomings and ambiguities in the original design are recognized and corrected. For example, the VAX-11 has already had several new queue instructions added to allow for interlocked queue access between multiprocessors. While this potentially allows architectural differences to develop, a good basic design generally prevents such an occurrence.

Second, as previously mentioned, new features such as caches, writeable control stores, high speed intelligent controllers, and parallel floating-point processors are added. Regardless of whether these features were anticipated in the original design, they must not endanger the architectural compatiblity. Indeed, it should be possible to reduce the cost of a given design by removing some of the features, such as the cache, while preserving the given architecture.

SUMMARY

In this chapter, we have examined some of the implementation choices made on the VAX-11/780 to enhance the performance of the VAX architecture. These features—the cache, translation buffer, and instruction buffer—are invisible to the user program, which thus sees a consistent architecture across all VAX-11 implementations. However, each designer can choose different components and internal structures to obtain a machine with different price/performance characteristics.

REFERENCES

More details specific to the VAX-11/780 implementation can be found in the *VAX-11/780 Hardware Handbook* and the *VAX-11 System Maintenance Guide*. The paper by Strecker (1976) describes the process of cache design in more detail, and the paper by Satyanarayanan and Bhandarkar (1980) discusses tradeoffs in VAX-11 translation buffer design.

EXERCISES FOR CHAPTER 11

1. Assuming that a reference to main memory (a cache miss) takes 1200 nanoseconds, while a cache hit takes 400 nanoseconds, graph the average access time versus cache hit rate for hit rates of 55, 65, 75, 85, and 95 percent.

2. Caches are often used to improve the access time to main memory by the CPU. What about using caches for I/O to and from main memory? What are the advantages and disadvantages of doing so?

3. Describe the similarities and differences between a main memory cache and a translation buffer. How can a translation buffer's performance be improved? Why might a 64-entry translation buffer be sufficient for the VAX?

4. Relate the effectiveness of the translation buffer to the implementation of process page tables on the VAX-11.

5. What must be done to the translation buffer following a process context switch operation and why?

6. Is it possible to build a VAX-11 machine without a cache, translation buffer, or instruction buffer? If you could have one, but not all three features, which one would you choose and why?

7. What is a computer family? Why are computer families useful?

APPENDIXES

Appendix A

VAX-11
Instruction Set Description

OPERAND SPECIFIER NOTATION LEGEND

The standard notation for operand specifiers is:

<name> . <access type> <data type>

where:

1. Name is a suggestive name for the operand in the context of the instruction. It is the capitalized name of a register or block for implied operands.

2. Access type is a letter denoting the operand specifier access type.

    a— Calculate the effective address of the specified operand. Address is returned in a pointer which is the actual instruction operand. Context of address calculation is given by data type given by <data type>.

    b— No operand reference. Operand specifier is branch displacement. Size of branch displacement is given by <data type>.

    m— Operand is modified (both read and written).

    r— Operand is read only.

    v— If not "Rn," same as a. If "RN," R[n + 1]R[n].

    w— Operand is written only.

3. Data type is a letter denoting the data type of the operand.

    b—byte
    d—double
    f—floating

l—longword
q—quadword
v—field (used only on implied operands)
w—word
x—first data type specified by instruction
y—second data type specified by instruction
∗—multiple longwords (used only on implied operands)

4. Implied operands, that is, locations that are accessed by the instruction, but not specified in an operand, are denoted in enclosing brackets,[ ].

CONDITION CODES LEGEND

. = conditionally cleared/set
— = not affected
0 = cleared
1 = set

OP	Mnemonic	Description	Arguments	Condition Codes N Z V C
9D	ACBB	Add compare and branch byte	limit.rb, add.rb, index.mb, displ.bw	. . . —
6F	ACBD	Add compare and branch double	limit.rd, add.rd, index.md, displ.bw	. . . —
4F	ACBF	Add compare and branch floating	limit.rf, add.rf, index.mf, displ.bw	. . . —
F1	ACBL	Add compare and branch long	limit.rl, add.rl, index.ml, displ.bw	. . . —
3D	ACBW	Add compare and branch word	limit.rw, add.rw, index.mw, displ.bw	. . . —
58	ADAWI	Add aligned word interlocked	add.rw, sum.mw	. . . .
80	ADDB2	Add byte 2-operand	add.rb, sum.mb	. . . .
81	ADDB3	Add byte 3-operand	add1.rb, add2.rb, sum.wb	. . . 0
60	ADDD2	Add double 2-operand	add.rd, sum.md	. . . 0
61	ADDD3	Add double 3-operand	add1.rd, add2.rd, sum.wd	. . . 0
40	ADDF2	Add floating 2-operand	add.rf, sum.mf	. . . 0
41	ADDF3	Add floating 3-operand	add1.rf, add2.rf, sum.wf	. . . 0
CO	ADDL2	Add long 2-operand	add.rl, sum.ml	. . . .
C1	ADDL3	Add long 3-operand	add1.rl, add2.rl, sum.wl	. . . 0
20	ADDP4	Add packed 4-operand	addlen.rw, addaddr.ab, sumlen.rw, sumaddr.ab, [R0-3.wl]	. . . 0

OP	Mnemonic	Description	Arguments	N	Z	V	C
21	ADDP6	Add packed 6-operand	add1len.rw, add1addr.ab, add2len.rw, add2addr.ab, sumlen.rw, sumaddr.ab, [R0-5.wl]	.	.	.	0
A0	ADDW2	Add word 2-operand	add.rw, sum.mw	.	.	.	.
A1	ADDW3	Add word 3-operand	add1.rw, add2.rw, sum.ww	.	.	.	0
D8	ADWC	Add with carry	add.rl, sum.ml	.	.	.	.
F3	AOBLEQ	Add one and branch on less or equal	limit.rl, index.ml, displ.bb	.	.	.	–
F2	AOBLSS	Add one and branch on less	limit.rl, index.ml, displ.bb	.	.	.	–
78	ASHL	Arithmetic shift long	count.rb, src.rl, dst.wl	.	.	.	0
F8	ASHP	Arithmetic shift and round packed	count.rb, srclen.rw, srcaddr.ab, round.rb, dstlen.rw, dstaddr.ab, [R0-3.wl]	.	.	.	0
79	ASHQ	Arithmetic shift quad	count.rb, src.rq, dst.wq	.	.	.	0
E1	BBC	Branch on bit clear	pos.rl, base.vb, displ.bb, [field.rv]	–	–	–	–
E5	BBCC	Branch on bit clear and clear	pos.rl, base.vb, displ.bb, [field.mv]	–	–	–	–
E7	BBCCI	Branch on bit clear and clear interlocked	pos.rl, base.vb, displ.bb, [field.mv]	–	–	–	–
E3	BBCS	Branch on bit clear and set	pos.rl, base.vb, displ.bb, [field.mv]	–	–	–	–
E0	BBS	Branch on bit set	pos.rl, base.vb, displ.bb, [field.rv]	–	–	–	–
E4	BBSC	Branch on bit set and clear	pos.rl, base.vb, displ.bb, [field.mv]	–	–	–	–
E2	BBSS	Branch on bit set and set	pos.rl, base.vb, displ.bb, [field.mv]	–	–	–	–
E6	BBSSI	Branch on bit set and set interlocked	pos.rl, base.vb, displ.bb, [field.mv]	–	–	–	–
1E	BCC	Branch on carry clear	displ.bb				
1F	BCS	Branch on carry set	displ.bb	–	–	–	–
13	BEQL	Branch on equal	displ.bb	–	–	–	–
13	BEQLU	Branch on equal unsigned	displ.bb	–	–	–	–
18	BGEQ	Branch on greater or equal	displ.bb	–	–	–	–
1E	BGEQU	Branch on greater or equal unsigned	displ.bb	–	–	–	–
14	BGTR	Branch on greater	displ.bb	–	–	–	–
1A	BGTRU	Branch on greater unsigned	displ.bb	–	–	–	–
8A	BICB2	Bit clear byte 2-operand	mask.rb, dst.mb	.	.	0	–

OP	Mnemonic	Description	Arguments	Condition Codes N Z V C
8B	BICB3	Bit clear byte 3-operand	mask.rb, src.rb, dst.wb	. . 0 –
CA	BICL2	Bit clear long 2-operand	mask.rl, dst.ml	. . 0 –
CB	BICL3	Bit clear long 3-operand	mask.rl, src.rl, dst.wl	. . 0 –
B9	BICPSW	Bit clear processor status word	mask.rw	. . . .
AA	BICW2	Bit clear word 2-operand	mask.rw, dst.mw	. . 0 –
AB	BICW3	Bit clear word 3-operand	mask.rw, src.rw, dst.ww	. . 0 –
88	BISB2	Bit set byte 2-operand	mask.rb, dst.mb	. . 0 –
89	BISB3	Bit set byte 3-operand	mask.rb, src.rb, dst.wb	. . 0 –
C8	BISL2	Bit set long 2-operand	mask.rl, dst.ml	. . 0 –
C9	BISL3	Bit set long 3-operand	mask.rl, src.rl, dst.wl	. . 0 –
B8	BISPSW	Bit set processor status word	mask.rw	. . . .
A8	BISW2	Bit set word 2-operand	mask.rw, dst.mw	. . 0 –
A9	BISW3	Bit set word 3-operand	mask.rw, src.rw, dst.ww	. . 0 –
93	BITB	Bit test byte	mask.rb, src.rb	. . 0 –
D3	BITL	Bit test long	mask.rl, src.rl	. . 0 –
B3	BITW	Bit test word	mask.rw, src.rw	. . 0 –
E9	BLBC	Branch on low bit clear	src.rl, displ.bb	– – – –
E8	BLBS	Branch on low bit set	src.rl, displ.bb	– – – –
15	BLEQ	Branch on less or equal	displ.bb	– – – –
1B	BLEQU	Branch on less or equal unsigned	displ.bb	– – – –
19	BLSS	Branch on less	displ.bb	– – – –
1F	BLSSU	Branch on less unsigned	displ.bb	– – – –
12	BNEQ	Branch on not equal	displ.bb	– – – –
12	BNEQU	Branch on not equal unsigned	displ.bb	– – – –
03	BPT	Break point fault	[–(KSP).w*]	0 0 0 0
11	BRB	Branch with byte displacement	displ.bb	– – – –
31	BRW	Branch with word displacement	displ.bw	– – – –
10	BSBB	Branch to subroutine with byte displacement	displ.bb, [–(SP).wl]	– – – –

OP	Mnemonic	Description	Arguments	Condition Codes N Z V C
30	BSBW	Branch to subroutine with word displacement	displ.bw, [–(SP).wl]	– – – –
1C	BVC	Branch on overflow clear	displ.bb	– – – –
1D	BVS	Branch on overflow set	displ.bb	– – – –
FA	CALLG	Call with general argument list	arglist.ab,dst.ab, [–(SP).w*]	0 0 0 0
FB	CALLS	Call with argument list on stack	numarg.rl,dst.ab, [–(SP).w*]	0 0 0 0
8F	CASEB	Case byte	selector.rb, base.rb, limit.rb, displ.bw-list	. . 0 .
CF	CASEL	Case long	selector.rl, base.rl, limit.rl, displ.bw-list	. . 0 .
AF	CASEW	Case word	selector.rw, base.rw, limit.rw, displ.bw-list	. . 0 .
BD	CHME	Change mode to executive	param.rw, [–(ySP).w*] y = MINU(E, PSLcurrent-mode)	0 0 0 0
BC	CHMK	Change mode to kernel	param.rw, [–(KSP).w*]	0 0 0 0
BE	CHMS	Change mode to supervisor	param.rw, [–(ySP).w*] y = MINU(S, PSLcurrent-mode)	0 0 0 0
BF	CHMU	Change mode to user	param.rw, [–(SP).w*]	0 0 0 0
94	CLRB	Clear byte	dst.wb	0 1 0 –
7C	CLRD	Clear double	dst.wd	0 1 0 –
D4	CLRF	Clear floating	dst.wf	0 1 0 –
D4	CLRL	Clear long	dst.wl	0 1 0 –
7C	CLRQ	Clear quad	dst.wq	0 1 0 –
B4	CLRW	Clear word	dst.ww	0 1 0 –
91	CMPB	Compare byte	src1.rb, src2.rb	. . 0 .
29	CMPC3	Compare character 3-operand	len.rw, src1addr.ab, src2addr.ab, [R0-3.wl]	. . 0 .
2D	CMPC5	Compare character 5-operand	src1len.rw, src1addr.ab, fill.rb, src2len.rw, src2addr.ab, [R0-3.wl]	. . 0 .
71	CMPD	Compare double	src1.rd, src2.rd	. . 0 0
51	CMPF	Compare floating	src1.rf, src2.rf	. . 0 0
D1	CMPL	Compare long	src1.rl, src2.rl	. . 0 .
35	CMPP3	Compare packed 3-operand	len.rw, src1addr.ab, src2addr.ab, [R0-3.wl]	. . 0 0
37	CMPP4	Compare packed 4-operand	src1len.rw, src1addr.ab, src2len.rw, src2addr.ab, [R0-3.wl]	. . 0 0
EC	CMPV	Compare field	pos.rl, size.rb, base.vb, [field.rv], src.rl	. . 0 .
B1	CMPW	Compare word	src1.rw, src2.rw	. . 0 .
ED	CMPZV	Compare zero	-pos.rl, size.rb, base.vb,	. . 0 .

OP	Mnemonic	Description	Arguments	Condition Codes N Z V C
0B	CRC	extended field Calculate cyclic redundancy check	[field.rv], src.rl tbl.ab, initialcrc.rl, strlen.rw, stream.ab, [R0-3.wl]	. . 0 0
6C	CVTBD	Convert byte to double	src.rb, dst.wd	. . . 0
4C	CVTBF	Convert byte to floating	src.rb, dst.wf	. . . 0
98	CVTBL	Convert byte to long	src.rb, dst.wl	. . . 0
99	CVTBW	Convert byte to word	src.rb, dst.ww	. . . 0
68	CVTDB	Convert double to byte	src.rd, dst.wb	. . . 0
76	CVTDF	Convert double to floating	src.rd, dst.wf	. . . 0
6A	CVTDL	Convert double to long	src.rd, dst.wl	. . . 0
69	CVTDW	Convert double to word	src.rd, dst.ww	. . . 0
48	CVTFB	Convert floating to byte	src.rf, dst.wb	. . . 0
56	CVTFD	Convert floating to double	src.rf, dst.wd	. . . 0
4A	CVTFL	Convert floating to long	src.rf, dst.wl	. . . 0
49	CVTFW	Convert floating to word	src.rf, dst.ww	. . . 0
F6	CVTLB	Convert long to byte	src.rl, dst.wb	. . . 0
6E	CVTLD	Convert long to double	src.rl, dst.wd	. . . 0
4E	CVTLF	Convert long to floating	src.rl, dst.wf	. . . 0
F9	CVTLP	Convert long to packed	src.rl, dstlen.rw, dstaddr.ab, [R0-3.wl]	. . . 0
F7	CVTLW	Convert long to word	src.rl, dst.ww	. . . 0
36	CVTPL	Convert packed to long	srclen.rw, srcaddr.ab, [R0-3.wl], dst.wl	. . . 0
08	CVTPS	Convert packed to leading separate	srclen.rw, srcaddr.ab, dstlen.rw, dstaddr.ab, [R0-3.wl]	. . . 0
24	CVTPT	Convert packed to trailing	srclen.rw, srcaddr.ab, tbladdr.ab, dstlen.rw, dstaddr.ab, [R0-3.wl]	. . . 0
6B	CVTRDL	Convert rounded double to long	src.rd, dst.wl	. . . 0
4B	CVTRFL	Convert rounded floating to long	src.rf, dst.wl	. . . 0

OP	Mnemonic	Description	Arguments	Condition Codes N Z V C
09	CVTSP	Convert leading separate to packed	srclen.rw, srcaddr.ab, dstlen.rw, dstaddr.ab, [R0-3.wl]	. . . 0
26	CVTTP	Convert trailing to packed	srclen.rw, srcaddr.ab, tbladdr.ab, dstlen.rw, dstaddr.ab, [R0-3.wl]	. . . 0
33	CVTWB	Convert word to byte	src.rw, dst.wb	. . . 0
6D	CVTWD	Convert word to double	src.rw, dst.wd	. . . 0
4D	CVTWF	Convert word to floating	src.rw, dst.wf	. . . 0
32	CVTWl	Convert word to long	src.rw, dst.wl	. . . 0
97	DECB	Decrement byte	dif.mb	. . . .
D7	DECL	Decrement long	dif.ml	. . . .
B7	DECW	Decrement word	dif.mw	. . . .
86	DIVB2	Divide byte 2-operand	divr.rb, quo.mb	. . . 0
87	DIVB3	Divide byte 3-operand	divr.rb, divd.rb, quo.wb	. . . 0
66	DIVD2	Divide double 2-operand	divr.rd, quo.md	. . . 0
67	DIVD3	Divide double 3-operand	divr.rd, divd.rd, quo.wd	. . . 0
46	DIVF2	Divide floating 2-operand	divr.rf, quo.mf	. . . 0
47	DIVF3	Divide floating 3-operand	divr.rf, divd.rf, quo.wf	. . . 0
C6	DIVL2	Divide long 2-operand	divr.rl, quo.ml	. . . 0
C7	DIVL3	Divide long 3-operand	divr.rl, divd.rl, quo.wl	. . . 0
27	DIVP	Divide packed	divrlen.rw, divraddr.ab, divdlen.rw, divdaddr.ab, quolen.rw, quoaddr.ab, [R0-5.wl,-16(SP): -1(SP).wb]	. . . 0
A6	DIVW2	Divide word 2-operand	divr.rw, quo.mw	. . . 0
A7	DIVW3	Divide word 3-operand	divr.rw, divd.rw, quo.ww	. . . 0
38	EDITPC	Edit packed to character string	srclen.rw, srcaddr.ab, pattern.ab, dstaddr.ab, [R0-5.wl]	. . . .
7B	EDIV	Extended divide	divr.rl, divd.rq, quo.wl, rem.wl	N . Z . . 0
74	EMODD	Extended modulus double	mulr.rd, mulrx.rb, muld.rd, int.wl, fract.wd	. . . 0
54	EMODF	Extended modulus floating	mulr.rf, mulrx.rb, muld.rf, int.wl fract.wf	. . . 0

OP	Mnemonic	Description	Arguments	Condition Codes N	Z	V	C
7A	EMUL	Extended multiply	mulr.rl, muld.rl, add.rl, prod.wq	.	.	0	0
EE	EXTV	Extract field	pos.rl, size.rb, base.vb, [field.rv], dst.wl	.	.	0	-
EF	EXTZV	Extract zero extended field	-pos.rl, size.rb, base.vb, [field.rv], dst.wl	.	.	0	-
EB	FFC	Find first clear bit	startpos.rl, size.rb, base.vb, [field.rv], findpos.wl	0	.	0	0
EA	FFS	Find first set bit	startpos.rl, size.rb, base.vb, [field.rv], findpos.wl	0	.	0	0
00	HALT	Halt (Kernel Mode only)	[-(KSP).w*]	.	.	.	.
96	INCB	Increment byte	sum.mb	.	.	.	.
D6	INCL	Increment long	sum.ml	.	.	.	.
B6	INCW	Increment word	sum.mw	.	.	.	.
0A	INDEX	Index calculation	subscript.rl, low.rl, high.rl, size.rl, entry.rl, addr.wl	.	.	0	0
5C	INSQHI	Insert at head of queue, interlocked	entry.ab, header.aq	0	.	0	.
5D	INSQTI	Insert at tail of queue, interlocked	entry.ab, header.aq	0	.	0	.
0E	INSQUE	Insert into queue	entry.ab, addr.wl	.	.	0	.
F0	INSV	Insert field	src.rl, pos.rl, size.rb, base.vb, [field.wv]	-	-	-	-
17	JMP	Jump	dst.ab	-	-	-	-
16	JSB	Jump to subroutine	dst.ab, [-(SP)+.wl]	-	-	-	-
06	LDPCTX	Load process context (only legal on interrupt stack)	[PCB.r*, -(KSP).w*]	-	-	-	-
3A	LOCC	Locate character	char.rb, len.rw, addr.ab, [R0-1.wl]	0	.	0	0
39	MATCHC	Match characters	len 1.rw, addr 1.ab, len2.rw, addr2.ab, [R0-3.wl]	0	.	0	0
92	MCOMB	Move complemented byte	scr.rb, dst.wb	.	.	0	-
D2	MCOML	Move complemented long	scr.rl, dst.wl	.	.	0	-
B2	MCOMW	Move complemented word	src.rw, dst.ww	.	.	0	-
DB	MFPR	Move from processor register (Kernel Mode only)	procreg.rl, dst.wl	.	.	0	-
8E	MNEGB	Move negated byte	src.rb, dst.wb	.	.	.	.
72	MNEGD	Move negated double	src.rd, dst.wd	.	.	0	0

OP	Mnemonic	Description	Arguments	N	Z	V	C
					Condition Codes		
52	MNEGF	Move negated floating	src.rf, dst.wf	.	.	0	0
CE	MNEGL	Move negated long	src.rl, dst.wl	.	.	.	.
AE	MNEGW	Move negated word	src.rw, dst.ww	.	.	.	.
9E	MOVAB	Move address of byte	src.ab, dst.wl	.	.	0	–
7E	MOVAD	Move address of double	src.aq, dst.wl	.	.	0	–
DE	MOVAF	Move address of floating	src.al, dst.wl	.	.	0	–
DE	MOVAL	Move address of long	src.al, dst.wl	.	.	0	–
7E	MOVAQ	Move address of quad	src.aq, dst.wl	.	.	0	–
3E	MOVAW	Move address of word	src.aw, dst.wl	.	.	0	–
90	MOVB	Move byte	src.rb, dst.wb	.	.	0	–
28	MOVC3	Move character 3-operand	len.rw, srcaddr.ab, dstaddr.ab, [R0-5.wl]	0	1	0	0
2C	MOVC5	Move character 5-operand	srclen.rw, srcaddr.ab, fill.rb, dstlen.rw, dstaddr.ab, [R0-5.wl]	.	.	0	.
70	MOVD	Move double	scr.rd, dst.wd	.	.	0	–
50	MOVF	Move floating	src.rf, dst.wf	.	.	0	–
DO	MOVL	Move long	src.rl, dst.wl	.	.	0	–
34	MOVP	Move packed	len.rw, srcaddr.ab, dstaddr.ab, [R0-3.wl]	.	.	0	–
DC	MOVPSL	Move processor status longword	dst.wl	–	–	–	–
7D	MOVQ	Move quad	src.rq, dst.wq	.	.	0	–
2E	MOVTC	Move translated characters	srclen.rw, srcaddr.ab, fill.rb, tbladdr.ab, dstlen.rw, dstaddr.ab, [R0-5.wl]	.	.	0	.
2F	MOVTUC	Move translated until character	srclen.rw, srcaddr.ab, escape.rb, tbladdr.ab, dstlen.rw, dstaddr.ab, [R0-5.wl]	.	.	.	.
BO	MOVW	Move word	src.rw, dst.ww	.	.	0	–
9A	MOVZBL	Move zero-extended byte to long	src.rb, dst.wl	0	.	0	–
9B	MOVZBW	Move zero-extended byte to word	src.rb, dst.ww	0	.	0	–
3C	MOVZWL	Move zero-extended word to long	src.rw, dst.wl	0	.	0	–
DA	MTPR	Move to processor register (Kernel Mode only)	src.rl, procreg.rl	.	.	0	–
84	MULB2	Multiply byte 2-operand	mulr.rb, prod.mb	.	.	.	0
85	MULB3	Multiply byte	mulr.rb, muld.rb,	.	.	.	0

OP	Mnemonic	Description	Arguments	N	Z	V	C
64	MULD2	3-operand Multiply double	prod.wb mulr.rd, prod.md	.	.	.	0
65	MULD3	2-operand Multiply double 3-operand	mulr.rd, muld.rd, prod.wd	.	.	.	0
44	MULF2	Multiply floating 2-operand	mulr.rf, prod.mf	.	.	.	0
45	MULF3	Multiply floating 3-operand	mulr.rf, muld.rf, prod.wf	.	.	.	0
C4	MULL2	Multiply long 2-operand	mulr.rl, prod.ml	.	.	.	0
C5	MULL3	Multiply long 3-operand	mulr.rl, muld.rl, prod.wl	.	.	.	0
25	MULP	Multiply packed	mulrlen.rw, mulradr.ab, muldlen.rw, muldadr.ab, prodlen.rw, prodadr.ab, [R0-5.wl]	.	.	.	0
A4	MULW2	Multiply word 2-operand	mulr.rw, prod.mw	.	.	.	0
A5	MULW3	Multiply word 3-operand	mulr.rw, muld.rw, prod.ww	.	.	.	0
01	NOP	No operation		–	–	–	–
75	POLYD	Evaluate polynomial double	arg.rd, degree.rw, tbladdr.ab, [R0-5.wl]	.	.	.	0
55	POLYF	Evaluate polynomial floating	arg.rf, degree.rw, tbladdr.ab, [R0-3.wl]	.	.	.	0
BA	POPR	Pop registers	mask.rw, [(SP)+.r*]	–	–	–	–
0C	PROBER	Probe read access	mode.rb, len.rw, base.ab	0	.	0	–
0D	PROBEW	Probe write access	mode.rb, len.rw, base.ab	0	.	0	–
9F	PUSHAB	Push address of byte	src.ab, [–(SP).wl]	.	.	0	–
7F	PUSHAD	Push address of double	src.aq, [–(SP).wl]	.	.	0	–
DF	PUSHAF	Push address of floating	src.al, [–(SP).wl]	.	.	0	–
DF	PUSHAL	Push address of long	src.al, [–(SP).wl]	.	.	0	–
7F	PUSHAQ	Push address of quad	src.aq, [–(SP).wl]	.	.	0	–
3F	PUSHAW	Push address of word	src.aw, [–(SP).wl]	.	.	0	–
DD	PUSHL	Push long	src.rl, [–(SP).wl]	.	.	0	–
BB	PUSHR	Push registers	mask.rw, [–(SP).w*]	–	–	–	–
02	REI	Return from exception or interrupt	[(SP)+.r*]	.	.	.	.
5E	REMQHI	Remove from head of queue, interlocked	header.aq, addr.wl	0	.	.	.

OP	Mnemonic	Description	Arguments	Condition Codes N Z V C
5F	REMQTI	Remove from tail of queue, interlocked	header.aq, addr.wl	0 . . .
0F	REMQUE	Remove from queue	entry.ab, addr.wl	. . . .
04	RET	Return from procedure	[(SP)+.r*]	. . . .
9C	ROTL	Rotate long	count.rb, src.rl, dst.wl	. . 0 –
05	RSB	Return from subroutine	[(SP)+.rl]	– – – –
D9	SBWC	Subtract with carry	sub.rl, dif.ml	. . . .
2A	SCANC	Scan for character	len.rw, addr.ab, tbladdr.ab, mask.rb, [R0-3.wl]	0 . 0 0
3B	SKPC	Skip character	char.rb, len.rw, addr.ab, [R0-1.wl]	0 . 0 0
F4	SOBGEQ	Subtract one and branch on greater or equal	index.ml, displ.bb	. . . –
F5	SOBGTR	Subtract one and branch on greater	index.ml, displ.bb	. . . –
2B	SPANC	Span characters	len.rw, addr.ab, tbladdr.ab, mask.rb, [R0-3.wl]	0 . 0 0
82	SUBB2	Subtract byte 2-operand	sub.rb, dif.mb	. . . .
83	SUBB3	Subtract byte 3-operand	sub.rb, min.rb, dif.wb	. . . 0
62	SUBD2	Subtract double 2-operand	sub.rd, dif.md	. . . 0
63	SUBD3	Subtract double 3-operand	sub.rd, min.rd, dif.wd	. . . 0
42	SUBF2	Subtract floating 2-operand	sub.rf, dif.mf	. . . 0
43	SUBF3	Subtract floating 3-operand	sub.rf, min.rf, dif.wf	. . . 0
C2	SUBL2	Subtract long 2-operand	sub.rl, dif.ml	. . . .
C3	SUBL3	Subtract long 3-operand	sub.rl, min.rl, dif.wl	. . . 0
22	SUBP4	Subtract packed 4-operand	sublen.rw, subaddr.ab, diflen.rw, difaddr.ab, [R0-3.wl]	. . . 0
23	SUBP6	Subtract packed 6-operand	sublen.rw, subaddr.ab, minlen.rw, minaddr.ab, diflen.rw, difaddr.ab, [R0-5.wl]	. . . 0
A2	SUBW2	Subtract word 2-operand	sub.rw, dif.mw	. . . .
A3	SUBW3	Subtract word 3-operand	sub.rw, min.rw, dif.ww	. . . 0
07	SVPCTX	Save process	[(SP)+.r*, –(KSP).w*]	– – – –

OP	Mnemonic	Description	Arguments	Condition Codes N Z V C
		context (Kernel Mode only)		
95	TSTB	Test byte	src.rb	. . 0 0
73	TSTD	Test double	src.rd	. . 0 0
53	TSTF	Test floating	src.rf	. . 0 0
D5	TSTL	Test long	src.rl	. . 0 0
B5	TSTW	Test word	src.rw	. . 0 0
FC	XFC	Extended function call	user defined operands	0 0 0 0
8C	XORB2	Exclusive OR byte 2-operand	mask.rb, dst.mb	. . 0 –
8D	XORB3	Exclusive OR byte 3-operand	mask.rb, src.rb, dst.wb	. . 0 –
CC	XORL2	Exclusive OR long 2-operand	mask.rl., dst.ml	. . 0 –
CD	XORL3	Exclusive OR long 3-operand	mask.rl, src.rl, dst.wl	. . 0 –
AC	XORW2	Exclusive OR word 2-operand	mask.rw, dst.mw	. . 0 –
AD	XORW3	Exclusive OR word 3-operand	mask.rw, src.rw, dst.ww	. . 0 –

INSTRUCTIONS IN NUMERIC ORDER

00	HALT	1D	BVS	3A	LOCC
01	NOP	1E	BCC,BGEQU	3B	SKPC
02	REI	1F	BCS,BLSSU	3C	MOVZWL
03	BPT	20	ADDP4	3D	ACBW
04	RET	21	ADDP6	3E	MOVAW
05	RSB	22	SUBP4	3F	PUSHAW
06	LDPCTX	23	SUBP6	40	ADDF2
07	SVPCTX	24	CVTPT	41	ADDF3
08	CVTPS	25	MULP	42	SUBF2
09	CVTSP	26	CVTTP	43	SUBF3
0A	INDEX	27	DIVP	44	MULF2
0B	CRC	28	MOVC3	45	MULF3
0C	PROBER	29	CMPC3	46	DIVF2
0D	PROBEW	2A	SCANC	47	DIVF3
0E	INSQUE	2B	SPANC	48	CVTFB
0F	REMQUE	2C	MOVC5	49	CVTFW
10	BSBB	2D	CMPC5	4A	CVTFL
11	BRB	2E	MOVTC	4B	CVTRFL
12	BNEQ,BNEQU	2F	MOVTUC	4C	CVTBF
13	BEQL,BEQLU	30	BSBW	4D	CVTWF
14	BGTR	31	BRW	4E	CVTLF
15	BLEQ	32	CVTWL	4F	ACBF
16	JSB	33	CVTWB	50	MOVF
17	JMP	34	MOVP	51	CMPF
18	BGEQ	35	CMPP3	52	MNEGF
19	BLSS	36	CVTPL	53	TSTF
1A	BGTRU	37	CMPP4	54	EMODF
1B	BLEQU	38	EDITPC	55	POLYF
1C	BVC	39	MATCHC	56	CVTFD

57 reserved	8F CASEB	C9 BISL3
58 ADAWI	90 MOVB	CA BICL2
59 reserved	91 CMPB	CB BICL3
5A reserved	92 MCOMB	CC XORL2
5B reserved	93 BITB	CD XORL3
5C INSQHI	94 CLRB	CE MNEGL
5D INSQTI	95 TSTB	CF CASEL
5E REMQHI	96 INCB	D0 MOVL
5F REMQTI	97 DECB	D1 CMPL
60 ADDD2	98 CVTBL	D2 MCOML
61 ADDD3	99 CVTBW	D3 BITL
62 SUBD2	9A MOVZBL	D4 CLRF,CLRL
63 SUBD3	9B MOVZBW	D5 TSTL
64 MULD2	9C ROTL	D6 INCL
65 MULD3	9D ACBB	D7 DECL
66 DIVD2	9E MOVAB	D8 ADWC
67 DIVD3	9F PUSHAB	D9. SBWC
68 CVTDB	A0 ADDW2	DA MTPR
69 CVTDW	A1 ADDW3	DB MFPR
6A CVTDL	A2 SUBW2	DC MOVPSL
6B CVTRDL	A3 SUBW3	DD PUSHL
6C CVTBD	A4 MULW2	DE MOVAF,
6D CVTWD	A5 MULW3	MOVAL
6E CVTLD	A6 DIVW2	DF PUSHAF,
6F ACBD	A7 DIVW3	PUSHAL
70 MOVD	A8 BISW2	E0 BBS
71 CMPD	A9 BISW3	E1 BBC
72 MNEGD	AA BICW2	E2 BBSS
73 TSTD	AB BICW3	E3 BBCS
74 EMODD	AC XORW2	E4 BBSC
75 POLYD	AD XORW3	E5 BBCC
76 CVTDF	AE MNEGW	E6 BBSSI
77 reserved	AF CASEW	E7 BBCCI
78 ASHL	B0 MOVW	E8 BLBS
79 ASHQ	B1 CMPW	E9 BLBC
7A EMUL	B2 MCOMW	EA FFS
7B EDIV	B3 BITW	EB FFC
7C CLRD,CLRQ	B4 CLRW	EC CMPV
7D MOVQ	B5 TSTW	ED CMPZV
7E MOVAD,	B6 INCW	EE EXTV
MOVAQ	B7 DECW	EF EXTZV
7F PUSHAD,	B8 BISPSW	F0 INSV
PUSHAQ	B9 BICPSW	F1 ACBL
80 ADDB2	BA POPR	F2 AOBLSS
81 ADDB3	BB PUSHR	F3 AOBLEQ
82 SUBB2	BC CHMK	F4 SOBGEQ
83 SUBB3	BD CHME	F5 SOBGTR
84 MULB2	BE CHMS	F6 CVTLB
85 MULB3	BF CHMU	F7 CVTLW
86 DIVB2	C0 ADDL2	F8 ASHP
87 DIVB3	C1 ADDL3	F9 CVTLP
88 BISB2	C2 SUBL2	FA CALLG
89 BISB3	C3 SUBL3	FB CALLS
8A BICB2	C4 MULL2	FC XFC
8B BICB3	C5 MULL3	FD reserved
8C XORB2	C6 DIVL2	FE reserved
8D XORB3	C7 DIVL3	FF reserved
8E MNEGB	C8 BISL2	

Appendix B

Abbreviations Used in the Text

AP	Argument Pointer
ASCII	American Standard Code for Information Interchange
AST	Asynchronous System Trap
CDC	Control Data Corporation
CLI	Command Language Interpreter
CPU	Central Processing Unit
CSR	Control and Status Register
DBR	Data Buffer Register
DEC	Digital Equipment Corporation
DMA	Direct Memory Access
FIFO	First In, First Out
FP	Frame Pointer
FPA	Floating Point Accelerator
IBM	International Business Machines
I/O	Input and Output
IPA	Instruction Physical Address register
IPL	Interrupt Priority Level
IRP	I/O Request Packet
LRU	Least Recently Used
LSI	Large Scale Integration
MBA	Massbus Adapter
MOS	Metal Oxide Semiconductor
NPR	Non-Processor Request
P0BR	P0 Base Register
P0LR	P0 Length Register
P1BR	P1 Base Register
P1LR	P1 Length Register

PC	Program Counter
PCB	Process Control Block
PCBB	Process Control Block Base register
PDP	Programmed Data Processor
PFN	Page Frame Number
PSL	Processor Status Longword
PSW	Program Status Word
PTE	Page Table Entry
QIO	Queue Input/Output service
RAM	Random Access Memory
SBI	Synchronous Backplane Interconnect
SBR	System Base Register
SCB	System Control Block
SCBB	System Control Block Base register
SILO	Service In Logical Order
SIRR	System Interrupt Request Register
SISR	System Interrupt Summary Register
SP	Stack Pointer
SPT	System Page Table
UBA	Unibus Adapter
UCB	Unit Control Block
VA	Virtual Address
VAX	Virtual Address eXtension
VMS	Virtual Memory System
VPN	Virtual Page Number
WCS	Writeable Control Store

Appendix C

VAX/VMS Terminal
Input/Output Routines

This appendix contains several routines for performing simple terminal input and output with the VAX/VMS operating system.

```
.TITLE VMS I/O Routines
     .SBTTL Introduction

;++
;
; This module contains some simple routines for performing
; single character and line-oriented terminal I/O on VAX/VMS.
; The routines available are the following:
;
; INIT_IO()
;
;     Initialize the I/O routines. Must be called once before
;     the following routines can be used.
;
; PUT_CHAR ( character_address )
;
;     Write a single character to the output device.
;
; PUT_CRLF()
;
;     Write a carriage return and line feed to the output device.
;
; PUT_LINE ( buffer_length , buffer_address )
;
;     Write a line to the output device. The line is preceded by a
;     carriage return and line feed.
;
; GET_LINE ( buffer_length , buffer_address , return_length_address )
;
;     Read a line from the input device.
;
;
;--
```

```
        .SBTTL   Data Definitions

        $RABDEF                      ; define Record Access Block offsets

;
; Data structures for VAX/VMS record management system
;

INFAB:  $FAB     FAC=GET,FNM=<SYS$INPUT>  ; define input file
INRAB:  $RAB     FAB=INFAB               ; define record access block
OUTFAB: $FAB     FAC=PUT,FNM=<SYS$OUTPUT>  ; define output file
OUTRAB: $RAB     FAB=OUTFAB              ; define record access block

;
; Define carriage return / line feed sequence
;

CRLF:   .BYTE    13,10
```

```
            .SBTTL    INIT_IO - Initialize I/O Routines
;++
;
; Functional Description:
;
;       This routine is called once at the start of
;       the program to initialize the data base
;       for the associated input and output routines.
;       The routine has no arguments.
;
; Calling Sequence:
;
;       CALLS    #0,INIT_IO
;
; Input Arguments:
;
;       none
;
; Output Arguments:
;
;       none
;--

INIT_IO::
        .WORD    0                          ; save no registers
        $OPEN    FAB=INFAB                  ; open input device
        $CONNECT RAB=INRAB                  ; and connect record access
      • $OPEN    FAB=OUTFAB                 ; open output device
        $CONNECT RAB=OUTRAB                 ; and connect record access
        RET                                 ; return to caller
```

```
        .SBTTL   PUT_CHAR - Write a single character

;++
; Functional Description:
;
;       This routine outputs a single character to the output
;       device.
;
; Calling Sequence:
;
;       PUT_CHAR( character_address )
;
; or
;
;       PUSHAB   CHARACTER
;       CALLS    #1,PUT_CHAR
;
; Inputs:
;
;       CHARACTER_ADDRESS - the address of the ASCII character to
;       output
;
;--

PUT_CHAR::
        .WORD   0                   ; save no registers
        $RAB_STORE RAB=OUTRAB,-     ; specify output record access block
             RBF=@4(AP),-           ; pass address of user's character
             RSZ=#1                 ; write one character
        $PUT    RAB=OUTRAB          ; output character
        RET                         ; return to user
```

```
            .SBTTL   PUT_CRLF - Write a carriage return and line feed
;++
;
; Functional Description:
;
;       This routine outputs a carriage return and line feed
;       to the output device.
;
; Calling Sequence:
;
;       PUT_CRLF()   or  CALLS #0,PUT_CRLF
;
; Parameters:
;
;       none
;
;--

PUT_CRLF::
        .WORD   0                       ; save no registers
        $RAB_STORE RAB=OUTRAB,-         ; specify output access block
                RBF=CRLF,-              ; specify CR/LF string address
                RSZ=#2                  ; specify length of 2 characters
        $PUT    RAB=OUTRAB              ; output two-char string
        RET
```

```
        .SBTTL   PUT_LINE - Write a line to the output device
;++
;
; Functional Description:
;
;       This routine outputs a line to the output device.
;       The output line is preceded by a carriage return, line feed.
;
; Calling Sequence:
;
;       PUT_LINE ( buffer_length , buffer_address )
;
;   or
;
;       PUSHAL   BUFFER
;       PUSHL    LENGTH
;       CALLS    #2,PUT_LINE
;
; Inputs:
;
;       buffer_length - the number of characters to output
;       buffer_address - the address of the buffer to output
;
;--

PUT_LINE::
        .WORD   0
        CALLS   #0,PUT_CRLF       ; begin output on new line
        $RAB_STORE RAB=OUTRAB,-   ; specify the record access block
                RBF=@8(AP),-      ; specify user buffer
                RSZ=4(AP)         ; specify string length
        $PUT    RAB=OUTRAB        ; output the string
        RET
```

```
                  .SBTTL   GET_LINE - Read a line from the input device
;++
;
; Functional Description:
;
;        This routine reads a single character from the input
;        device.
;
; Calling Sequence:
;
;        GET_LINE ( buffer_length , buffer_address ,
;        return_length_address)
;
; or
;
;        PUSHAL   RETURN_LENGTH
;        PUSHAB   BUFFER
;        PUSHL    BUFFER_LENGTH
;        CALLS    #3,GET_LINE
;
; Inputs:
;
;        buffer_length - the size in characters of the user input buffer
;        buffer_address - the address of the buffer to receive the
;                         characters read from the input device
;        return_length_address - address of a longword to receive the
;                         number of characters actually read
;
;--

GET_LINE::
            .WORD    0                        ; save no registers
            $RAB_STORE RAB=INRAB,-            ; specify record access block
                  UBF=@8(AP),-               ; specify user's buffer
                  USZ=4(AP)                  ; specify buffer length

            $GET     RAB=INRAB                ; read the line
            MOVZWL   INRAB+RAB$W_RSZ,@12(AP)  ; return length to caller
            RET
      .END
```

Bibliography

Abrams, M. D., and Stein, P. G., *Computer Hardware and Software: An Interdisciplinary Introduction,* Addison-Wesley, Reading, MA, 1973.

Aho, A. V., Hopcroft, J. E., and Ullman, J. D., *The Design and Analysis of Computer Algorithms,* Addison-Wesley, Reading, MA, 1976.

Barron, D. W., *Recursive Techniques in Programming,* American Elsevier, New York, 1968.

Belady, L. A., "A Study of Replacement Algorithms for Virtual Storage Systems," *IBM Systems Journal,* Vol. 5, No. 2, pp. 78–101, 1966.

Bell, C. G., and Newell, A., *Computer Structures: Readings and Examples,* McGraw-Hill, New York, 1971.

Bell, C. G., Mudge, J. C., and McNamara, J., *Computer Engineering, A DEC View of Hardware Systems Design,* Digital Press, Maynard, MA, 1978.

Berztiss, A. T., *Data Structures—Theory and Practice,* Academic Press, New York, 1971.

Bhandarkar, D., and Rothman, S., "The VAX-11, DEC's 32-Bit Version of the PDP-11," *Datamation,* Feb. 1979.

Brinch Hansen, P., *Operating System Principles,* Prentice-Hall, Englewood Cliffs, NJ, 1973.

Burr, W. E., and Smith, W. R., "Comparing Computer Architectures," *Datamation,* Vol. 23, pp. 48–52, Feb. 1977.

Chapin, N., *360 Programming in Assembly Language,* McGraw-Hill, New York, 1968.

Daley, Robert C., and Dennis, Jack B., "Virtual Memory, Processes, and Sharing in MULTICS," *CACM,* Vol. 11, No. 5, pp. 306–312, 1968.

Denning, P. J., "Third Generation Computer Systems," *Computing Surveys,* Vol. 3, No. 4, 1971.

Denning, P. J., "The Working Set Model for Program Behavior," *CACM,* Vol. 11, No. 5, pp. 323–333, 1968.

Donovan, J. J., *Systems Programming,* McGraw-Hill, New York, 1972.

Eckhouse, R. H. Jr. and Morris, L. R., *Minicomputer Systems: Organization, Programming, and Applications,* Prentice-Hall, Englewood Cliffs, NJ, 1979.

Foster, C. C., *Computer Architecture, 2nd ed.,* Van Nostrand Reinhold, New York, 1976.

Gear, C. W., *Computer Organization and Programming, 2nd ed.,* McGraw-Hill, New York, 1974.

Gill, A., *Machine and Assembly Language Programming of the PDP-11,* Prentice-Hall, Englewood Cliffs, NJ, 1978.

Haberman, A. N., *Introduction to Operating Systems Design,* Science Research Associates, Chicago, 1976.

Hamacher, V. G., Vranesig, F. G., and Zaky, S. G., *Computer Organization,* McGraw-Hill, New York, 1978.

Hayes, J. P., *Computer Architecture and Organization,* McGraw-Hill, New York, 1978.

Hellerman, H., *Digital Computer System Principles, 2nd ed.,* McGraw-Hill, New York, 1973.

Holt, R. C., *Structured Concurrent Programming with Operating Systems,* Addison-Wesley, Reading, MA, 1978.

Katzan, H. Jr., *Computer Organization and the System/370,* Van Nostrand Reinhold, New York, 1971.

Katzan, H. Jr., *Operating Systems—A Pragmatic Approach,* Van Nostrand Reinhold, New York, 1973.

Kent, W., "Assembler-Language Macroprogramming," *Computing Surveys,* Vol. 1, No. 4, 1969.

Knuth, D. E., *The Art of Computer Programming, Vol. 1: Fundamental Algorithms,* Addison-Wesley, Reading, MA, 1968.

Lewis, T. G., and Smith, M. Z., *Applying Data Structures*, Houghton Mifflin, Boston, 1976.

Maurer, H. H., *Data Structures and Programming Techniques*, Prentice-Hall, Englewood Cliffs, NJ, 1977.

Organick, E. I., *The MULTICS System: An Examination of Its Structure*, MIT Press, Cambridge, MA, 1972.

Presser, L., and White, J. R., "Linkers and Loaders," *Computing Surveys*, Vol. 4, No. 3, 1972.

Ralston, A., *Introduction to Programming and Computer Science*, McGraw-Hill, New York, 1971.

Randall, B., and Kuehner, C. J., "Dynamic Storage Allocation Systems," *CACM*, Vol. 11, No. 5, pp. 297–306, 1968.

Ritchie, Dennis M., and Thompson, Ken, "The UNIX Time-Sharing System," *CACM*, Vol. 17, No. 7, pp. 365–375, July 1974.

Satyanarayanan, M., and Bhandarkar, D., "Design Tradeoffs in VAX-11 Translation Buffer Organization," correspondence to authors.

Shaw, A. C., *Logical Design of Operating Systems*, Prentice-Hall, Englewood Cliffs, NJ, 1974.

Spirn, J., *Program Behavior: Models and Measurements*, American Elsevier, New York, 1977.

Stone, H. S., and Siewiork, D., *Introduction to Computer Organization and Data Structures*, McGraw-Hill, New York, 1975.

Stone, H. S., *Introduction to Computer Architecture*, Science Research Associates, Chicago, 1975.

Strecker, W. D., "Cache Memories for the PDP-11 Family Computers," *Proc. 3rd Annual Symposium on Computer Architecture*, ACM, pp. 155–158, 1976.

Strecker, W. D., "VAX-11/780—A Virtual Address Extension to the DEC PDP-11 Family," *Proceedings of the NCC*, AFIPS Press, Montvale, NJ, 1978.

Struble, G., *Assembler Language Programming: The IBM System/360*, Addison-Wesley, Reading, MA, 1969.

Tannenbaum, A. S., *Structured Computer Organization*, Prentice-Hall, Englewood Cliffs, NJ, 1976.

Vickers, F. D., *Introduction to Machine and Assembly Language: Systems/360/370*, Holt Rinehart and Winston, New York, 1971.

Watson, R. W., *Timesharing System Design Concepts*, McGraw-Hill, NY, 1970.

IBM Series/1 Model 5 Processor and Processor Features Description, 3rd ed., IBM Corp., White Plains, NY, 1977.

IBM Series/1 Base Program Preparation Facilities Macro Assembler Programmer's Guide, 1st ed., IBM Corp., White Plains, NY, 1976.

IBM System/370 Principles of Operation, 5th ed., IBM Corp., White Plains, NY, 1976.

Introduction to VAX-11 Concepts, Digital Equipment Corp., Maynard, MA, 1978.

PDP-11 Peripherals Handbook, Digital Equipment Corp., Maynard, MA, 1979.

PDP-11/04/34/45/55/60 Processor Handbook, Digital Equipment Corp., Maynard, MA, 1978.

Terminals and Communications Handbook, Digital Equipment Corp., Maynard, MA, 1978.

Translation Buffer, Cache, and SBI Control Technical Description (VAX-11/780 Implementation), Digital Equipment Corp., Maynard, MA, 1978.

VAX-11 Architecture Handbook, Digital Equipment Corp., Maynard, MA, 1979.

VAX-11 Command Language User's Guide, Digital Equipment Corp., Maynard, MA, 1979.

VAX-11/780 Hardware Handbook, Digital Equipment Corp., Maynard, MA, 1979.

VAX-11 Linker Reference Manual, Digital Equipment Corp., Maynard, MA, 1979.

VAX-11 Macro Language Reference Manual, Digital Equipment Corp., Maynard, MA, 1979.

VAX-11 Primer, Digital Equipment Corp., Maynard, MA, 1979.

VAX-11 Software Handbook, Digital Equipment Corp., Maynard, MA, 1978.

VAX-11 Symbolic Debugger Reference Manual, Digital Equipment Corp., Maynard, MA, 1979.

VAX-11/780 System Maintenance Guide, Digital Equipment Corp., Maynard, MA, 1978.

VAX-11 Technical Summary, Digital Equipment Corp., Maynard, MA, 1979.

Index